UNROOTED
CHILDHOODS

UNROOTED CHILDHOODS

MEMOIRS OF GROWING UP GLOBAL

FAITH EIDSE AND NINA SICHEL, EDITORS

Published by Nicholas Brealey Publishing in association with
Intercultural Press in 2004

53 State Street, 9th Floor
Boston, MA 02109, USA
Tel: + 617-523-3801
Fax: + 617-523-3708

3-5 Spafield Street, Clerkenwell
London, EC 1R 4QB, UK
Tel: +44-(0)-207-239-0360
Fax: +44-(0)-207-239-0370

www.nicholasbrealey.com

© 2004 by Faith Eidse and Nina Sichel

Printed in the United States of America

17 16 15   8 9 10

ISBN: 1-85788-338-1

Library of Congress Cataloging-in-Publication Data
Unrooted childhoods: memoirs of growing up global/edited by Faith
Eidse and Nina Sichel.—1st ed.
        p. cm.
Includes bibliographical references.
    ISBN 1-85788-338-1 (alk. paper)
    1. Hybridity (Social sciences) 2. Identity (Philosophical concept)
    3. Affiliation (Psychology) 4. Social interaction. I. Eidse, Faith.
    II. Sichel, Nina.

    HM1272.U57 2003
    306—dc21
                        2003050913

To our far-flung families.

.

Permissions

Grateful acknowledgment is made to the following individuals and publishers for allowing us to include their work in our collection:

Isabel Allende, excerpt from *Paula.* Copyright © 1994 by Isabel Allende. Translation copyright © 1995 by HarperCollins Publishers.

Kathleen Anderson, for "A Minnesota Girl in the Holy Land."

Marie Arana, excerpt from *American Chica.* Copyright © 2001 by Marie Arana. Used by permission of The Dial Press/Dell Publishing, a division of Random House, Inc. and by permission of International Creative Management, Inc.

Tara Bahrampour, excerpt from *To See and See Again: A Life in Iran and America.* Copyright © 1999 by Tara Bahrampour. Reprinted by permission of Farrar, Straus and Giroux, LLC and by permission of the Karpfinger Agency.

Clark Blaise, for "Memories of Unhousement," which first appeared in 1985 in *North American Review* and was selected that year for the Pushcart Prize.

Pat Conroy, whose essay first appeared in 1991 as the introduction to Mary Edwards Wertsch's *Military Brats.* Reprinted by permission of Aletheia Publications, Inc., http://members.aol.com/AlethPub.

Ariel Dorfman, excerpt from *Heading South, Looking North.* Copyright © 1998 by Ariel Dorfman. Reprinted by permission of Farrar, Straus and Giroux, LLC and by permission of The Wylie Agency (UK) Ltd.

Eileen Drew, for "Snakes and Angels."

Anora Egan, for "Breath Roots."

Faith Eidse, whose essay "Embers" first appeared in 1999 in *Rhubarb*.

Carlos Fuentes, essay "How I Started to Write." Excerpt from *Myself with Others*. Copyright © 1988 by Carlos Fuentes. Reprinted by permission of Farrar, Straus and Giroux, LLC and by permission of Brandt & Hochman Literary Agents, Inc.

Nancy Henderson-James, for "Diving In."

Pico Iyer, for "Living in the Transit Lounge."

Lisa Suhair Majaj, for "Beyond Silence," which first appeared in 1996 in *Homemaking*, by Garland Publishing, Inc.

Peter Ruppert, for "Displacements."

Nina Sichel, for "Going Home."

Sara Mansfield Taber, for "Rain Light."

Camilla Trinchieri, for "A String of Beads."

Ruth Van Reken, whose excerpt from *Letters Never Sent* is now available from the author at "Letters," P.O. Box 90084, Indianapolis, IN 46290-0084.

Mary Edwards Wertsch, whose excerpt from *Military Brats* first appeared in 1991. Reprinted by permission of Aletheia Publications, Inc., http://members.aol.com/AlethPub.

Contents

Acknowledgments

This book was conceived ten years ago after a Global Nomads International (GNI) meeting near Boston, and for that we thank Anora Egan. We also thank Norma McCaig for founding GNI and David Pollock and Ruth Van Reken for being among its early leaders. Each submission was affirmation of the need for this collection, and we thank our contributors for sharing their stories.

The book's gestation was measured in years, starting with our parents who gave us international childhoods. Early coaches were the creative writers at Florida State University: Patricia Foster, Wendy Bishop, Sheila Ortiz Taylor, Janet Burroway, and Hunt Hawkins. We are grateful for the assistance and advice of our writer's group in Tallahassee: Nancy Hubener, Betsy Kellenberger, and Lynn Peterson. Special thanks for the continual support, love, and encouragement of our spouses and children go to Phillip, Anthony, and Stefan Kuhns and to Mark, Lisa, and Dylan Silva.

The book's ultimate delivery team was Intercultural Press: Judy Carl-Hendrick, Toby Frank, and Patty Topel. In their expert hands, our project came to life.

Introduction

They are perpetual outsiders, millions of children around the world, born in one nation, raised in others, flung into global jet streams by their parents' career choices and consequent mobility. Some move often, from place to place, country to country. Others establish semipermanent lodgings on foreign soil, returning to the place their parents call home for vacations or family events. Their parents are educators, international businesspeople, foreign service attachés, missionaries, military personnel. The children shuttle back and forth between nations, languages, cultures, and loyalties. They live unrooted childhoods.

Nomadic children are like epiphytes, plants that live on the moisture and nutrients in the air, blown in the wind and propped impermanently in host trees. Lifted from one home and set down in another, these children learn not to attach too deeply. Yet despite their resistance to rooting, these children need a sense of belonging, a way to integrate their many cultural selves and find a place in the world. Like all children, they need a secure sense of self, a stable identity.

Growing up global, nomadic children often enjoy an expanded worldview but may lack a particular national identity. Though their parents may have strong ties to their home countries, these children often feel as though they are citizens of the world and must grow to define home for themselves. They belong everywhere and nowhere—they are "other" wherever they find themselves—and in their search for common ground, they often gravitate toward those whose childhoods have been similarly unrooted, often finding affinity in blended cultural groups. Even into adulthood, they are bound by perennial outsider status, by memories of frequent moves, and by the benefits and challenges a mobile childhood has granted them.

Decades of studies have begun to shed light on the complex identity formation of nomadic children. Sociologist Ruth Hill Useem coined the term *Third Culture Kid* (TCK) and compared their identity development process to pressing a musical record, laying down one note (or track) upon another to produce a multi-toned chord. The tracks include the home culture they are born into and the second (and third, fourth, fifth) host culture, or cultures, they live in. The unique blend, the chord, is a combination of all the cultural influences they make their own. Sometimes the chord is rich and melodic; sometimes it's shrill and discordant.

In their timely study, *Third Culture Kids: The Experience of Growing Up Among Worlds*, David Pollock and Ruth Van Reken describe the TCK as

> *one who has spent a significant part of his or her developmental years outside the parents' culture. The TCK builds relationships to all of the cultures, while not having full ownership in any. Although elements from each culture are assimilated into the TCK's life experience, the sense of belonging is in relationship to others of similar background. (1999, 19)*

Cultural Composites: Enrichment

The usual clues that identify a person don't apply to globally nomadic children. Language, place, family, and community shift for these children with each geographic move. Self-image is slippery; they refuse or are unable to conform to standard definitions of who they are. Lebanese in Iowa, Argentine in New York, they are never wholly one or the other. They are composites, bits and pieces added with each relocation, each new cultural influence.

Unrooted children absorb fragments of the many cultures they are exposed to and develop kaleidoscopic identities. They wiggle their toes in African soil, tip their faces to equatorial sun, then abruptly relocate to snowbound Canada. They attend American schools on foreign soil, learning to pledge allegiance to the U.S. flag and then sing the Venezuelan national anthem. They adopt the wooden shoes of Holland and the saffron robes of Tibet. They speak many languages; their tables are set with silver brought over land and sea, packed and unpacked from La Paz to Beirut. Their mobility allows them to sample experiences around the globe and to move among cultures and identities—and be enriched by them—while they are young, pliant, and still forming their personalities.

Paradox: Estrangement

For some, adaptation to many cultures comes easily, and they welcome the opportunities and the expanded understanding of the world provided by their frequent moves. But the paradox of nomadism is that its benefits are always tied to losses. A child raised abroad cannot form permanent roots in the host culture, and this can feel both liberating and isolating. Roots bind children to a place and time and help them define who they will become. Mobile children may lack long-term relationships or a strong national identity. Often their needs for emotional ties and support are met in a heightened connection to immediate family. But there are times when unrooted children ache for the comforts of extended family, the rhythms and rituals of tradition, an ongoing circle of friends who know them and can take their measure over time. Loneliness may be a frequent companion.

At other times, feeling different allows unrooted children to remain safely uncommitted. They are free of ties, free of patriotism, free to interpret others as separate from themselves. Because they must move often, they learn to adapt quickly. They explore the surfaces of the places they live in, fall in love with their surroundings temporarily. They find they can survive even if they partake only briefly of this culture or that. They learn that no home is permanent and that frequent moves can be a gift.

Entering new cultures young, willing, open, and vulnerable often exposes children to adventure and danger. To leave the security of one's home culture is to risk physical exposure in new places and psychological exposure among strangers. In each new culture, so much depends on getting one's bearings early. There can be drama in every new move, excitement at discovering new places to go, new people to be. But there can also be intense pain in severing the familiar, in the physical and emotional distancing of loved ones.

Where Is Home? Rootlessness

Millions of nomadic children who grow up beyond their national borders return to their parents' home countries. They are expected to integrate smoothly, to assimilate a culture they've been taught is theirs, to camouflage the numerous cultures they've accumulated while living abroad. For many, the transition is difficult. The assumptions they have made about their home community may only partially fit reality. They feel more like new arrivals or hidden immigrants than travelers coming home, and their sense of displacement and culture shock can be extreme.

Children raised as foreigners often question the whole concept of home, never feeling that they quite belong anywhere. They wonder who they are and whether they can settle anywhere permanently. Some seek the security of roots in adulthood and teach themselves to stop in one place. Others keep traveling, a learned restlessness working against their choosing a career, establishing a family, or creating a sense of permanence. Every year, more children grow up crossing borders, blending cultures, following their parents around the world. Often, they find that the only permanence is in memory and in the stories they tell.

Who Am I? Identity

In a nomadic world, telling our stories is one way to establish our place in time, especially when ties to extended family and community become tenuous and personal histories may be fragmented by moves, scripted by family mission, or silenced by the need to conform. Finding a voice can be difficult when language and location are always changing. Adept at learning new languages and understanding new cultures, many mobile children are able to adjust quickly to changing circumstances and often have a distinct advantage over more rooted children. Choosing among their many languages is often a first step toward embracing identity.

Unrooted children have myriad encounters to write about, many cultures to report from, and constant transitions to chronicle. Telling our stories binds us in an act of remembrance. This anthology reveals a community of writers, bound by the recurrent motif of creating an identity while growing up global.

Collected here are twenty essays by adults who lived unrooted childhoods. Their memoirs are grouped thematically, progressing from the adventure and enchantment of moving among worlds to the losses and feelings of estrangement from family, friends, and community to the restlessness of the unrooted child to the creation of a portable cultural identity.

Pico Iyer opens the anthology with the premise that a nomadic childhood provides a solid foundation for life in an increasingly interdependent, multicultural world. Like many adults who had mobile childhoods, he continues to relocate often and to relate to many cultures.

In Section I, "Enrichment," Sara Mansfield Taber, Kathleen Anderson, and Eileen Drew describe international pasts enriched by a nomadism that elicits mostly happy recollections. Isabel Allende's sparkling warmth and humor are woven into her memories of childhood moves in South America and the Middle East.

Section II, "Estrangement," probes the losses tied to these benefits. For many children, frequent transitions are jarring, even painful, as personal ties are ruptured. Camilla Trinchieri steels herself for each new move by concentrating on the place, not the people, she will leave behind. Pat Conroy and Mary Wertsch explore some of the lifelong implications of moving among military bases. Faith Eidse, Ruth Van Reken, and Nancy Henderson-James question their centrality and importance to parents who are dedicated to their missionary work.

Section III, "Rootlessness," explores the difficult search for home among unrooted children. Restlessness stirs the writings of Nina Sichel and Tara Bahrampour. Anora Egan attempts to immerse herself in several host cultures, but is never able to completely assimilate. Clark Blaise settles on a Canadian identity, even as he continues to reside in the United States.

Section IV, "Identity," illustrates the process of finally embracing a cultural self, a task often connected with language choice. Peter Ruppert and Lisa Suhair Majaj endure years of childhood difficulties with speech before finding voices that fit. Ariel Dorfman dons one identity when he writes or speaks in Spanish and another when he communicates in English. Carlos Fuentes establishes his identity only after exploring many other cultures—sharing, reading, growing, exchanging information. Marie Arana considers herself a bridge between cultures, facilitating mutual understanding of each to the other.

This anthology is a unique fusion that presents a world rich in texture, image, and symbol, a gathering of writers who were raised internationally. They sing to us, blending stories of longing and loss, growth and healing. These are memoirs of childhoods spent packing. They reflect on formative years of pain and hope, of the loneliness of the outsider, of restlessness and resilience, and on the gift of a flexible worldview.

Pico Iyer has made a career of his internationalism. He grew up shuttling between England and California, the son of Indian immigrant parents. Keenly aware of the privilege bestowed upon him by a life spent traveling, he describes the adult he has become as the "product of a movable sensibility...a multinational soul on a multicultural globe, where more and more countries are as polyglot and restless as airports."

For Iyer, impermanence is largely a gift, not a burden. His transitory childhood led to a nomadism he considers liberating, enabling him to feel at home everywhere in the world. Sent to boarding schools from the age of nine, he has long been accustomed to a life independent of family, place, or even cultural identity. A confirmed outsider, his roots are in ideas and language rather than place. A professional observer, he is an expert at dispassion, a stranger to belief. His mobile life has granted him emotional distance from the ties of patriotism or deep commitment.

In this essay he identifies himself as a member of a new tribe of intercontinental wanderers whose home is an airport transit lounge, whose worldview is relative rather than absolute, and whose identity is chosen from "a wardrobe of selves." He celebrates the freedom and mobility he cherishes as the product of his unrooted childhood. Comfortable everywhere, he is a true citizen of the world.

Living in the Transit Lounge

Pico Iyer

By the time I was nine, I was already used to going to school by
trans-Atlantic plane, to sleeping in airports, to shuttling back and
forth, three times a year, between my parents' (Indian) home in
California and my boarding school in England. Throughout the
time I was growing up, I was never within 6,000 miles of the nearest relative—and came, therefore, to learn how to define relations
in non-familial ways. From the time I was a teenager, I took it for
granted that I could take my budget vacations (as I did) in Bolivia
and Tibet, China and Morocco. It never seemed strange to me that
a girlfriend might be half a world (or ten hours' flying time) away,
that my closest friends might be on the other side of a continent
or sea.

It was only recently that I realized that all these habits of mind
and life would scarcely have been imaginable in my parents' youth;
that the very facts and facilities that shape my world are all dis-
tinctly new developments, and mark me as a modern type.

It was only recently, in fact, that I realized that I am an example, perhaps, of an entirely new breed of people, a transcontinental
tribe of wanderers that is multiplying as fast as IDD lines and
IATA flights. We are the Transit Loungers, forever heading to the
Departure Gate, forever orbiting the world. We buy our interests
duty-free, we eat our food on plastic plates, we listen to the world
through borrowed headphones. We pass through countries as

through revolving doors, resident aliens of the world, impermanent residents of nowhere. Nothing is strange to us, and nowhere is foreign. We are visitors even in our own homes.

This is not, I think, a function of affluence so much as of simple circumstance. I am not, that is, a jet-setter pursuing vacations from Marbella to Phuket; I am simply a fairly typical product of a movable sensibility, living and working in a world that is itself increasingly small and increasingly mongrel. I am a multinational soul on a multicultural globe where more and more countries are as polyglot and restless as airports. Taking planes seems as natural to me as picking up the phone or going to school; I fold up my self and carry it round with me as if it were an overnight case.

The modern world seems increasingly made for people like me. I can plop myself down anywhere and find myself in the same relation of familiarity and strangeness: Lusaka, after all, is scarcely more strange to me than the foreigners' England in which I was born, the America where I am registered as an "alien," and the almost unvisited India that people tell me is my home. I can fly from London to San Francisco to Osaka and feel myself no more a foreigner in one place than another; all of them are just locations— pavilions in some intercontinental Expo—and I can work or live or love in any one of them. All have Holiday Inns, direct-dial phones, CNN, and DHL. All have sushi and Thai restaurants, Kentucky Fried Chicken and Coke. My office is as close as the nearest fax machine or modem. Roppongi is West Hollywood is Leblon.

This kind of life offers an unprecedented sense of freedom and mobility: tied down to nowhere, I can pick and choose among locations. Mine is the first generation that can go off to visit the Himalayas for a week, or sample life in the distant countries we have always dreamed about; ours is the first generation to be able to go to Kenya for a holiday to find our roots—or to find they are not there. At the lowest level, this new internationalism also means that I can get on a plane in Los Angeles, get off a few hours later in Jakarta, and check into a Hilton, and order a cheeseburger in English, and pay for it all with an American Express card. At the next level, it means that I can meet, in the Hilton coffee shop, an Indonesian businessman who is as conversant as I am with Michael Kinsley and Magic Johnson and Madonna. At a deeper level, it means that I need never feel estranged. If all the world is alien to us, all the world is home.

I have learned, in fact, to love foreignness. In any place I visit, I have the privileges of an outsider: I am an object of interest, and even fascination; I am a person set apart, able to enjoy the benefits of the place without paying the taxes. And the places themselves seem glamorous to me—romantic—as seen through foreign eyes: distance on both sides lends enchantment. Policemen let me off speeding tickets, girls want to hear the stories of my life, pedestrians will gladly point me to the nearest Golden Arches. Perpetual foreigners in the transit lounge, we enjoy a kind of diplomatic immunity; and, living off room service in our hotel rooms, we are never obliged to grow up, or even, really, to be ourselves.

We learn too the lesser skills of cosmopolitan life. We become relativists, sensitively aware that what goes down in Casablanca will not go down well in Cairo. We become analysts, able to see every place through an outsider's eyes, and even our homes through foreign spectacles. We become professional correspondents, adept at keeping up friendships through the mail, our affinities and sympathies scattered across all borders.

We learn, indeed, to exult in the blessings of belonging to what feels like a whole new race. It is a race, as Salman Rushdie says, of "people who root themselves in ideas rather than places, in memories as much as in material things; people who have been obliged to define themselves—because they are so defined by others—by their otherness; people in whose deepest selves strange fusions occur, unprecedented unions between what they were and where they find themselves." We learn to enjoy the fruits of international coproductions—Bertolucci movies, Peter Brook plays, Derek Walcott poems. All of us are international coproductions these days, global villages on two legs. All of us flaunt the United Colors of Benetton, with our English shoes, Japanese watches, and American terms. And when people argue that our very notion of wonder is eroded, that alienness itself is as seriously endangered as the wilderness, that more and more of the world is turning into a single synthetic monoculture, I am not worried: a Japanese version of a French fashion is something new, I say, not quite Japanese and not truly French. *Comme des Garçons* hybrids are the art form of the time.

And yet, sometimes, I stop myself and think. What kind of heart is being produced by these new changes? And must I always be a None of the Above? When the stewardess comes down the aisle with disembarkation forms, what do I fill in? Am I an Asian-American? Even though I feel not very Asian and not at all American? An Indian American? An ambiguous term in any case, not least for one who has never lived in India, and lives in America only because it feels so little like home. My passport says one thing, my face another; my accent contradicts my eyes. Place of Residence, Final Destination, even Marital Status are not much easier to fill in; usually I just tick "Other."

And beneath all the boxes, where do we place ourselves? How does one fix a moving object on a map? I am not an exile, really, nor an immigrant; not deracinated, I think, any more than I am rooted. I have not fled the oppression of war, nor found ostracism in the places where I do alight; I scarcely feel severed from a home I have scarcely known. Is "citizen of the world" enough to comfort me? And does "feeling at home anywhere" make it easier to sleep at night?

Alienation, we are taught from kindergarten, is the condition of the time. This is the century of exiles and refugees, of boat people and statelessness; the time when traditions have been abolished, and men become closer to machines. This is the century of estrangement: more than a third of all Afghans live outside Afghanistan; the second city of the Khmers is a refugee camp; the second tongue of Belfast is Chinese. The very notion of nation-states is outdated; many of us are as cross-hatched within as Beirut.

To understand the modern state, we are often told, we must read Naipaul, and see how people estranged from their cultures mimic people estranged from their roots. Naipaul is the definitive modern traveler in part because he is the definitive symbol of modern rootlessness; his singular qualification for his wanderings is not his stamina, nor his bravado, nor his love of exploration—it is, quite simply, his congenital displacement. Here is a man who was a foreigner at birth, a citizen of an exiled community set down on a colonized island. Here is a man for whom every arrival is enigmatic, a man without a home—except for an India to which he stubbornly returns, only to be reminded of his distance from it. The strength of Naipaul is the poignancy of Naipaul: the poignancy of a wanderer who tries to go home, but is not taken in, and is accepted by another home only so long as he admits that he's a lodger there.

There is, however, another way of apprehending foreignness, and that is the way of Nabokov. In him we see an avid cultivation of the novel: he collects foreign worlds with a connoisseur's delight, he sees foreign words as toys to play with, and exile as the state of kings. This touring aristocrat can even relish the pleasures of Lo culture precisely because they are the things that his own high culture lacks: the motel and the summer camp, the roadside attraction and the hot fudge sundae. I recognize in Nabokov a European's love for America rooted in America's very youthfulness and heedlessness and a historicity; I recognize in him the sense that the newcomer's viewpoint may be the one most conducive to bright ardor (a sixteen-year-old may be infinitely more interesting to a forty-year-old than to a fellow teenager). The hideous suburb that looks so vulgar from afar becomes a little warmer when one's in the thick of it. Unfamiliarity, in any form, breeds content.

Nabokov shows us that if nowhere is home, everywhere is. That instead of taking alienation as our natural state, we can feel partially adjusted everywhere. That the outsider at the feast does not have to sit in the corner alone, taking notes; he can plunge into the pleasures of his new home with abandon.

We airport-hoppers can, in fact, go through the world as through a house of wonders, picking up something at every stop, and taking the whole globe as our playpen, or our supermarket (and even if we don't go to the world, the world will increasingly come to us: just down the street, almost wherever we are, are nori and salsa, tiramisu and naan). We don't have a home, we have a hundred homes. And we can mix and match as the situation demands. "Nobody's history is my history," Kazuo Ishiguro, a great spokesman for the privileged homeless, once said to me, and then went on, "Whenever it was convenient for me to become very Japanese, I could become very Japanese, and then, when I wanted to drop it, I would just become this ordinary Englishman." Instantly, I felt a shock of recognition: I have a wardrobe of selves from which to choose. And I savor the luxury of being able to be an Indian in Cuba (where people are starving for yoga and Tagore), or an American in Thailand; to be an Englishman in New York.

And so we go on circling the world, six miles above the ground, displaced from Time, above the clouds, with all our needs attended to. We listen to announcements given in three languages. We confirm our reservations at every stop. We disembark at airports that are self-sufficient communities, with hotels, gymnasia and places of worship. At customs we have nothing to declare but ourselves.

But what is the price we pay for all of this? I sometimes think that this mobile way of life is as novel as high-rises, or the video monitors that are rewiring our consciousness. And even as we fret about the changes our progress wreaks in the air and on the airwaves, in forests and on streets, we hardly worry about the changes it is working in ourselves, the new kind of soul that is being born out of a new kind of life. Yet this could be the most dangerous development of all, and not only because it is the least examined.

For us in the Transit Lounge, disorientation is as alien as affiliation. We become professional observers, able to see the merits and deficiencies of anywhere, to balance our parents' viewpoints with their enemies' position. Yes, we say, of course it's terrible, but look at the situation from Saddam's point of view. I understand how you feel, but the Chinese had their own cultural reasons for Tiananmen Square. Fervor comes to seem to us the most foreign place of all.

Seasoned experts at dispassion, we are less good at involvement, or suspensions of disbelief; at, in fact, the abolition of distance. We

14

are masters of the aerial perspective, but touching down becomes more difficult. Unable to get stirred by the raising of a flag, we are sometimes unable to see how anyone could be stirred. I sometimes think that this is how Rushdie, the great analyst of this condition, somehow became its victim. He had juggled homes for so long, so adroitly, that he forgot how the world looks to someone who is rooted—in country or belief. He had chosen to live so far from affiliation that he could no longer see why people choose affiliation in the first place. Besides, being part of no society means one is accountable to no one, and need respect no laws outside one's own. If single-nation people can be fanatical as terrorists, we can end up ineffectual as peacekeepers.

We become, in fact, strangers to belief itself, unable to comprehend many of the rages and dogmas that animate (and unite) people. Conflict itself seems inexplicable to us sometimes, simply because partisanship is; we have the agnostic's inability to retrace the steps of faith. I could not begin to fathom why some Moslems would think of murder after hearing about *The Satanic Verses,* yet sometimes I force myself to recall that it is we, in our floating skepticism, who are the exceptions, that in China and Iran, in Korea and Peru, it is not so strange to give up one's life for a cause.

We end up, then, like non-aligned nations, confirming our reservations at every step. We tell ourselves, self-servingly, that nationalism breeds monsters, and choose to ignore the fact that internationalism breeds them too. Ours is not the culpability of the assassin, but of the bystander who takes a snapshot of the murder. Or, when the revolution breaks out, hops on the next plane out.

In any case, the issues, in the Transit Lounge, are passing; a few hours from now, they'll be a thousand miles away. Besides, this is a foreign country, we have no interests here. The only thing we have to fear are hijackers—passionate people with beliefs.

Sometimes, though, just sometimes, I am brought up short by symptoms of my condition. They are not major things, but they are peculiar ones, and ones that would not have been so common fifty years ago. I have never bought a house of any kind, and my ideal domestic environment, I sometimes tell friends (with a shudder) is

15

a hotel room. I have never voted, or ever wanted to vote, and I eat in restaurants three times a day. I have never supported a nation (in the Olympic Games, say), or represented "my country" in anything. I refer to everyone in the third person, and seldom use the first person plural. Even my name is weirdly international, because my "real name" is one that makes sense only in the home where I have never lived.

I choose to live in America in part, I think, because it feels more alien the longer I stay there (and is, of all places, the one most made up of aliens and, to that extent, accommodating to them). I love being in Japan because it reminds me, at every turn, of my foreignness. When I want to see if any place is home, I must subject the candidates to a battery of tests. Home is the place of which one has memories but no expectations.

If I have any deeper home, it is, I suppose, in English. My language is the house I carry round with me as a snail his shell; and in my lesser moments I try to forget that mine is not the language spoken in America, or even, really, by any member of my family.

Yet even here, I find, I cannot place my accent, or reproduce it as I can the tones of others. And I am so used to modifying my English inflections according to whom I am talking to—an American, an Englishman, a villager in Nepal, a receptionist in Paris—that I scarcely know what kind of voice I have.

I wonder sometimes if this new kind of non-affiliation may not be alien to something fundamental in the human state. The refugee at least harbors passionate feelings about the world he has left—and generally seeks to return there; the exile at least is propelled by some kind of strong emotion away from the old country and towards the new—indifference is not an exile emotion. But what does the Transit Lounger feel? What are the issues that we would die for? What are the passions that we would live for?

Airports are among the only sites in public life where emotions are hugely sanctioned, in block capitals. We see people weep, shout, kiss in airports; we see them at the furthest edges of excitement and exhaustion. Airports are privileged spaces where we can see the primal states writ large—fear, recognition, hope. But there are some of us, perhaps, sitting at the Departure Gate, boarding passes in hand, watching the destinations ticking over, who feel neither the pain of separation nor the exultation of wonder; who alight with the same emotions with which we embarked; who go down to the baggage carousel and watch our lives circling, circling, circling, waiting to be claimed.

Section I
Enrichment

To children who successfully navigate a lifetime of change, the world is a garden of exotic gifts, a house of treasures to explore and take in. Transferred from place to place, young and porous, they collect and absorb experience, their personalities amalgams of those cultures they internalize and claim as their own. Perched for a while in a new environment, they experience each move as an occasion for growth, a chance to blossom in new ways.

These children see the world in all its richness and variety. Theirs is a privileged life, filled with opportunities to extend and enhance their knowledge of the earth and its people. Bilingual or even multilingual at an early age, immersed in an interrelated, interdependent world community, they are able to enjoy a broader and more mature perspective than many of their more rooted peers. Theirs is a global education. Though they may regret the loss of a unifying tradition or history, they are grateful for the variety of experiences to which they have been exposed.

The authors in this section adapted fairly quickly to the changes their parents' choices necessitated for them. They were young, girls on the cusp of adolescence, and the world was theirs to savor. Open to adventure, secure in close family relationships, they accepted the pangs of relocation pragmatically, understanding that the benefits of living a new life would compensate for the loss of the familiar. Moving among places, one sampled the thin, high air of La Paz and the swirling streets of Beirut, far from the comforts of her ancestral home in Chile. Another tasted the dense ocean breeze blowing through a Guinean foreign compound, scurrying down the beach to safe haven during an evacuation. One's feet stirred sand in a Palestinian school yard as she learned to belly-dance in the shadow of Israeli soldiers; another's splashed through puddles in soggy Holland to her cozy attic retreat under the pitched eaves of a burgher home.

They are the children whose lives have been enriched by change. Aware that they will never fully belong to one or another of the traditions they sample, they become cultural composites, finding ways to be accepted despite their differences, developing an intercultural understanding unusual in children so young. "The world I breathed in was a borrowed world," writes Sara Taber, and she determines to make the most of her stay in Holland. Her pampered passage aboard an ocean liner from New York to Le Havre buffers the pain of the week-long separation from her father. Her fears upon arriving in an unknown place fade as she becomes accustomed, despite the taunting of boys in the street, to the life, ways, and language of her new home. Within a year, her family is settled in an old brick house "as though we'd always lived there and always would."

Transitions herald new opportunities to explore a fascinating world and to make connections across cultures. Kathleen Anderson feasts her senses on the sights and sounds of Ramallah, enamored of the landscape and embraced by the hospitality of her Palestinian friends and the mysteries of their ancient ways. High in a tree, "taking in the Holy Land," she writes, "I felt the presence of all time." Even the dangers and restrictions of frequent curfews imposed by Israeli soldiers only serve to strengthen her bond to Palestine and its people.

Eileen Drew, visiting her New York relatives, embellishes the facts of her Guinean experience, knowing her cousins cannot comprehend her way of life or her way of thinking. "Fiction is, sometimes, the only truth," she muses, recalling the days when she and her brothers played on her cousins' gullibility and ignorance. Aware that her experience abroad has amplified her in ways beyond her ability to express or theirs to understand, she resorts to telling stories that confirm her belief in the equality of people and the universality of truth. She determines to become "a citizen of the world, a disciple of life."

Isabel Allende celebrates a world rich in sensory delight. Her nomadic childhood teaches her perspective and the relativity of point of view. Born into a family fueled by passion and intelligence and a lack of conformity, her childhood wanderings and her secret readings of *A Thousand and One Nights* nurture her imagination. She claims, "The contrast between the puritanism of my school, where work was exalted and neither bodily imperatives nor lightning flash of imagination allowed, and the creative idleness and enveloping sensuality of those books branded my soul." Her world is a tapestry of exoticism, sensuality, and artistry; her search that of the individual finding her way through the bustle and clash of civilizations.

These authors, largely, are comfortable in their transient lives. Like orchids that inhabit a tree's high branches, these writers flourish in unusual environments, gathering strength from their hosts but taking sustenance from the very air about them. Not permitted by their mobile parents to sink roots, their lives are adventures lived moment by moment, built place by place. In exchanging the security of roots for the diversity of nomadism, their lives are filled with change, their perspectives broadened, their childish souls opened to the wisdom new experience brings.

Sara Mansfield Taber *is a writer, memoirist, and a cross-cultural development specialist who teaches in Chevy Chase, Maryland. The daughter of a U.S. Foreign Service officer, her childhood was spent in the Far East, Europe, and the United States. When she was nine years old, her family was transferred to Holland.*

Even a child who is used to constant change is deeply affected by repeated moves. Taber writes here of struggling to balance her conflicting loyalties to the United States and the many other places she has become attached to. She seeks stability in the rhythms of her new home, in the patterns of attending school, making new friends, learning yet another language. Suspended between childhood clamor and adolescent urgency and uncertainty, sheltered by her close family ties, she assuages the loneliness of the outsider by immersing herself in her new surroundings. She finds calm in hours spent reading English novels to the steady thrum of rain on a peaked Dutch roof.

Rain Light

Sara Mansfield Taber

The rain spatters at first, and then pelts down as I walk. It gushes from puddles up the sides of my black rubber boots. There is a gravelly, crunching sound as my feet hit the hard, wet bricks. My nose and cheeks itch from the wet. My braids begin to drip. Save for the brick of the dwellings that line the street, the air is almost colorless. The dominant color is that of cold stone.

Home is a red brick row house built by The Hague burghers. The building, with its square-block shape, its wide, staunch front balcony, its three full stories and broad red slate roof, is solid.

If I kept walking beyond the house, down the wet-flushed tree- and fence-lined street, and jogged a little to the left, I would come to the baker's shop. There, I could buy a cream puff. And if I continued to walk straight on for about twenty minutes, I would come to the North Sea.

Another day, I will get a pastry or walk to the sea, I decide. Today, I turn in at my house. I walk up to the large brick house where I know, with the certainty that this is rain, that my mother will be waiting for me with two siroopwafels, *the cookies I love best this year that I am ten, on a blue pottery plate.*

We are standing on the sports deck of the *S. S. America*, a ship of grand lounges and varnished wood, built in the forties, just before it is to set sail across the North Atlantic. The nine-hundred-foot ocean liner is docked next to one of the enormous, bustling and clanging garbage-strewn warehouses that make up the port of New York. The four members of my family have climbed up to the very top of the ship and are positioned near the three red funnels and the captain's quarters. We are alone on the flat, gray plain of deck. No other passengers have ventured out into the damp March wind.

Perched on the deck of a ship, headed for an unknown place, we—brother and sister—are, in one sense, in our element. Born in Japan, weaned in Greece, and toilet trained in Taiwan, we have been bred to change countries, at the U.S. government's whim, on a week's notice. The packing of suitcases and the boarding of a ship is second nature to us. We have been living in Washington, D.C., for the last two years, but we are prepared to move on. To be on the way somewhere feels familiar, like old shoes.

I am nine and Andy is seven, and we are beginning our journey to Holland, following my father to his newest post with the Foreign Service. The year is 1964.

I am excited, and Andy has an impish grin on his face as we stand in the wind. I am wearing a buckskin jacket that makes me feel brave as a Sioux. Andy is thrilled at the prospect of a week-long ship voyage. He will imagine himself on a troop ship crossing the Atlantic for Portsmouth and D-Day.

My mother's face is in a half-smile, streaked from weeping. She loves the leisure and dalliance of ship crossings, while my father travels ahead of us by plane, but she dreads the loss of his presence for even a short time.

I stand off to one side, alone: a skinny girl on a wet, gray platform surrounded by railings, overhung with teepees of cables, and spotted with puddles. On this surface, for now, I am steady on my feet. In a moment, though—the moment we leave the dock—the boat will begin to pitch and I will have to gain new footing.

Now my mother, my brother, and I stand on the lower promenade deck and wave to my father far down below. He is being jostled in the mass of people gathered against the immense dark maw of the dockhouse. My throat thickens as I watch my father in his dark suit walk down the long, steep, cloth-roofed gangplank after the "All ashore who're going ashore" is shouted out. He is the

handsome "diplomat" whose secret, important political work at
foreign embassies inflates my chest with pride. His title—political
attaché—and the mysterious aura that wafts around his activities
burnish the edges of my gypsy childhood with grandeur.

The passengers kiss and laugh in glamorous, flowing wool
coats, holding silver cups of coffee handed out by the stewards.
Andy and I munch sugar-glazed pastries. Children blow on party
horns. Confetti fills the air.

The fog horn blasts three times. And the ship lumbers out,
pulled by three tugs. We hurl three or four streamers, in turn,
toward my father. They all land in the water, except for one. That,
my father catches and holds up in his leather-gloved hand. He
waves his tweed cap. My mother puts on her dark glasses. Andy
and I wave until our hands flop, as the distance of dark water
between us and the dock grows. We wave until we can no longer
see my father's thin gray figure.

After we pass the Statue of Liberty, my mother suggests that
we go down to the cabin. She begins to brighten as we descend
into the spacious, gleaming elegance of the ship. We peek at the
ballroom, with its magnificent, polished oak floor and gaze into
the chandeliered lounges with their grand, brocade, down-filled
couches where we will watch movies, falling back into the billow-
ing softness of the feathers, during the rough days of the voyage.

Our porter is waiting for us on B deck, and ushers us into our
stateroom with a kindly and competent wave of his white glove. We
enter what I immediately decide is the perfect living space. Every
surface—the writing desk, the bureaus, the portholes—sparkles
with cleanness. Three beds are made up with crisp soldier-smooth
sheets and soft, peach-colored blankets. The tiny bathroom has a
container of soaps and lotions and toothbrushes and perfumes all
wrapped in smooth white paper with the ship's red and navy insig-
nia. I dab each wrist with yellow-green perfume from a miniature
bottle. On the bureau there is a silver bowl of fresh fruit.

I get the top bunk, since I am older (this has been prenegoti-
ated), so I clamber up. I sit there, smug and happy, eating a pear
from the bowl, and swinging my legs back and forth off the edge

so that they brush my brother's head below. "Mom, can I have my Indian jacket back now?" he says. I fling it down to the floor.

The crossing itself is rough. When we walk on deck, the boat pitches up and down almost vertically. We hang on to thick, crimson, silk cords that the stewards—an innumerable battalion of friendly elves—suspend all along the passageways. My mother keeps a brave face, but it's clear she doesn't like it when the boat leans way up on a wave. She's made mostly Pacific crossings before; that sea is a pond to this cataract. Sometimes she suggests that we stay in the stateroom for our meal, and at these times I notice, she orders only mashed potatoes. One day, queasy myself, I put in the same meager order.

When I descend into the deep bowl-belly of the ship another day, my mother leading the way down through the maze of cramped aisles of the second- and third-class sections of the ship, for a swim in the pool, the depth of the water at the shallow end swings with each roll of the ship, from one to eight feet. Swimming is a precarious matter. Though an expert swimmer, I feel like a little dog, paddling madly just to keep my head above water, as the waves of the North Atlantic toy with my sense of surety.

A vague, low-lying border of land enlarges and enlarges as the *S. S. America* carries us across the gray water to the edge of France. During the last hours of our voyage, Andy and I stand at the rail watching the land grow and gobbling pastries from the steward's silver tray. My mother sips coffee from a silver cup. Relieved to be nearing my father, she does not once remove her eyes from the shore.

The atmosphere that caresses my cheeks is moist as I lean over the rail toward land. As this sweet interval of the ship crossing draws to a close, I suck in the new, European air, trying to see into my life ahead. A cool, delicate fog makes it difficult to piece together any feature on the shore.

My father meets us at the dock in Le Havre with a mackintosh over his arm. I throw myself at his chest and Andy clings to his side while our parents kiss above us, my mother weeping again. We travel by train to The Hague. Rain streaks the views of geometrically placed brick houses and green cow pastures the whole journey.

A taxi transported us to our new home, a yellow brick row house in a vast new suburban development of identical houses at the raw edge of The Hague. Small, low-walled gardens stood to the front and rear of each narrow, upright house, along broad streets with recently planted thin trees.

In this house in suburban Wassenaar, where we lived for a year or so, my room, one of three on the upper story, was sharp-cornered and white-walled. During the daytime I sat within its clean space and happily drew pictures of trolls, but every night, in the bed in that room, my entire nine-year-old body trembled as I gazed at those white walls. The shaking only stopped when my mother or father had checked under the bed and in the closets and inside the chest of drawers and behind the curtains for kidnappers. Some nights, paralyzed by this fear that appeared my first night in Holland, I needed them to check two or three times before I could settle down to sleep. It was as though my body remembered, even if my mind did not, that change, though rhythmic and regular, is still a ransacking and a threat.

The neighborhood around the yellow brick house was, in actuality, quite risk-free, and my mother permitted us a new free-dom. In the clearness of daylight I was reinvigorated, and from the narrow walkway leading up to the house Andy and I set out on grand bicycle excursions. Cycling side by side—a stick-thin girl in white Keds and a shaggy-headed boy in shorts with hidden pockets and five zippers—we were each other's primary companions. We looked after each other.

A blur of hand-shaking made up our first weeks of life in the yellow brick house, as we met other embassy families and Dutch dignitaries. Andy and I were installed in a school—a small American school in the old heart of The Hague. There, for several days, I stood at the edge of the blacktop, pretending to be interested in my fingers and swallowing tears. Then, and many times thereafter, it seemed to me that my whole life had consisted just of this: standing at the edge of the blacktop, swallowing tears.

Gradually, life took on a form. Routines were established, I made tentative forays into new friendships, and I tried on a new language that sounded as though everyone was hawking all the time. My parents bought us the rubber boots all the Dutch children wore and led us on walks and bicycle outings to the surrounding canals and little shops and horse fields to acquaint us with the neighborhood. After a couple of months of these excursions, and of accustoming my ears to the squeaks and clomps of Holland and my body to the rhythms of my new school, the bedtime fears, so vivid and haunting during my first months, gradually faded, like butterflies into the drizzly air.

Turned loose in the afternoons and on weekends, Andy and I explored. First on an outing we would stop at the candy shop around the corner. We had quickly learned the Dutch names for our favorite sweets. At the shop, I would buy a candy necklace to consume, one bead at a time, as we rode around. Andy would buy long strings of *dubbel zout* licorice, and we would put the last of our *gulden* together to purchase a big bottle of Seven-Up. Thus prepared, we would set out to fish with sticks in the canal, or to simply race around the neighborhood. Our most common goal on these wanderings, however, was to discover ponies. Holland was a country of riders, and the possibility of a pony or a horse appearing in a back yard, paddock, or vacant lot was a source of unending delight to us.

If not in the mood for cycling, we hung around the house. With his neighborhood friend, Jan, Andy dug up the back yard, in endless archaeological excavations to China, his turtle named Egbert standing by, while I became an expert at roller skating and walking on stilts.

On weekends we took trips around Holland. Singing "Anchors Aweigh M' Boys" or "The Caissons Go Rolling Along," we made our way, in our new Volkswagen bug, to museums and castles and dikes. At one castle in Friesland, where we ate the most delicious breakfast of our lives—seven kinds of breads and rolls, an array of peppery meats and cheeses, and a crowning touch of chocolate sprinkles for our bread—we spent the day ambushing our parents from behind the tall trees that lined the lanes of the castle park.

From the Wassenaar house to our school in The Hague proper was an hour's journey. For four months in the winter my brother and I left home in the dark and arrived at school just as a gray dawn was rising over the brick blocks of the city. We rode home in the same utter blackness. Although we made this journey in a fancy tour bus and didn't mind the ride, my mother hated it for us. I believe it was this cold, black ride that motivated her to seek out the old, wonderful, red brick house on Duinweg, in the heart of the city, to which we moved within a year of our arrival. There, instantly, and for the next four years, we nestled into our rooms, as though we'd always lived there and always would.

Klompen. Even the word was wonderful—the challenge of trying to say it right, with the *n* there but barely heard, and giving the *o* the right half-closed mouth sound. And the minute I saw a pair of grass- and mud-stained wooden shoes on the large feet of a farmer feeding his horse grain from a bucket, I loved them and wanted them. They were my parents' first purchase for me in Holland, and I spent my first year wearing them as often as possible. Even though I seldom saw anyone in the suburban streets wearing klompen, except for the occasional farmer buying a newspaper from a little shop or a farm boy who'd raced in on his bike to exchange some coins for some chocolates at the candy shop, they were the emblem of my attachment to, and identification with, my new country.

I once watched a klompen maker at work. Out of a block of wood set on a pedestal, he chiseled, with smooth, deft moves of his large hands, a shoe like something out of a fairy tale—a smooth wooden slipper that fit like a sock, with an up-turned elfin toe.

The Dutch shoe fit my parents and brother as well. My parents took to biking in the rain, wheels splattering their coattails as they pedaled. My father loved roaming Dutch villages, scanning for war monuments. My mother, for the first time, had found a language she could make her own, and with astonishing speed was translating Dutch for the embassy. And both of them took great glee in reading the latest naughty Dutch novels. And as for my brother, rain just added to the richness of his dirt-digging. He was meant for a mud wallow.

Holland filled up the romantic openness of my heart. I'd heard of Hans Brinker, of course, and of the boy with his finger in the dike, but it was more than that: the mossy-banked canals with the small boys and men in caps fishing from their banks; the dilapidated stone windmills thrumping away in the wind; the *pannekoeken* houses at the bends in winding country roads; the cows grazing in the flat, green fields and solid horses loping everywhere; the homely princesses, who lived only a few miles from me, riding their ponies in the queen's woods, where I also rode.

In the towns we visited, people sometimes wore old-fashioned costumes—bright, long skirts, and aprons, and up-curled lace bonnets. The Dutch children had blond hair and red cheeks that really were like apples, and the boys' legs were as chapped as their cheeks, as they wore short pants all through the winter. The mounted policemen who strolled the streets on their immense chestnuts seemed friendly despite their towering bulk. The dogs—everywhere—sat calmly by diners in restaurants. And no one seemed to mind the dog-doo all over the sidewalks. At least one person on any walk outside managed to step in something. A certain dignity was wonderfully lost. A strolling queen and a muddy-faced boy were equal in the face of a Dutch sidewalk.

On wet days in Holland, there were the soggy green fields or hunched and hooded cyclists to look out upon. On bright ones, the tulips and hyacinth and daffodils were like scarlet and yellow and blue bedspreads on the ground. The tulips, sold everywhere in buckets for the price of a candy, seemed the perfect antidote to rain.

By the end of three months in The Hague, I could walk on stilts in my klompen. It was with great satisfaction that I used to demonstrate this to my parents' guests and to any child who might happen by. Even a lot of Dutch kids, I reckoned, probably couldn't do that. And this meant, in a kind of way, that I measured up, that I belonged.

When I put on my klompen that first month in Holland, I sprouted an attachment like that of cows to grass.

The March when I was plopped into The Hague American School, I found myself in Dutch class, never having read or spoken a Dutch word in my life, reading a book called *Jan-Jaap en Zijn Beesten*, a story about a girl and a boy and their turtle. The little Dutch family in the book, turtle and all, exactly matched my own. With some hard work, I was actually able to follow the guttural noises and grunts and thumps of the language, and loved to say such words as *lopen, fietspad*, and *lekker*, onomatopoeic words for "walk," "bike path," and "delicious." Then and there, in that narrow classroom, I fell in love with the earthiness of the Dutch language, and with all things Dutch.

Mine was split loyalty, however, and constantly tested. One night, on my way home from buying eggs for my mother at the candy shop, some neighborhood boys taunted me for being an American and tossed rocks at me. While running away, I jolted the eggs. At home, with a basket full of broken eggs, I wept to my mother about the mean boys, calling them "Dutchies," as I had heard other American children do. My mother patted me, in sympathy, while telling me never to use the term *Dutchie* again. She then loped off, herself, to buy another dozen eggs.

I sat stiffly on the couch during the time my mother was gone. While trying to focus on my book, I felt an acute, red-hot shame—a mixture of anger and chagrin that reflected my split response to being a foreigner in Holland. On the one hand, my chest burst with fierce pride in being an American—the unadulterated pride that only a grade-school child can have—and, in my arrogance, I wanted to sic some big American boys on my tormenters to show them whose country was the stronger. On the other hand, I hated not being able to understand what the Dutch boys had said to me and would have liked to be on their side of the vacant lot—and that part of me wished, ardently, that I were Dutch.

We ended the school year without finishing the slim Dutch storybook, and the next year we were to be switched over to French. In the final days of school, I asked my parents if I could attend Dutch school the following academic year, but they considered Dutch an impractical language to know and made the decision to keep me in the American school. With that, and the closing of the little Dutch volume, I was left with a little lump of feeling, which has remained in my belly ever since, that, somehow, an important chapter of my life had gone unfinished, a self left off, half-begun.

In the small, attic library of The Hague American School, feeding on British children's books (I couldn't read Dutch sufficiently well to indulge there), I honed a taste for broad, soggy landscapes. In its small room, lined floor-to-ceiling with shelves, and with a view out over rooftops, I curled up with the likes of Enid Blyton, Arthur Ransome, and Frances Hodgson Burnett. As I turned the thumb-softened pages of these books (flicking my retainer with my tongue), I was transported to downs and moors and fens and bottomlands where children roamed, parentless, engaging in every manner of daring deed—from rescuing people to exploring wrecked houses, ships, lighthouses, and caves, to meeting crotchety old fishermen or gypsies and, by turns, either helping or outwitting them. There was the smell of wild primroses, the tangle of roses gone astray, and, always, rain that turned all the colors soft and vivid and blackened the earth.

By way of my hours spent in that library, with rain pattering safely overhead, a soggy countryside with long vistas and dotted with cottages entered my imagination and took up permanent residence. This vision melded with the land and seascapes that flowed into my eyes whenever I looked out of the window, or ran outdoors to play. Holland, to my mind, was just a blonder, wetter, heartier, more outgoing and stubborn England. Those days in the library forged a longing for a certain look of land that is like a lodger that came to the inn of my heart and never moved away.

The brick house downtown, where I spent most of my five years in Holland, was the best home I ever had. To think of its big, leaky bedrooms with fireplaces, its ballroom-size bathrooms, its furniture-stuffed attics—despite the glamour and grace of the Bornean and Japanese and Vietnamese houses to come—is to bring me a sensation of sleepy protectedness. A canopy that holds fast even under drumming rain. That home has for me what Patricia Hampl calls "the radiance of the past," for it was home the way it is when you are young: the home your parents give you.

Holland houses my image of what childhood should be: freedom, bikes, canals, and fields. It was the time in my life when nothing seemed hidden, when words and actions held nothing underneath. Puberty was an inconceivable world away, life was immediate and bright like Dutch coins, and home was a simple and sufficient thing: my dog, my family, a big, drafty house. I thought when I was nine and ten and eleven that this life would never end.

My life in Holland was one of pause and of grace, a five-year hammock suspended between the clamorings of earliest childhood and the urgencies and uncertainties of adolescence. Like life on shipboard, Holland was a time out of time, and yet a time packed with possibility. Every day there was the chance of a cream puff, a walk by the sea, or a pony around a corner.

The world I breathed in was a borrowed world, in a way. (For, unbeknownst to me, I would leave it far behind.) But most of all, my girlhood world was a Dutch world: a world where french fries are served with mayonnaise, where noses are red and damp, and where the best shoes are made of wood. Dutch hues and flavors came to constitute the sense of Home—both harborage and bunker—to which I would return forevermore.

A terrain of flat, green, sodden fields, pastures of cows and red brick burgs. A land overhung by delicate, gray-white skies, aflutter with rising and falling flocks of pigeons. A town and a countryside continually rinsed by flashes of rain.

Here, under the shell-colored glow of rainlight, I pieced together a girlhood and breathed in the world around.

*Professor and nonfiction writer **Kathleen Anderson** teaches Victorian literature at Palm Beach Atlantic University. The daughter of academics, her childhood was spent partly in Palestine, Japan, and England. Transported from Minnesota to Ramallah at age nine so her parents could teach at Birzeit University, Anderson still thrills, as an adult, to the sound of the Muslim evening call to prayer, finding in it the beauty and intensity she discovered in the Palestinian people.*

The experience of living abroad at an early age can open a child up to a sense of wonder and a sophisticated acceptance of other ways of life. Anderson befriended the local girls in her school and was invited into their homes and their lives, sharing with them the feast of Ramadan, learning to bellydance, deepening her attachment to the land and its people. Her status as a foreigner grants her privileges unavailable to her friends and a sense of personal safety they cannot take for granted. Distressed at her return to the United States, where she no longer feels completely at home, she clings to her memories of Palestine as a place of warmth, laughter, and welcoming generosity.

A Minnesota Girl in the Holy Land

Kathleen Anderson

On my ninth birthday, I held a carved olive-wood camel against the sunset, balancing the camel's feet on the horizon. The wails of evening prayer rang out from a nearby mosque. I thought the prayer sounded like a cry of pain, but the more I listened, the more its beautiful intensity was a deep affirmation. It seemed to say, "We are here. And we dare to thank God for it."

My family lived in the Palestinian city of Ramallah, in one of a small neighborhood of white stone houses with green metal shutters and barred windows like jails. Our house was perched at the end of a rough circle drive filled with trees, brush, and large hunks of rock. My parents taught at Birzeit University, and my older brothers and I attended the local Friends Schools run by British Quakers.

I loved walking to school alone at daybreak, feasting my senses on the awakening desert city. The pastry shop's display window had been transformed into a kingdom of delights in preparation for the Muslim holiday of Ramadan. A special kind of candy appeared in the display window: crystal clusters of ice in stacks of pastel pink, blue and yellow.

At the butcher's shop, I paused nervously, preparing for a contrasting horror of reds. In the window, three gigantic, blood-stained carcasses hung suspended from hooks. Somehow challenged by the shop's new display of carnage, I entered to investigate. The smell of flesh and blood was thick. Tubs of animal parts lined the floor. The goats' and calves' heads stared at me with terrified eyes while flies buzzed and feasted on the contents of the tubs. Worst of all, long, grotesque snakes of fatty intestines curled round and round inside of buckets. Feeling brave and sick, I stumbled out of the butcher's shop.

As the sun rose, the streets began to flow with colorful crowds. Shopkeepers stood proudly before their shops, joining in loud conversation with clusters of men wearing white shirts, dark pants and black-and-white, diamond-checked headdresses called *kafiyas*. Cabdrivers shouted out their destinations: "Amman, Amman! You want to go Amman?" Women in becoming Palestinian dresses glided by as I passed the shouting cabbies. Their gold-embroidered draperies flowed about them as they performed a graceful balancing act, carrying giant baskets of laundry on their heads, and shopping bags and babies in their arms, all the while keeping track of small children. The occasional car looked silly wandering through a sea of chattering pedestrians and noisy livestock, its driver honking and gesturing.

At the Friends School for girls, I wore a crisp blue uniform with large pleats that flapped like fabric planks as I walked. The only bully quickly discovered me. Zane had very long, straight, light brown hair, a delicately chiseled face and cat eyes. She smiled suavely and introduced herself. "I've heard all about you," she said in a knowing tone. Something in Zane's eyes worried me. Her best friend told me a story that turned my worry into terror. She had told Zane she was a Christian, just to see what would happen. Zane threw her down the stairs.

"Why?" I asked in wide-eyed bewilderment.

"Because she believed I was a Christian," her sidekick explained.

"But why did that matter?"

"She hates Christians!"

"Why does she hate Christians?"

"Because she just does!"

"But why?"

"I don't know. She just does."

In Minnesota, people did not throw each other down the stairs because of religious differences. My family attended both a Catholic and an Episcopal church, and no one at either church had ever been tossed, that I knew of. I kept waiting for Zane to pounce on me in an enraged frenzy and throw me out a schoolroom window or pitch me over the stone walls surrounding the school. I imagined my bloody martyrdom in all its potential forms and had violent nightmares of Zane's cat-face laughing as she plunged her claws into my heart again and again. In reality, she did little more than make snide comments or stare at me with a look of wild-eyed deviance.

My teacher in the English-speaking section of the fourth grade was an American who let us call her Leslie. She had long brown hair and walked with a limp. She always wore clogs and elegant hippie outfits like jeans, ponchos, embroidered blouses, and beaded sweaters. She and her Palestinian husband had a leather goods shop, in which she reigned, queen of handmade shoulder bags, wallets, vests, and shoes.

"Numbers came from the Arabs," Leslie boasted as we worked out our math problems. She expected that this information would inspire us to be better mathematicians. My favorite subject was Arabic. I enjoyed scrawling the swooping words over and over in my little blue copybook. The words were too pretty to be real; they seemed like made-up, Spirograph shapes. Lots of swoops and upside-down *u*s and curly *j*s, with accents and dots here and there for added spice.

On rare occasions, a bellydancing ritual occurred at recess. The first time it happened, I knew I was being initiated into a secret mystical society of Palestinian women. Several tall girls invited me to join them in a circle that was forming in the walled garden behind the school. The girls folded their kafiyas into large triangles, and tied them around their hips. The embroidered black and white or red and white diamond shapes on the kafiyas provided a colorful contrast to the navy jumpers. One of the girls found an extra kafiya for me and showed me how to tie it around my little hips. I tried it twice, until she nodded her approval.

The girls began to sing a wild, wailing song as they swayed from side to side. One girl started it, then another joined in, until everyone was singing by turns and together. It wasn't sad, but fiercely mysterious, a cry of the triumphant secret knowledge of these girls who were really women in disguise. We swirled our arms through the air, swishing our hips around and around in irregular ovals to the downbeat of the song. We gyrated and clapped as we faced each other with exultant solemnity. Then we locked arms and did a jump and skip to the right and to the left, right and left, over and over. For once, the language barrier was totally irrelevant: we were dancing women. The older girls looked radiant, with their long black hair released to flow in the wind, in synch with their graceful figures. I was in an ecstasy of gratitude at being included in this earnest sunlight song of womanhood.

Suddenly, the "Green Men" were there, the Israeli soldiers, who are dotted through my memory of the Holy Land, like aliens invade our otherwise pleasant dreams. They had crept up on us and leapt onto the stone wall. They stood in a row towering above us as they unstrapped their giant guns, flexed and gaped.

The circle was broken. This was not a place for men, least of all those men. Their grins were wrong and made my spine bristle. The girls began to run toward the school. They didn't stop to untie their scarves or pin up their hair. Their draperies rustled in the wind as they ran, and I heard muffled sobs. I was frozen in my tracks. The last girls called out to me to run. One waited for me a moment, pulling on my arm, and then ran on when she saw I was immovable. My companions disappeared so quickly, and the schoolyard was silenced so suddenly, that I wondered whether the dance had ever occurred.

I turned to face the soldiers, my hands clenched into tight fists on my hips. I glared at them as fiercely as I could, shaking my head. Why had they come? How dare they upset my dearest friends, who had done nothing to them? Rage surged through me. When I had shown my disapproval as severely as I could, I turned and marched slowly toward the school door, to show that it was disgust rather than fear that inspired our retreat. The soldiers had violated our sacred rite, and I would not forgive them for that. We prayed, huddled together in the gym, some crying silently while others hugged and comforted them. I hated feeling powerless to help my friends. Their courage and generosity touched me, especially when they made gestures to comfort me. I always innately knew that I was not the target of interest, my yellow and blue paleness somehow absolution from the kind of harassment my friends, neighbors and even my olive-skinned brother sometimes experienced.

Whenever curfew was announced during school, everyone seemed to disappear into thin air. I walked home alone through the deserted streets, sometimes walking backwards to feel safer. The town felt dead. Suddenly, I was filled with hope. There were campfires in the distance; visions of roasting marshmallows in the Minnesota woods danced in my head. But as I walked closer, I realized they were little fires in black tires. What did it mean? My rage must have leapt out of me and lit up the street.

As I neared my neighborhood, I saw a group of Green Men blocking the sidewalk. I walked along as casually as possible and tried to pass them. One of the soldiers stepped toward me and beckoned for me to go to him. I strode up to the group of men, who looked smug and plastic in their ugly uniforms as they grimaced smiles at me, their machine guns swaying at my eye level.

"Little girl, where you live?" said the soldier. I turned on the cutesy routine, full strength.

"Oh, around," I said, acting as if I had fully answered the question and they would have no interest in specifics.

"Around here?" the soldier persisted.

"Yes. In this area," I answered, and my eyelashes batted furiously as I smiled sweetly up at the soldiers and tilted my head to one side in my best flirtatious pose.

"Oh, ah-hah," the soldier responded vaguely, nodding his head while his hand stroked his five-o'clock shadow. He seemed unable to help smiling back at me, although I could tell he was dissatisfied.

"Well, I better go now. Goodbye," I called out. I implied that for a good little girl, it was time to get home. Rather than passing the soldiers and entering my circle drive, I casually walked back down the street the way I had come. When I saw from my peripheral vision that the men could no longer see me, I ducked into a side street and ran. Faster and faster, past the smell of suppers cooking, snatches of an old couple's conversation and a baby's squall. Down a grassy alley with morning glories clinging to trellises, glowing in the sunset like fiery trumpets. In places, the walls were low enough that I could catch a glimpse of a backyard, with its flowers, trees, scattered pottery, rocks, and flapping laundry on low lines. I climbed the wall at the back of my yard, dashed to the door and into the house, hoping that I wasn't seen in the twilight by any lingering soldier.

My heart sank whenever I heard the nasal voice announcing curfew over a loudspeaker from a truck that wove through the streets. Trapped in our house, sometimes for up to three weeks at a time, my brothers and I tired of playing popcorn catch, varied by marshmallow catch and grape catch. I crammed my face against the window bars, trying to get outside or at least to breathe the air. At night, the Green Men drove around shooting their machine guns, sometimes accompanying this with the nasal taunts over the loudspeaker. They wandered around on foot as well. When I slept alone in my room, I lay awake listening to the guns going off. Sometimes, I heard the crunch of soldiers' boots nearby, as they snuck around among the houses. I stayed perfectly still in my bed, holding my breath, waiting for the footsteps to fade.

After a curfew, my brothers and I rushed outside. We wandered through the weeds and stones, discovering the shiny golden souvenirs left to us in the night by the Green Men. I picked one up and held it to the light: it was an empty shell casing, one of hundreds that were scattered around us like seeds. We ran from house to house, visiting the neighbors to make sure they were all right. It was like a family reunion after many years of separation. My father and I were typical non-touchy Midwesterners, protective of our personal space, but we hugged our neighbors back and all laughed with relief as we looked into each other's faces. Each one's own suffering was downplayed. "We're fine. Just fine." We worried when Majed, the dashing, hot-blooded son of our neighbors, went missing. A few days later, after his parents' persistent negotiations with Israeli authorities for his release, he visited us to prove that he had lived through another confrontation. I always hoped he wouldn't run out of lives. Considering how often Majed went to jail, I wondered how he could always be in such a good mood. He ruffled my dignity by grabbing me up, laughing and tickling, and tossing me high into the air.

After a curfew, it was wonderful to be outside again, roaming among the grasses and shiny stone bricks. My brothers and I dared each other to hop from one irregular granite rock to another, wherever it happened to lie (moving rocks closer together was cheating). All three of us earned bloody gashes and bruises from landing funny on a slanted stone, our legs crumbling and bodies crashing down upon it. The knowledge of such possibilities added a perverse attraction to the game. Cool stones felt good in the swirling heat. I climbed trees, played "spy" with my brother Tim, and chased sheep when they flocked into our circle drive to graze. No one grazed sheep in my yard in Minnesota. I wished they would. I spent a lot of time trying to hug a sheep, but they knew how to stay just out of reach.

Tim and I went hiking in the desert sometimes, searching for undiscovered scrolls hidden in caves that were tucked into the hillsides. Somewhere, there was a secret message waiting for us. I loved the sight of Bedouins, their robed silhouettes floating across the horizon like mirages. As we hiked along, simple stone cottages appeared, with strings of colorful clothes and white linens waving beside them. Some hills were decorated with tiered rows of stones in horizontal stripes, like strands of beads around a proud woman's neck or the layers of a wedding cake. Everything seemed closer to heaven out here in the desert than anywhere else. I remembered the mournful procession of black figures that sometimes passed by our house in town. Once I saw them carrying a coffin about my size. I hoped they would carry it out of the city and way up the layers of hillside so God could whisk the child to heaven more quickly.

My best buddy from the Friends School was named Fideh. We had many adventures together. She was a friendly giant of a girl, with shaggy hair that was cut short at the neck and stuck out on top like a palm tree. Her round face contained black slanted eyes that were set far apart, and a large, laughing mouth. She was not nervous like me, so I felt comfortable and reassured around her. She always made me laugh, whether she intended to or not. I visited Fideh and her family for the Muslim holiday of Ramadan.

"Hi, Kathy!" Fideh hollered in her raspy voice and clobbered me on the back. She grabbed my hand with her sweaty, fat fingers and led me into the backyard to introduce me to her family. I learned never to ask my friends about their dads, because so many of them seemed to be dead or mysteriously away. However, I was glad to see that Fideh had a dad, a robust-looking man with a bushy mustache who welcomed me in rough English. He couldn't contain his pride in the livestock scampering around us. I tried to pet the calf that bleated from behind a tree.

Fideh was the oldest in her family and had several younger sisters. She mothered them in a blunt, tomboyish way that suited her personality. She gave matter-of-fact answers to the youngest child, assuming her capacity for reason with a touching show of respect. Fideh was not one to flaunt her superiority. She ruffled the girls' hair by way of caress. I thought maybe she was trying to make her sisters' hair as wildly out of control as her own.

Fideh, her closest sister Renee, and I sat primly in the living room drinking tea with lots of milk and sugar, and munching dates and nuts. Then Fideh suggested showing me their bedroom. We marched upstairs to a small corner room. It contained a double bed, small dresser, wardrobe, and one window. A homey child's quilt was draped across the bed. I complimented them on the room, and peeked out the window into the backyard, where Fideh's father was gesticulating while engaged in boisterous conversation with her uncle.

In the evening, as we were getting ready for bed (I was to spend the night there), I asked where the smaller children slept, and Fideh told me she and her three sisters shared the room. Four girls in one room! I had always had my own room, with everything neatly in place where I wanted it, down to the barrettes lined up in colored pairs on my dresser.

"Where does everyone sleep?" I inquired, dumbfounded.

"In the bed," Fideh said, matter-of-factly.

I looked at the bed. "How?"

"We lie across the bed like this," she explained, drawing sections across the width of the bed with her arm, "and that way, there's room for each of us."

"Oh," I said, and was so surprised that I just shut my mouth, afraid I would say something that would offend the honor of the family.

Fideh, Renee, and I sat up and talked for awhile after the others fell asleep. Renee and I brushed our long hair in the dim light of the moon.

I got little sleep that night, even though all the girls unanimously decided to give me the coveted end spot on the bed. We were lined up like a row of sausages. I could hear each person's breathing, and feel the rise and fall of the bed with each breath. The bed squeaked with every slight turn or move I made, so I lay frozen in place, staring into the darkness and feeling my nervous stomach rumble.

The next day, we spent most of our time in the backyard where the animals were being prepared. When we went out into the sunny morning, Fideh's father was there, busy with the various parts of the animals he had slaughtered with his brother's help. I knew what the sight of those buckets meant.

Fideh was excited to show me what was on display in the row of buckets. I pretended to be preoccupied with enjoying the morning air and the view of the sky, until I couldn't put off her pressing invitation any longer. I swallowed hard and followed her toward the first bucket. It contained a calf's head, with jagged fur at the base where it had once connected to a neck and a body. The marble-white eyeball was lolling back in its head, as if the calf were trying to look into its own brain for the answer. My stomach groaned. Fideh assured me that all the animals were dead. I had always thought calves were cute, especially if they were drinking from a large baby bottle.

We paraded from bucket to bucket, animal part to animal part in the morning breeze. Flies were everywhere, violating the heads and innards of the dead. It seemed a particular insult when they perched on the eyes. I stood up for a moment and looked over the walls on both sides of the backyard, hoping the sight of the neighbors' yards would provide some relief to my senses. More livestock, buckets upon buckets, flies upon flies.

When we came to the end of the buckets and stepped back from the display, Fideh's father and relatives looked at me, as if expecting a pronouncement.

"You've got a lot of stuff here," I said briskly, trying to imply a compliment. I wandered toward the back door and stumbled up the steps into the house. I ran to the bathroom. It was lonely vomiting away from home.

Something exciting always happened when I socialized with my Arab friends. I loved Palestinian hospitality. The best of whatever our hosts had was showered upon us. Most of my parents' students at Birzeit University could not afford to entertain guests, but this did not stop them. A student of my mom's invited our entire family to his home one day. He was very handsome and sweet, and looked like a prince with his perfect olive complexion, chiseled features and deep-set brown eyes. When we arrived, he showed us into his house. It was nothing more than a cave. We walked along a surface of rock, and there it was: a hollowed-out nest. Knitted shawls were draped across low chairs and a small coffee table was set with red coffee cups and saucers. It was a cozy bungalow from a storybook, and I half-expected a talking rabbit to appear. The prince spoiled me with a ride on his donkey before tea, a jet-black, silky brayer that twisted and tossed its back while my giggles made me lose hold. He walked alongside me like a prince should, chuckling at my fits of laughter as I clutched the donkey.

We sat down to a royal feast in the prince's hideaway. His mother poured the thick, pasty Turkish coffee into the delicate red cups. We nibbled on pastel-colored Jordan almonds, dates, figs, raisins, and doll-sized cookies. I loved the elegance, sophistication and yet joviality of socializing in our friends' homes. Everything good the hosts had was spread before us in the most inviting way. It amazed me what children were allowed to do. They sat with the adults, drank coffee out of china cups and ate adult snacks. In Minnesota, kids were encouraged to play outside or in a basement playroom, and to have pop and chips at a separate, sturdy card table, with plastic table settings featuring Big Bird.

If soldiers weren't around and things seemed peaceful, my parents would sometimes let me visit Birzeit University. The beautiful campus of Birzeit contained old stone buildings and walkways lined by stone walls, and was sprinkled with exotic desert plants. Hanan Ashrawi was Chair of the English Department at the time. When my parents introduced me to her, she gazed at me with an earnest directness that made me blush with surprise that an adult would consider me worthy of serious attention. She asked me brief, to-the-point questions as she lit up another cigarette.

"And how do you like school?" she inquired as she puffed the cigarette.

I could see her intelligent eyes shining through the curls of smoke. "Um, fine. I like it a lot."

"Ah. And what is your favorite subject?"

I blushed as I answered her, increasingly mesmerized by the grace and style with which she smoked. I had never had a conversation with an Arab woman wearing a suit, who was enjoying a cigarette. I couldn't tell her opinion of my responses, but she half-smiled in an affirming way as she breathed a swirl of incense, and my admiration was sealed for this woman of mysterious strength and savvy. I was also impressed that if she wandered by where my brothers and I were hiding in the trees, she pretended not to see us, though I suspected she always knew we were there. My brothers and I preferred the blackberry trees, plucked the plumpest berries and munched away while looking out over the landscape. I was in the sky, eating sweetness and taking in the Holy Land. I felt the presence of all time.

I wasn't ready to return home. I found myself in the airport at Tel Aviv, watching a Green Man behead my white-haired, smiling doll. I had politely asked him not to do it. I said, "Please." I wanted to scream at him and snatch my doll from his grip, but habit made me ask in a repressed voice, "Do you have to do it?"

"Yes, those are the rules," said the soldier, as if he were talking to a dog or a hanging carcass. The Green Man tore the helpless doll in two, and examined her insides. My mother's words of comfort trailed off, as she cradled the doll's remains. I looked away, clutching my wooden camel tightly in my hand.

In Minnesota, everything was too green. The desert, caves, scrolls, and Bedouins were gone. There were no mysteries, and I was expected to be a child again and to play volleyball, go to cartoon movies, like cute boys and eat peanut butter. Everyone in St. Cloud had a house, a couple of cars, and a dad. They went to the mall on Saturdays and ate at Country Kitchen.

I looked down at the camel in my hand. The chain along its graceful neck crushed a pattern into my palm. I examined the majestic, varied grain of the camel's wooden body, and its face, which held neither a smile nor a frown. I held it close and shut my eyes. I saw the holy desert and dancing, feasts and burning tires, ancient olive trees and tanks, settlements and Green Men. I tasted bitter coffee-paste and sweet layers of baklava. I felt heat and fear, hugging and kissing on both cheeks, loud laughter, friendly arguing, wails of worship and sorrow. Happy, anxious eyes. Sweet figs. Fideh. And more dancing.

Eileen Drew *extended a nomadic childhood into adulthood, volunteering for the Peace Corps, where she served in Congo. The child of a U.S. Foreign Service officer, she was born in Morocco and lived in several African nations, in Korea, and in Washington, D.C. She is author of a novel and a book of short stories and contributed to a collection of Peace Corps memoirs. She currently resides in California.*

Like many children raised internationally, she finds it difficult to explain her foreign life to those who haven't lived abroad. Returning to the United States following evacuation from Guinea, she is frustrated in her attempts to share a complex worldview with her New York cousins, disdainful of their ignorance and their stereotyping of others, and unforgiving of their religious bigotry. A foreigner at home, a multicultural composite, she finds in storytelling the ability to share the greater truths that she has learned in her unrooted life.

Snakes and Angels

Eileen Drew

"We lived in a tree house," I told my cousins in New York. They had just finished imping a cannibal dance in their living room, hands tapping mouths like Indians, pretending to shoot darts. Then they'd asked what Africa was like.

"Yeah," my brother nodded, playing along. "We had to climb a rope ladder up." He elaborated naturally, nostalgically; teasing was his territory, not mine. I never lied. Yet he hadn't batted an eye at my fib; in this, in Africa, we were a team.

Richard was eleven, I was nine; my three cousins ranged in age from eleven to fourteen. As the punk, I was eager to please, and a bit of a goodie-goodie to boot; nobody expected me to lie. The story grew.

"We swam in a stream to wash."

"We had mosquito nets over our beds."

"We ate elephant."

"We got to school by jumping from branch to branch; we didn't have to walk on the ground."

"You never walked on the ground?" Karen frowned.

"No. We could; we did get down when we wanted to, but we didn't have to. We could go all the way through trees."

"The school was a tree house?"

"No, idiot, the school was on the ground, in a regular building, like the embassy." A master at dissembling, my brother knew when to pull back.

"What about snakes?" asked Kevin, the eldest.

"We had a pet snake," Richard said. "Not poisonous, just a python. This long," he demonstrated with his arms spread wide.

"What did you do with it when you left?"

Richard gave me a histrionic look. "Should we tell them?"

"Only if you promise not to tell our parents." I had no idea what.

Kevin, Karen, and Kim agreed, coolly. Although they seemed to believe our scenario, they had yet to act impressed. They were never impressed. Sassy and street-smart, initiates of their own Irish tribe, they were urban yet provincial, wary of anything foreign, their caution expressed as disdain. African, Native American, Amazonian—it was all the same to them, and so they'd gone whooping in a circle, spouting mumbo-jumbo, shooting invisible darts—Africa to them was anything they'd ever seen about natives on TV.

Why wouldn't we live in a tree house? Have a pet snake? Richard was stalling, pretending to not trust them with our secret while he decided what it was. We all waited in suspense.

He tightened his eyebrows, fixing each cousin in turn with a threatening look. Then relaxed. "It's in Eileen's suitcase," he confided quietly.

"In my Pan Am bag," I corrected.

"Where?" Karen, Kevin, and Kim looked alarmed.

"In your room," I said to the girls.

Now the bedlam was American, genuine alarm. Whether or not they believed us anymore, they were mad. The idea of a snake underfoot was ghastly, but if the story were false, they'd been duped. Kevin went to pin Richard on the carpet, but I was laughing, ready to tell the truth.

It was Christmastime, snowing, and mostly my cousins were kind, showing us how to shape snowballs and skate. But I could not forgive their ignorance, their offhand dismissal of my beautiful palm trees and beaches and people, their lack of compassion for poor children who were black.

My family had just been evacuated from Conakry, Guinea. My father was an economist for the Department of State, and his job in Conakry was one of many overseas stints. His two-year tour at the Conakry embassy, however, had been interrupted by political unrest. It was 1966, and I admit that my own impression of the place we'd left was childishly rosy, based on what, at nine, I knew.

I knew that Barry, our houseboy, had always been gentle, moving slowly in his starched shorts, his yellow eyes solicitously watchful. My mother and father once discussed whether he should be let go, for fear that he was jaundiced and could infect us kids, and I worried he'd go away sick. But as I recall, he stayed.

What else did I know? I knew the Guinean kids' wary curiosity—not unlike that of the New York Irish tribe—as we examined each other's toys. They showed us how to propel scrap bicycle wheels with sticks—a street game of race and chase—and we offered our bikes to ride. My encounters with them were abortive and sporadic; short of common words, our talk and play would fizzle out. Perhaps their mothers, like ours, cautioned them against alien playmates. Their bare bellies were bloated like basketballs, the navels convex, but they ran and danced and laughed. Their world was like a club I wanted to join. Perhaps I was too shy. Richard was better. Not that he cultivated any real pals, but he did tag along with the boys who fished from the rocks behind our house, tossing makeshift hooks on strings, gathering catch in rusty coffee cans.

I knew the swimming pool behind our house, the ocean behind that, a lagoon to the side, where miniature crabs thrived. Sometimes—maybe low tide, maybe after rain, maybe at dusk; I'm not sure—if you went out there quietly, you'd see the silty beach alive, a carpet of swift, tiny angles. If disturbed, the crabs jerked out of sight en masse, skidding inside multiple holes, as if tugged underground simultaneously by strings. I knew how to pry mussels off the rocks, break open their shells, and swallow them: salty, slick. I knew riding in motorboats to "the island" where, on Sundays, expatriates swam.

I knew the extreme sweetness of locally grown bananas, the squeaky coconut. I knew the green, green bush. The rain showers like waterfalls. I knew waking to roosters, going to sleep to drums.

I knew our exotic house, a colonial imitation *paillotte*, a three-bedroom home with circular walls and a great thatch roof. It was a child's fantasy; I might as well have lived in a tree. Inside, our rooms were air-conditioned, yet the roof rose like an upside-down funnel. Our cat sat on top.

I knew the French ladies next door, who taught me to crochet lace.

I knew the freedom my brother and I enjoyed riding our bikes across the neighborhood to American kids' homes, the Guinean compounds we passed, shirtless women pounding yams, babies lolling on straw mats, goats tethered in patches of shade.

I knew the humid evenings at the home of Americans who hosted films, the kids all sprawling sleeveless in shorts on the floor, our parents seated behind, the Cokes we were served between reels, James Bond finagling escape as the embassy projector hummed and clicked.

I knew my father's sailboat, how he tacked out of the harbor, how, once, he sailed past our house.

I knew playing "Truth or Dare" with girlfriends from the American school. Jessica Doe, the daughter of the Liberian ambassador, was a classmate; she had us all over to a slumber party, where we sat confiding under the stars on her roof patio—which boys we liked, which hands to hold. I didn't think twice that she was African; her parents were middle class, her accent American, her kitchen staffed with a Guinean cook.

I knew twisting to the Beatles, stomping to Nancy Sinatra— "these boots are made for walking"—at another friend's where we went for summer lessons in French. I knew her civet, her African cat. I knew our dog's puppies, the kittens of our cat—a fertile multitude of pets. We had no snakes.

Even now I find it hard to tell the truth. I give infinite details, but you can't know what it was like, what it was about Conakry

I loved. I can't recall giving any of these details to my cousins in New York. Stories are easier to tell. Fiction is, sometimes, the only truth.

There was a bigger picture of Conakry, the hints of which reached me merely as the props of an *007* adventure—for my world, if geographically wider than my cousins,' was framed by the same Hollywood movies that had given them *Tarzan* and *Swiss Family Robinson*. It was Cold War time, the Russians were the enemies, and the Guineans, under Sekou Toure, were on the wrong side. President Toure denounced the U.S. presence in his country. Group by group—Peace Corps, Pan Am, A.I.D.—he threw us out. The embassy was the last to go, except for the missionaries who stayed.

But nobody I knew got hurt. People simply packed and left in a hurry; kids were suddenly permanently absent from school. For a while, school closed; my brother and I welcomed the holiday. A Halloween party was cancelled; we had all the Hershey's Kisses to ourselves. Under house arrest, we spied on the armed guard outside our fence, passed him candy through the wire. He said *merci* but didn't smile. Nobody was mean; no one shouted, no one shot. As kids, we experienced the threat as a game: adopting the new rules, we improvised.

The school break lasted a couple weeks, house arrest a few days. A lorry full of sleepy soldiers in fatigues arrived early in the morning, letting off one or two men to stay at our gate, spelling them in the evening with a change of guard. My father kept going to work, talking his way out, returning at lunch. The house arrest was for our protection, we were told, to keep us safe from angry mobs. The servants—cook, gardener, *guard de nuit*—stayed away. Richard and I were not allowed outside the yard.

I did not know then that a mob did attack the ambassador's residence, that his wife hid upstairs in a closet while the house was trashed, that my father got her out. Armed by bravado, he pushed his way past. The first I heard of this story was a year or so later, when, at a ceremony in Washington, he got an award.

I do remember our walk down the beach. Perhaps the same day the Guineans stormed the ambassador's house—it must have seemed that things were coming to a head—my mother told us we were going down the beach. It was a secret; the guards were not to know. She'd had instructions from my father at some point when he was home; a plan had been hatched. She made sandwiches, got her purse; Richard and I each had a basket, as if for a picnic, to fill with things to do. I took my attempt to crochet lace; Richard took Corgi toy cars. Into each basket my mother dropped Baggies of Halloween treats.

No guard had been posted at the gate onto the beach. We walked quickly across the patio, past the pool, my mother telling us to hush. Like all kids, my brother and I were used to sneaking around, but not with my mother in charge.

"Walk normally," she said, "as if nothing's wrong."

She locked the gate behind us with a gentle snap. We balanced our way across the rocks, strode quietly on the sand. It did not feel like running away. I didn't understand that there was much at stake until, catching sight of his fishing friends, my brother took off to call hello.

"No!" my mother said, "not now!"

Surprisingly, my brother obeyed, hanging back.

"We don't want anyone to know we're out here, we're supposed to be at home," she explained. "Those guards have guns."

I didn't see any guards, just the kids, but I kept waiting to hear the buzz of bullets as I had in films. Richard waved as if nothing were wrong; curiously, the kids waved back. I'd seen my mother angry often enough, but never afraid. Even now there was more fight than flight in her urgency, her pace determined, each step evenly sinking as she fixed the horizon with a squint. She hadn't held my hand on walks for years; she didn't hold it now.

We had a destination: the home of a colleague of my father's where all nearby Americans were to wait. There was a group of ten or fifteen; some had come by beach, some, somehow, by car. A two-way radio blasted static and garbled voices from the embassy; now and then a lady at our end radioed back. There were mostly women there, a couple of men; Richard and I were the only kids. Everyone spread out, rambling through these people's home: either holed up in an air-conditioned room, arrayed in chairs set up against the walls as if for a dance, or roaming the humid living room. Drinks were served; people smoked. I crocheted my lace as best I could. Everyone was calm, tense, mostly bored, complaining about the inconvenience, how they needed to get to the market, missing the help.

I felt suspense as one does in a movie, with no immediate danger, no fear. We didn't even spend the night. By evening things had resolved themselves and we were driven home. I don't remember telling my cousins this story at all. I do remember one of them asking me if Africans all went to hell. As Catholics we were taught that anyone not baptized was damned; I could think only of Guineans who were good. Not even the guards outside our gate were mean.

I began to doubt my religion that Christmas, age nine. My cousin's question about the state of grace of Africans left me rebellious—against my cousins, against their white righteousness, their God. Over the next few years, the question nagged. At Catholic school in northern Virginia, I meekly asked the nuns. They condemned the villagers to hell. Only conversion by missionaries, baptism by priests, could save African souls. Babies went to purgatory, I was told—but what about the kids chasing bicycle wheels in the street? What about the old man who'd come running when, once, I fell?

He lived in a compound around the corner from my house, up a hill. We passed it often riding bikes, turning at the top, coasting down. There was a band of little kids who often chased a soccer ball we had to dodge. Hardly more than toddlers, they stayed close to home, sprinting hectically after their homespun ball of cloth. Their compound was like any other: behind the low brick wall, squat cement buildings surrounded a courtyard studded with trees. Older girls and women in busily printed cloth—some patterns faded, others marvelously bright—chatted lazily in their clipped diphthongs as they chopped and pounded and milled around their cook fires. The only man I ever saw there was old; the others must have been at work. He sat regally on a wood stool in the shade of an acacia.

I was used to coasting down recklessly on my Schwinn; I knew just when to punch the pedal brakes. But this day I was trying out the bike of a friend, an impressive model like nothing I'd ever seen. It was futuristic, foreign, pink. It had big handlebars, small wheels. It looked fast.

Generously, the girl waited outside my house while I took my spin. I was wearing sunglasses; I'd had surgery that summer in Germany on my crossed eyes and they were still sensitive to light. I don't know how I must have looked to the Guineans: a prissy white child in movie star sunglasses perched on a pink bike. I don't know if they knew what movie stars were.

Going uphill was nothing special; I circled to head down. Before I knew it, I was hurtling over potholes and rocks, kids turning slow-motion to look, faces blurring past. The world, for a moment, held its breath. Out of control, the handlebars and front wheel shuddered, gyrating side to side; alarmed, I hit the brakes. And flew into a heap—immobile, stunned. I heard the barefoot scrape of someone at a run, an African exclamation, the hiss of a gasp. My skewed glasses were removed, and a narrow dark face blocked the sun. Like a halo, white hair capped his backlit head.

Lifted in his arms, I felt the jounce and swing as he ran me downhill. By this time I was howling, frightened more by the emergency than pain. My mother met us outside my house, taking over as the man set me gingerly in the drive; I was perfectly able to stand. She examined the blood running evidently from my eye, took the glasses from his hand. Someone else showed up with the bike. Later my girlfriend apologized, "That bike isn't safe going fast."

There was nothing wrong, actually, with my eye; the American doctor sewed up my eyebrow where my glasses' nosepiece had cut. There was no concussion, and I'm glad now that I did keep my consciousness, so that this image of a guardian angel—an elderly Guinean between me and the sun, the halo of his white hair—

could be forever etched in my mind. It made it impossible for me to imagine him in hell.

I did not walk away from God those few years later, just away from the priests and nuns and the mumbo jumbo of the church. If I didn't know anymore what to call God, I always had faith.

I had to believe that people lived on after death; ghosts and souls and animism appealed. I told my father I wanted to quit church when I was thirteen; when I was eleven my mother had died. It helped to think of her as Bantu Africans do of their ancestors—watching from the afterworld, protecting me from harm. She might as well have been a guardian angel with wings.

The only difference I could see between the afterworld and heaven was that the afterworld was democratic, home to the unfortunate as well as the blessed. I saw everyone as innocent, victims of experience rather than original sin. And I could not believe Guineans burned in hell because they'd never heard of Christ.

When I explained this to my father, he nodded thoughtfully, and that was that. We were living in Accra, Ghana, then; my mother had died of cancer in the States. He'd made sure I got to church each Sunday since, although he wasn't Catholic, himself. My brother, in boarding school, hadn't gone to church for months.

Catholic, Animist; American, Guinean: spiritually, all the same. I could not deny anybody's god, not anybody's skin or clothes or language or dance. I could never laugh at African stereotypes in the States; when my cousins played Generic Native, stomping their xenophobic circles in New York, I could only laugh at them.

I was lucky. I'd had the good fortune in Conakry to be exposed to nothing bad. Had my father been slaughtered by that angry mob at the ambassador's, I might have grown up bitter and mistrustful and vengeful toward blacks. Instead I picture kids happily swarming after wheels and balls, an old man toothlessly smiling as I wave, recovered, passing by on my bike.

Of course, I was not exposed to *nothing* bad. I witnessed the same dilemmas and injustices of any kid growing up. One night I heard a neighbor child screaming, being beaten. I asked my parents if they couldn't help, and they answered, sadly, "No." I can still hear the cries curdling the night. I understood this injustice as a universal, though—a random sort of cruelty that could also occur in the States. Violence was an aberration, I thought, whether in Conakry or Washington, D.C.; I didn't understand historical anger or societal fear, nor why citizens might riot, tribe against tribe.

I never felt very American in the States. Each time we returned from a tour in Africa, culturally, we had to catch up. Arriving in New York from Conakry that winter, we went straight to my cousins', our clothes out of season, out of date. My cousin wore kooky white go-go boots, but "these boots are made for walking" was an oldie no one sang. We'd never heard of the Monkees, didn't know any new TV. My brother, the extrovert, fared better than I, coming off as exotic rather than estranged. Always, he stuck up for the States—later, in Accra, when our English friends would tease, he'd say, "If your country is better, why do the Beatles sing in an American accent?" For his first job, he joined the Marines; the Peace Corps was my choice.

My brother had nothing to explain; I kept trying, telling lies, making stories from truth—trying to figure out why heathens seemed more Christian than those who went to church. I was trying to become more than American, a citizen of the world, a disciple of life.

It was not a bad way to grow up.

*Renowned author and memoirist **Isabel Allende** writes of her youth with characteristic humor and intensity of feeling. Her early childhood was spent in Chile, where she lived in her grandfather's house until the age of ten. This excerpt from her memoir,* Paula, *describes Allende's years in Bolivia and then Lebanon, where her stepfather, Tío Ramón, was general consul to several Arab nations over the years. She captures both the upheaval of those seminal years and the sensory-rich feast they provided, which nurtured her creative soul.*

Life for Allende is a continuous adventure, an opportunity to feed an extraordinarily rich imagination. Even within the diplomatic community, she always felt different. Her family's unusual status, their poverty in comparison with other diplomats, her rebellion against the rigidity of her "English" education, all led her to a closer relationship with her brothers and to the early recording of her life in notebooks and journals she has maintained through the years. Her sense of roots is not in a place, she's said, but "in my memories, in my books."

Arabian Nights

Isabel Allende

La Paz is an extraordinary city, so near heaven, and with such thin air that you can see the angels at dawn. Your heart is always about to burst, and your gaze is lost in the consuming purity of endless vistas. Mountain chains, purple hills, rocks and splashes of earth in saffron, violet, and vermilion tones encircle the long, narrow valley from which this city of contrasts spills. I remember narrow streets rising and falling like party streamers, little hole-in-the-wall shops, broken-down buses, Indians dressed in bright wool, the ever-present wad of coca leaves staining their teeth green. The bell towers of hundreds of churches, and the courtyards where Indian women sat to sell dried yucca and purple maize and little mounds of dried llama fetuses for curative poultices, all the while fanning away flies and nursing their babies. The smells and colors of La Paz are inscribed in my memory as an inseparable part of the slow and painful awakening of adolescence. The ambiguity of my childhood ended at the precise moment we moved from my grandfather's house.

The night before we left [Chile for Bolivia], I crept out of bed, went downstairs, carefully avoiding the treads that creaked, and felt my way through the dark ground floor to the drawing room drapes where Memé was waiting to tell me that I must not be sad because she had nothing more to do in that house and was ready to go with me; she said that I should get her silver mirror from Tata's desk, and take it with me. I will be there from now on, she added, always with you. For the first time in my life, I dared to open the door of my grandfather's room. Light from the street filtered through the slats of the shutters, and my eyes were by now accustomed to the darkness. The grandfather clock struck three. I could see Tata's motionless body and austere profile; he was lying on his back, rigid as a corpse in that room filled with funereal furniture. I would see him exactly like that thirty years later, when he came to me in a dream to reveal the ending for my first novel. Ever so quietly, I glided toward his desk—passing so close to his bed that I could sense his widower's loneliness—and opened his drawers one by one, terrified that he would wake and catch me in the act of stealing. I found the baroque-handled mirror next to a tin box I did not dare touch. I took it in both hands and tiptoed out of the room. Safely back in bed, I peered into the shining glass where I had so often been told demons appear at night; I suppose I saw my ten-year-old face, round and pale, but in my imagination I saw Memé's sweet image, telling me good night. Early the next morning I added the last touch to my mural, a hand writing the word *adiós*.

That day was filled with confusion, contradictory orders, hasty farewells, and superhuman efforts to fit the suitcases on top of the automobiles that were to drive us to the port to take the ship north. The rest of the journey would be undertaken on a narrow-gauge train that climbed toward the heights of Bolivia at the pace of a millenarian snail. The sight of my grandfather—in his mourning, and with his cane and his Basque beret—standing at the door of the house where I grew up marked the end of my childhood.

Evenings in La Paz are a conflagration of stars, and on moonless nights you can see them individually, even those that died millions of years ago and those that will be born tomorrow. Sometimes I used to lie on my back in the garden to gaze at those awe-inspiring skies and feel the vertigo of death, falling and falling toward the depths of an infinite abyss. We lived in a compound of three houses that shared a common garden; in front of us was a celebrated oculist, and behind, a Uruguayan diplomat who was rumored to be homosexual. We children thought that he suffered from an incurable disease. We always said hello with great sympathy and once were so bold as to ask him whether "homosexuality" hurt very much. After school, I sought solitude and silence in the paths of that large garden; I found hiding places for the notebook with the record of my life and secret places to read, far away from the noise of the city. We attended a coeducational school; until then my only contact with boys had been my brothers, but they didn't count. Even today I think of Pancho and Juan as asexual, like bacteria.

For her first history lesson, the teacher lectured on Chile's nineteenth-century wars against Peru and Bolivia. In my country I had been taught that the Chileans won battles because of their fearless valor and the patriotism of their leaders, but in that class I learned about the atrocities committed by my compatriots against civilian populations. Chilean soldiers, drugged on a mixture of liquor and gunpowder, swept into occupied cities like barbarian hordes. With fixed bayonets and slaughtering knives, they speared babies, gutted women, and mutilated men's genitals. I raised my hand to defend the honor of our armed forces—not yet suspecting what they are capable of—and was greeted by a hail of spitballs. I was sent from the room, amid hisses and catcalls, and told to stand in the corridor with my face to the wall. Holding back my tears, so no one would see my humiliation, I fumed for forty-five minutes. During that traumatic time, my hormones—until then totally unknown to me—erupted with the force of a volcano. "Erupt" is not an exaggeration: that day I had my first menstrual period. In the opposite corner, also facing the wall, stood a fellow culprit, a tall boy, skinny as a broom, with a long neck, black hair, and enormous, protruding ears that from the rear gave him the air of a Greek amphora. I have never seen more sensual ears. It was love at first sight; I fell in love with those ears before I ever saw his face, with such vehemence that in the next months I lost my appetite and then, from eating so little and sighing so much, became anemic. My romantic rapture was devoid of sexuality; I did not connect what had happened in my childhood—the pine forest beside the sea, and the warm hands of a young fisherman—with the pristine sentiments inspired by those extraordinary appendages. I was a victim of that chaste, and therefore much more devastating, love for two years.

I remember that time in La Paz as a succession of fantasies in our shady garden, ardent pages in my notebooks, and storybook daydreams in which a pitcher-eared knight rescued me from the maws of a dragon. To top everything off, the entire school knew of my enslavement, and because of my infatuation and my unarguable nationality, I became the prime victim of the most offensive schoolyard pranks. My love was destined for failure; the object of my passion treated me with such indifference that I came to believe I was invisible in his presence. Not long before our final departure from Bolivia, a fight broke out on the playground in which—I shall never know how—I ended up with my arms around my idol, roiling in a dust devil of fists, hair-pulling, and kicking. He was much larger than I and, although I put into practice every trick I had learned at the Teatro Caupolicán wrestling matches with my grandfather, I was bruised and bloody-nosed at the end. In a moment of blind fury, however, one of those ears came within range of my teeth and I had the satisfaction of stealing an impassioned nip. For weeks I walked on air. That was the most erotic encounter of a long lifetime, a combination of intense pleasure from the embrace and no-less-sharp pain from the pummeling. Given that masochistic awakening of lust, another, less fortunate woman might today be the complaisant victim of a sadist's whip, but as it worked out, I never again had occasion to practice that particular hold.

Shortly after, we left Bolivia forever, and I never saw the ears again. Tío Ramón flew directly to Paris, and from there to Lebanon, while my brothers and mother and I made the long descent by train to a port in the north of Chile; from there we took an Italian steamer to Genoa, then a bus to Rome; and from there we flew to Beirut. It was a journey of two months, and I believe it was a miracle my mother survived. We traveled in the last car of the train, in the company of an enigmatic Indian who never spoke a single word and spent the entire trip kneeling on the floor beside a small stove, chewing his coca, scratching his lice, and gripping an archaic rifle. Day and night his small, oblique eyes watched us, his expression impenetrable. We never saw him sleep. My mother was sure that at some unguarded moment he would murder us, even though she had been assured he had been hired to protect us. As the train moved slowly across the desert, inching past dunes and salt mines, my brothers often jumped down and ran alongside. To upset my mother, they would fall behind, feigning exhaustion, and then yell for help because the train was leaving them behind. On the ship, Pancho caught his fingers so often in the heavy metal hatches that finally no one would respond to his howls, and Juan caused an uproar one day by disappearing for several hours. While playing hide-and-seek, he had fallen asleep in an unoccupied state-room; he wasn't found until a blast from the ship's whistle waked him, just as the captain was prepared to back down the engines and lower lifeboats to search for him; in the meantime, two brawny petty officers were forcibly restraining my mother to prevent her from diving into the Atlantic. I fell in love with all the sailors with a passion nearly as violent as that inspired by my young Bolivian, but I suspect they had eyes only for my mother. Although those slender young Italians stirred my imagination, even they could not cure me of my shameful vice of playing with dolls. Locked tight in my stateroom, I rocked them, bathed them, gave them their bottles, and sang in a low voice—in order to hear anyone coming—while my fiendish brothers threatened to take my dolls up on the deck and expose them to the crew. However, when we disembarked in Genoa, both Pancho and Juan, loyal under fire, were carrying a suspicious, towel-wrapped bundle under one arm while I hung behind, sighing, to bid the sailors of my dreams goodbye.

We lived in Lebanon for three surreal years, which allowed me to learn some French and to travel to most of the surrounding countries—including the Holy Land and Israel, which in the decade of the fifties, as now, existed in a permanent state of war with the Arabs. Crossing the border by car, as we did more than once, was a sobering experience. We lived in a large, ugly, modern apartment.

From the terrace, we could look down on a market and the Guard Headquarters that played important roles later when the violence began. Tío Ramón set aside one room for the consulate and hung the shield and flag of Chile on the front of the building. None of my new friends had ever heard of that country; they thought I came from China. In general, in that time and in that part of the world, girls were confined to house and school until the day of their marriage—if they had the misfortune to marry—the moment at which they exchanged a paternal prison for a conjugal one. I was shy, and kept very much to myself.

I rode the school bus every day, the first to be picked up in the morning and the last to be left off in the afternoon. I spent hours circling around the city, an arrangement I liked because I didn't much want to go home. When I was eventually delivered, I often found Tío Ramón sitting in his undershirt beneath the ceiling fan, trying to move more air with a folded newspaper and listening to boleros.

"What did the nuns teach you today?" he would ask.

I particularly remember one day replying, sweating, but phlegmatic and dignified in my dreadful uniform, "They're not nuns, they're Protestant ladies. And we talked about Job."

"Job? That idiot God tested by sending every calamity known to mankind?"

"He wasn't an idiot, Tío Ramón, he was a saintly man who never denied the Lord, no matter how much he suffered."

"Does that seem right? God makes a bet with Satan, punishes poor Job unmercifully, and wants to be loved by him besides. That is a cruel, unjust, and frivolous God. A master who treated his servants that way would deserve neither loyalty nor respect, much less adoration."

Tío Ramón, who had been educated by Jesuits, was intimidatingly emphatic and implacably logical—the same skills he used in squabbles with my mother—as he set out to prove the stupidity of the biblical hero whose attitude, far from setting a praiseworthy example, demonstrated a personality disorder. In less than ten minutes of oratory, he had demolished all Miss St. John's virtuous teachings.

"Are you convinced that Job was a numbskull?"

"Yes, Tío Ramón."

"Will you swear to that in writing?"

"Yes."

The consul of Chile crossed the couple of yards that separated us from his office and composed on letterhead paper a document with three carbons saying that I, Isabel Allende Llona, fourteen years old, a Chilean citizen, attested that Job, he of the Old Testament, was a dolt. He made me sign it, after reading it carefully—"because you must never sign anything blindly"—then folded it and put it in the consulate safe. He went back to his chair beneath the ceiling fan and, heaving a weary sigh, said,

"All right, child, now I shall prove that you were correct in the first place, and that Job was a holy man of God. I shall give you the arguments you should have used had you known how to think. Please understand that I am doing this only to teach you how to debate, something that will be very helpful in life." And he proceeded to dismantle his previous arguments and convince me of what I had firmly believed in the first place. In a very few minutes, I was again defeated, and this time on the verge of tears.

"Do you accept that Job was right to remain faithful to his God despite his misfortunes?"

"Yes, Tío Ramón."

"Are you absolutely sure?"

"Yes."

"Would you sign a document?"

And he composed a second statement that said that I, Isabel Allende Llona, fourteen years old, a Chilean citizen, was retracting my earlier opinion and instead agreeing that Job acted correctly. He handed me his pen, but just as I was about to sign my name at the bottom of the page he stopped me with a yell.

"*No!* How many times have I told you not to let anyone twist your arm? The most important thing in winning an argument is not to vacilate even if you have doubts, let alone if you are wrong!"

That is how I learned to defend myself; and years later in Chile I participated in an intramural debate between our girls' school and San Ignacio, which was represented by five boys with the mien of criminal lawyers and two Jesuit priests whispering instructions to them. The boys' team arrived with a load of books they consulted to support their arguments and intimidate their opponents. My only resource was the memory of those afternoons with Job and my Tío Ramón in Lebanon. I lost, of course, but at the end my team paraded me around on their shoulders as our macho rivals retreated haughtily with their cartload of arguments. I do not know how many statements with three carbons I signed in my adolescence on topics as wildly diverse as biting my fingernails and the threatened extinction of whales. I believe that for a few years Tío Ramón kept some of them—for example, the one in which I swear that it is his fault that I will never meet any men and will end up an old maid. That was in Bolivia, when at age eleven I threw a tantrum because he did not let me go to a party where I thought I would see my beloved Big Ears.

Three years later I was invited to a different party, this one in Beirut at the home of the U.S. ambassador and his wife. That time I had the good sense not to want to go because the girls had to play the part of passive sheep; I was sure that no boy in his right mind would ask me to dance, and I could not think of a worse humiliation than being a wallflower. That time my stepfather forced me to attend because, he said, if I did not overcome my complexes I would never have any success in life. The day before the party, he closed the consulate and dedicated the afternoon to teaching me to dance. With single-minded tenacity he made me sway to the rhythm of the music, first holding the back of a chair, then a broom, and finally him. In several hours I learned everything from the Charleston to the samba. Then he dried my tears and drove me to buy a new dress. As he left me at the party, he offered a piece of unforgettable advice, one I have followed at crucial moments of my life: *Remember that all the others are more afraid than you.* He added that I should not sit down for a second but should take up a position near the record player...oh, and not eat anything, because it takes tremendous courage for a boy to cross a room and go up to a girl anchored like a frigate in her chair and with a plate of cake in her hand. Besides, the few boys who know how to dance are the same ones who change the records, so you want to be near the player.

At the entrance to the embassy, a cement fortress in the worst fifties style, there was a cage of huge black birds that spoke English with a Jamaican accent. I was greeted by the ambassador's wife—in some sort of admiral get-up and with a whistle around her neck for giving instructions to the guests—and led to an enormous room swarming with tall, ugly adolescents with pimply faces, all chewing gum, eating french fries, and drinking Coca-Cola. The boys were wearing plaid jackets and bow ties, and the girls had on circle skirts and angora sweaters that left a flurry of hair in the air but revealed enviable protuberances on their chests. I, on the other hand, had nothing to put in a brassiere. They were all wearing bobby socks. I felt totally alien; my dress was a disaster of taffeta and velvet, and I didn't know a soul there. Panic-stricken, I stood and fed cake crumbs to the black birds until I remembered Tío Ramón's instructions. Trembling, I removed my shoes and headed toward the record player. Soon I saw a male hand stretched in my direction and, unable to believe my luck, was borne off to dance a sugary tune with a boy who had flat feet and braces on his teeth and was not half as graceful as my stepfather. It was the time when everyone danced cheek-to-cheek, a feat usually denied me even today, since my face comes about to a normal man's breastbone; at this party, barely fourteen and not wearing my shoes, my head was at the level of my partner's belly button. After that first ballad, they played a whole record of rock 'n' roll. Tío Ramón had never even heard of that, but all I had to do was watch the others for a few minutes and apply what I had learned the afternoon before. For once, my size and my limber joints were a plus: it was a breeze for my partners to toss me toward the ceiling, twirl me through the air like an acrobat, and catch me just before I broke my neck on the floor. I found myself performing arabesques, lifted, dragged, whipped around, and bounced by a variety of youths who by this point had shed their plaid jackets and bow ties. I had no complaint. I was not a wallflower that night, as I had dreaded, but danced until I raised blisters on my feet, in the process acquiring the assurance that it is not so difficult to meet men after all, and that certainly I would not be an old maid. I did not, however, sign a document to that effect. I had learned not to let anyone twist my arm.

Tío Ramón had a three-sectioned wardrobe that could be taken apart when we moved, in which he locked his clothes and treasures: a collection of erotic magazines, cartons of cigarettes, boxes of chocolates, and liquor. My brother Juan discovered a way to open it with a bent wire, and we became expert sneak thieves. If we had taken only a few chocolates or cigarettes, he would have noticed, but we would sneak an entire layer of chocolates and reseal the box so perfectly it looked unopened, and we filched entire cartons of cigarettes, never a few, or a pack. Tío Ramón first became suspicious in La Paz. He called us in, one by one, and tried to get us either to confess or to inform on the guilty party. Neither gentle words nor threats were any good: we thought that to admit to the crime would be stupid and, in our moral code, betrayal among siblings was unpardonable. One Friday afternoon when we got back from school, we found Tío Ramón and a man we didn't know waiting for us in the living room.

"I have no patience with your disregard for the truth; the least I can expect is not to be robbed in my own home. This gentleman is a police detective. He will take your fingerprints, compare them with the evidence on my wardrobe, and we will know who the thief is. This is your last chance to confess the truth."

Pale with terror, my bothers and I stared at the floor and clamped our jaws shut.

"Do you know what happens to criminals? They rot in jail," Tío Ramón added.

The detective pulled a tin box from his pocket. When he opened it, we could see the black inkpad inside. Slowly, with great ceremony, he pressed each of our fingers to the pad, then rolled them onto a prepared cardboard.

"Have no worry, Señor Consul. Monday you will have the results of my investigation," the man assured Tío Ramón as he left.

Saturday and Sunday were days of moral torture; hidden in the bathroom and the most private corners of the garden, we whispered about our black future. None of us was free of guilt; we would all end up in a dungeon, on foul water and dry bread crusts, like the Count of Monte Cristo. The following Monday, the ineffable Tío Ramón called us into his office.

"I know exactly who the thief is," he announced, wiggling thick, satanic eyebrows. "Nevertheless, out of consideration for your mother, who has interceded in your behalf, I shall not incarcerate anyone this time. The culprit knows I know who he or she is. It will remain between the two of us. I warn all of you that on the next occasion I shall not be so softhearted. Do I make myself clear?"

We stumbled from the room, grateful, unable to believe such magnanimity. We did not steal anything for a long time, but a few years later in Beirut I thought about it again and was struck by the suspicion that the purported detective was actually an embassy chauffeur—Tío Ramón was quite capable of playing such a trick. Bending a wire of my own, I again opened the wardrobe. This time, in addition to the predictable treasures, I found four red leather-bound volumes of *A Thousand and One Nights*. I deduced that there must be some powerful reason these books were under lock and key, and that made them much more interesting than the bonbons, cigarettes, or erotic magazines with women in garter belts. For the next three years, every time Tío Ramón and my mother were at some cocktail party or dinner, I read snatches of the tales, curled up inside the cabinet with my faithful flashlight. Even though diplomats necessarily suffer an intense social life, there was never enough time to finish those fabulous stories. When I heard my parents coming, I had to close the wardrobe in a wink and fly to my bed and pretend to be asleep. It was impossible to leave a bookmark between the pages and I always forgot my place; worse yet, entire sections fell out as I searched for the dirty parts, with the result that innumerable new versions of the stories were created in an orgy of exotic words, eroticism, and fantasy. The contrast between the puritanism of my school, where work was exalted and neither bodily imperatives nor lightning flash of imagination allowed, and the creative idleness and enveloping sensuality of those books branded my soul.

For decades I wavered between those two tendencies, torn apart inside and awash in a sea of intermingled desires and sins, until finally in the heat of Venezuela, when I was nearly forty years old, I at last freed myself from Miss St. John's rigid precepts. Just as in my childhood I hid in the basement of Tata's house to read my favorite books, so in full adolescence, just as my body and mind were awakening to the mysteries of sex, I furtively read *A Thousand and One Nights.* Deep in that dark wardrobe, I lost myself in magical tales of princes on flying carpets, genies in oil lamps, and appealing thieves who slipped into the sultan's harem disguised as old ladies to indulge in marathon love fests with forbidden women with hair black as night, pillowy hips and breasts like apples, soft women smelling of musk and eager for pleasure. On those pages, love, life, and death seemed like a gambol; the descriptions of food, landscapes, palaces, markets, smells, tastes, and textures were so rich that after them the world has never been the same to me.

Section II
Estrangement

Being raised in the global jet stream creates enormous complexities for children. They slipstream around the world, tucking into areas of least resistance, shedding old cultures, donning new. They retain fleeting memories of people and places, live through drama and displacement behind actors' masks, and learn the natural guile of the chronic newcomer. Wherever they land, they must start over. They select cultural totems, and they observe and follow local customs. They learn to silence the loss and pain of frequent separation, and to pretend bravado.

"Certain things happen to make these people encounter great difficulty with who they are, where they're going, and what they want to be," says Dr. Ruth Hill Useem, the sociologist-anthropologist who coined the term *Third Culture Kid*. These children struggle with answering simple questions like "Where are you from?" They belong nowhere. They contend with migratory urges and the conflicting desire to root. Travel, adventure, and danger cause them to mature early, yet they continue to experience confusion about identity, direction, and belonging. Estranged from their parents' home culture and disconnected from their host culture, they proceed through the world identified as chronic outsiders, known only superficially to those around them, longing, in each new home, to establish connection, yet fearful of becoming too attached. The result is a cultural changeling, alienated from self and aloof from others.

"You grow up knowing no one well, least of all yourself," writes Pat Conroy, whose military family was relocated more than twenty times in his childhood. He realized that children learn who they are by "testing and measuring" themselves against friends over many years. But if those measures and friends are always changing, who are you? "I was always leaving behind what I was just about ready to become," he writes, echoing the identity confusion so common to nomadic children.

Camilla Trinchieri's narrative shows the child's ability to survive personal loss and ruptured identity. Born in war-torn Europe to an Italian father and an American mother, her family was continually fractured due to her father's diplomatic assignments, the displacements of war, and her mother's descent into paranoid schizophrenia. Buffeted among countries, shunted among relatives, she endures by remembering the places she lived in but forgetting many of the people she left.

Children of missionaries or military officers are raised to conform to a group identity forged by their parents. Members of the "perfect family," they are expected to be committed, dedicated, patriotic. Moved often, they have little faith in permanence, and may identify completely only with other nomads. Practiced at parting with best friends, unwilling to look back, they seldom write or exchange forwarding addresses. They may inherit their parents' sense of mission, yet they often experience deep loneliness and can feel orphaned by their parents' dedication to God or country. An uneasy restlessness marks them, whether they are missionary kids or military brats.

Life on American military bases is structured by a similitude that feels rigid to many children. Plucked like hothouse flowers from one post and set in a carbon-copy base a state or a continent or an ocean away, theirs is an invisible nation without a capital, a world of unquestioned rules and unbending social status. Pat Conroy, whose autobiographical novel, *The Great Santini*, exploded the myth of the idealized military family and exposed brutality at its core, is among the first voices of the Cold War's child victims. Shuttled from one U.S. military base to another, he suffers "as an act of patriotism" the chronic loneliness of not being permitted to root. He clearly articulates the military child's lack of choice about participating in his parents' mission and his ongoing emotional struggle with the fallout of years of upheaval and personal abuse.

Mary Wertsch, raised on American bases abroad, states candidly, "For the military brat, each time the family moves, the world dissolves and is swept away." She experiences such estrangement as an outsider that she finds she can bond only with other outsiders, and for years she loses herself in relationships with foreign men she knows can only be temporary. Seized by the need to move often, she chafes at the regularity of a stable civilian lifestyle and feels most "at home" with constant change.

In contrast to the cultural isolation of many military families, missionary parents seek connection with local communities, but it often comes at the expense of their own children's emotional needs. Faith Eidse enjoyed the rhythms of African village life and living on the land, as do many missionary children raised in developing nations, but she often felt superseded by the urgency of her parents' mission and their dedication to the needy people around them. Like many others, she was sent away to boarding school at a young age. The experience resulted in a denial of feelings and a chronic fear of commitment to either place or people.

Ruth Van Reken's epistolary story makes immediate the suppressed pain of the child subsumed by the parents' mission. Not allowed by her teachers to write about her loneliness in her letters home from boarding school, she avoids telling the truth about her feelings for years. Silence results, as the child fears ruining her parents' careers by revealing her pain to those who know her best. Instead, she mimics the sacrifice that is modeled so well for her. The protective shell she builds against attachment, loss, or emotions of any kind cracks in her young adulthood. When she is finally able to articulate her anguish, she can confront the pain that consumed so much of her childhood.

Despite her obvious foreign status as a missionary kid in Angola, Nancy Henderson-James attempted to absorb "home" by learning the several languages spoken around her. At age fourteen, she also begged her distracted parents for, and received, an orphan to care for. In this way she hoped to create love, family, and home after years of independent living at boarding school. So seriously did Henderson-James take these cultural imperatives that she sometimes became despondent. But decades later, after war and disconnection, she embraces those years for forming in her a solid identity.

The process of writing is redemptive, helping authors face, understand, and accept a complicated reality. The writers in this section find new connection in writing about their unrooted lives.

Camilla Trinchieri *lives with her husband in Greenwich Village, New York. As Camilla T. Crespi, she has published seven HarperCollins mysteries in The Trouble With series. Words, she's learned, are relatively stable. Born in Prague in the midst of World War II, Trinchieri collects memories of her many childhood homes as though they were beads on a string, and describes the act of writing as "stringing one word after another."*

Trinchieri's family is split and reunited, settled and relocated, many times in her childhood. By the time she is twelve, she has lived in seven cities in six countries. Her memories are "moss," a slippery ground shifting too quickly with language and people. She survives near-constant upheaval and the pain of separation by depersonalizing her memories. She copes with tragedy by developing the "skills" of selective memory, distancing, and denial. She forgets people but not places, which are immovable. "My heart grows impenetrable," she writes. She focuses on what she can take with her: appreciation for place, a facility with language, a cosmopolitan sophistication, and an ability to produce tough skins to match her new surroundings. Though she finds other nomads, she remains an outsider at her core.

A String of Beads

Camilla Trinchieri

"Hey, take me to Siberia and I'll survive," I liked to brag with the shaky bravado of the new kid in town. Thanks to my Italian diplomat father and other vicissitudes, I had lived in seven cities in six countries and learned four languages by the time I was twelve. The memory of these places and the people I met in them are fleeting, snatched as if from a speeding train.

My first stop in life is Prague, Czechoslovakia, the day the Germans destroy the town of Lidice and all its male inhabitants in retaliation for the assassination of Reinhard Heydrich, the protectorate's governor, who was known as the butcher of Bohemia. My American mother, Cathleen, claims she first breast-fed me to the sound of machine gunfire outside the hospital window as the Nazis ambushed Heydrich's killers barricaded inside the church across the street. The dates don't match, but my mother thrives on dramatic stories that will give her life resonance. The Lidice part is true, though.

I went back to Prague ten years ago. It has the faded colors of an old print someone has forgotten to dust. The rush of the Vlatva River filled my ears. The blackened statues of the Charles Bridge filled my nose with the smell of coal that kept my mother warm in this city during the winter when America entered the war. The place evoked no memories, and yet it filled me with great sadness because it was here, in my birthplace, that the threads that held my family together fell apart.

Three months after my birth our mother moves us—three sisters and a brother. My father has taken up his new post in Osijek in the German puppet state of Croatia. A long train ride takes us to Milan (where my father's sister lives to the sound of air-raid sirens and exploding bombs). A few weeks later another train deposits us in the apricot glow of Rome, where the nearby presence of the Vatican will supposedly protect us from Allied bombings. When the Allies bomb Rome, we leave the mewing of the starving Roman cats (who will soon end up on the dinner table as chicken) and head for the Tuscan hills, as many vacationers have done before and since.

We move to the town of Cortona, famous for its steepness and Fra Angelico's *Annunciation*. Before the Germans overrun Italy in September of 1943 and close off the frontier, my brother Paolo, the oldest, and my sister Franca join my father, who is now safe on the warless island of Majorca. He begs for us all to join him, but our mother wants no part of my father. She has also been parting ways with reality since her stay in Prague, but she still clings to us, the baby and Carolita, her "good children." My oldest sister conquers her own fears with obedience and order and is therefore an ideal daughter. She is also gracefully pretty. I cry a lot and refuse to eat, which is a plus with no food around.

The Allies land in Sicily, but contrary to the American movies our mother misses sorely, the "cavalry" doesn't move up the peninsula in a dust cloud to the sound of the bugle. She takes matters into her own hands and hires a taxi to take her north. *"La signora è pazza,"* the neighbors whisper. She is crazy, crazy enough to think the walls have been wired and Hitler hears her; crazy enough to know that if she opens her mouth, her distorted vowel sounds will betray her as an *americana*, the enemy; crazy enough not to wait the ten months that it will take her GIs to march up the boot.

She is crazy enough to have the guts to get us out.

A long expensive taxi ride, which she pays for with all her jewelry and fine clothes, then a quiet stay in a village, Brunate, clustered high above Lake Como, while our mother breathes in the calm of the lake to gather strength. One winter night, guided by a "passer," we walk up the snow-covered Bisbino Mountain, which rises from the other side of the lake. The "passer" digs a ditch in the snow and we scramble under the barbed wire that divides Italy from Switzerland. Twelve-year-old Carolita drags the one suitcase, our mother holds me and the belief that she has walked to safety.

In Switzerland we are met with food, delousing, and quarantine camp.

I have gone back to search for the place and found a school, high above Lake Lugano, which was once a displaced persons camp. I cannot be sure this is where they kept us locked for three months for reasons I still don't understand. Were the Swiss afraid we might taint their own population? With what? Hunger, hopelessness, their own sense of guilt for having turned so many away?

I take a walk around the perimeter of the school and imagine the high fence my mother scaled at night to find eggs—the only food I would eat. It is a pretty place where the air is laced with cool sunlight and the sweetness of pine sap. This is the camp, I decide. I claim it as one of the glass beads on the string that is my life.

After the war is over in Europe, we gather in Rome. My father is left out of this reunion by our mother's orders. I am three years old, which gives me a legitimate excuse for not remembering the meeting at the Rome train station, but perhaps I am already developing a certain skill at selective memory. Momentous occasions do not stay with me, I discover years later in a therapist's office. A parent, a sister is there, then isn't. A friend is for life, then isn't. The ground underneath my feet shifts too quickly, the players and the language change. I am left with the moss of memory, but I will shake that off too when remembering becomes uncomfortable. As I write this, the air around me thins, as if I were suddenly high on a mountaintop. I find it hard to breathe.

Rome after the war is the time of comic-strip food. Cheese is orange and comes from dull green cans. I develop a love for pink-speckled Spam; my sister Franca, three years older, a lifelong hatred for split-pea soup. Carolita and Paolo, both in their teens, go to parties and have a new love each month. Oleander trees line the streets. I pick the fallen flowers off the pavement and wear them in my hair. No one warns me that chewing a leaf can stop my heart. Franca is told by the nuns never to look into a mirror unless she wants to see the devil. Those same nuns tell my mother that I write with the hand of the devil—I am left-handed—but they teach me to embroider and I love them for it. We live mostly in Italian, but when our mother sees Hitler peering at her from the wallpaper, she screams in English.

During our second winter in Rome, our mother disappears. Years later I will discover she was placed in the first of many mental clinics. Paolo and Carolita also disappear, sent to a fancy boarding school in Florida, their tuition paid for by our American grandparents. Franca and I leave the nuns and board a train to Geneva, where my father is posted. We attend a French school. Franca is nine and I am six; we learn the language quickly. I play house with a new metal tea set, red with white polka dots. My father's apartment is compact, neat, filled with the smell of the Russian cigarettes he is always smoking. The dining room is flanked by two rows of tall, leather-covered chairs. He stands by the window, backlit like a saint, holding up a bar of Nestlé chocolate in each hand. Switzerland becomes the brown and silver of the chocolate bars. Brown and silver and red with white polka dots.

I don't remember running away from school in Geneva. My father will tell me years later, one of the few memories he will share from those days. The police were called. My father roamed the city until hours later he found me sitting barefoot by the lake. Why did I run away? Because the lake was beautiful, I told my baffled father. Six years old, I was already keenly aware of place. Place is solid, definable. I can reproduce it with my colored pencils. Badly but recognizably. Place has visible borders. Its history and language are learnable.

Place can be conquered.

In the summer I will lose my footing in the same lake I found so beautiful. The current takes me away from the shore. I don't know how to swim and as I flail and swallow water, I fix my eyes on a white dot growing on the horizon until it is so near I can suddenly float again and the dot has transformed itself into the bathing cap on Carolita's head.

My mother doesn't get better. My father suggests Jung, who is in Switzerland at this time. Her parents instead decide to bring her back to the States with Franca and me. In the Genoa hotel room, the night before embarking on the ship that will take us (including a governess, Giulia) to the States, our mother piles all the furniture of the room against the door. I don't know if she is warding off Hitler or stopping herself from joining her husband who still longs for her, for all of us, back in Geneva.

Leaving my father is another white space in my mind. I imagine he bends over me, lifts me up to hug me tighter. His cheek is rough and smells of the lemony cologne he wore until his death to cancer twenty-one years later. My feet dangle and the skirt of my dress bunches up under his grip. I fill my head with the thought that my underpants must be showing. To think anything else is unbearable.

Of the ocean crossing I remember only a specific moment: a man puffing on his cigarette, extending his arm, and smiling as he pops first Franca's, then my balloon. A melodramatic memory, I admit. My mother would approve.

Next stop is Ancon, the American zone of Panama, where our mother grew up, where my grandfather is an ear, eye, nose, and throat doctor at Walter Reed Hospital, where my two sisters and brother were born.

My grandfather is a balding, round man with sagging eyes and a cigar permanently attached to his teeth. His tobacco-soaked drawl goes straight to my heart. We call him Daddy. My grandmother prefers to be called Mother. She is thin, brittle, with lips she has sucked in for so long they are barely visible. A hair net tightens over her gray head like a hair shirt for the brain. Mother is permanently attached to the Bible and disapproval.

Our mother is nowhere. We ask no questions, afraid of answers. It is hot in Panama. My long hair is cut off, and although I now decide I look hideous, I much prefer ugliness to having to endure hours of hair-pulling by Giulia. Giulia is a large woman, who slaps me when I put my finger between my legs for the first time and, filled with wonder, offer her my exotic smell. She also listens to me, fanning herself on the balcony with a dried palm leaf as I reel off stories I make up as I go along. The heat will defeat her. She takes to wandering through the house in underpants, great big breasts swinging braless. After two months my grim grandmother ships her back to Italy. I miss her only briefly.

Letting go is a skill I am learning to master. As an adult I insult friends by paying no attention when they say goodbye, my mind already focused on what will come next. I am like an animal intent on molting. I learn to shed skins with great agility, remaining naked only long enough to drink in my surroundings, to decide which new skin I should produce. Despite my efforts, what I finally come up with in each new place doesn't quite match the native skin. It doesn't make the grade. I remain the visitor, the stranger. Other. I learn to wear that new, nonmatching skin like a magical dress that shines in the dark. I chatter, I offer opinions based on little fact. I know. I am strong. Sticks and stones can't hurt my bones. My heart grows impenetrable.

Franca and I have never lived in a house before Panama. I am fascinated by the number of empty rooms, small hot rooms where spiders swing in corners and cobwebs glow in the sweep of sunlight. I learn caution and stop walking barefoot. Before going to sleep, I check underneath the pillow for tarantulas. The garden has snakes and a mysterious-looking man with the black hair of a Sicilian and skin the color of the syrup Daddy pours over Sunday pancakes. Pancakes, syrup, and the Indian gardener are part of my new discoveries.

So are Jane, Dick, and Spot. "See Spot run," I read and relate. I am comfortable at school. English is fun. I don't think twice about switching languages. English at school and at home, Spanish everywhere else. Learning a new language gives me the illusion I will win something, even if it's only a gold star on my report card. Too new, too wary, I don't make friends.

I do want to win attention. One morning I announce to the class that it's my birthday. The teacher must know that I'm lying (I'm a June baby—after school is over), but she stands me up in a chair and instructs the class to sing "Happy Birthday" to me. Expecting to be gloriously happy, all I feel is shame.

On Christmas Eve, from the first-floor landing, Franca and I watch Daddy and Mother wrap presents in the living room. The myth of Santa Claus is dispelled in a cloud of cigar smoke. We retreat to our room for a quick powwow. Our new knowledge— well, it's a relief, really. One less surprise, say I. Perhaps, sitting on my Panama bed, I recognize a need to stand on firm ground. Be it good news or bad, I still, in my fifties, want to know what to expect. To make contingency plans. To steel myself. To pretend that, really, it's no big deal. "Hey, take me to Siberia..." It might also explain why I am happiest when barefoot. I feel the ground underneath my feet.

Panama is dark, moist, heavy with cigar smoke. Silent. Sheets of green leaves press against the schoolroom windows. My grand-parents' garden is overrun with banana trees, the underbrush dense with plants whose names I don't bother to learn. Maybe I suspect our stay will last only four months.

By January Franca and I are in a boarding school, this time in Miami. My grandfather has bought a home in Coral Gables—a ranch-style house with rooms white with sunlight. I live for the weekend, when Daddy comes to pick us up. I rush to him, hug him hard around the soft cushion of his belly. I inhale his cigar smell and ask for my weekly present. I want a doll, a pin, a book, anything I can squeeze in my hand, then place in a drawer where, tomorrow, I will find it again, unscathed, exactly as I had left it. I believe only in tangibles.

On Sundays we attend a Southern Baptist service. This is an American religion. Democratic. Everyone joins in the singing. We drink grape juice together and shake our neighbor's hand at the end of the service. This sharing makes me uncomfortable. I miss the statues of the saints, the protectors, the intercessors to whom you can make requests. I miss the pomp and the ritual that keeps the worshipper at an adoring distance. A few years later, back in Italy, I will declare my intention to become a nun, attracted more by the absolutes of Catholicism and the idea of belonging to a tight-knit community than by any communion with God.

I learn to love money. Franca discovers that I squirrel away the nickel Daddy gives me each Sunday morning for the poor box. She is horrified, but when she runs out of money, which is often, she comes to me and I hand out those nickels with a lord's largesse. I will continue to save money; it makes me feel safe. When I am thirty-eight and desperate to leave a bad relationship, money will allow me to cross the ocean and start all over. I become a spend-thrift only when it comes to presents. I suspect they are a way of marking my path through people's lives.

At the Miami boarding school I'm chosen to perform as one of the second-grade class clowns for the end-of the-year festivities. I'm ecstatic until I discover I'll have to turn a somersault. "I don't know how," I protest. "My head will split open!" A teacher sits down on the grass and shows me a new way. Her attention lures me. I find myself crossing my legs, leaning forward. I close my eyes. Her hand presses the small of my back. For an instant I seem to fall off the world. Then the sun is on my face again. I open my eyes. I am sitting upright. Safe, with a giddy sense of accomplishment. It is my first positive lesson in trust. Hopelessly in love, I tell myself that this woman with brown hair curling behind her ears will be my teacher. Next year and the year after that. For always maybe.

In a hospital up north, doctors give my mother's behavior a name: paranoid schizophrenia. Daddy decides spending money for a nonexistent cure makes no sense. Our mother is shipped home to the Florida ranch house. My brother and sister are also in Florida, in boarding school, but I don't recall their presence. Again my memory supplies only melodrama: my mother slapping Daddy's secretary for dressing me improperly, whacking Franca's head for talking to Hitler on the street corner.

Slowly it dawns on my grandparents that ours is a center that cannot hold. The younger children have to go.

My mind goes blank again. School was out, I was told years later. Carolita and Daddy's secretary packed our things and we were whisked off to New York and a ship. My mother, unsuspecting, was told ours was only a summer visit to our father. Later in life she will claim she was locked in her room and was told nothing.

Carolita takes Franca and me to Europe on the ship *Sobieski*. She is much in demand by men who wear carnations in the lapel of their white dinner jackets. I watch her going off to a dance in a gray and pink tulle dress, her blonde hair neatly turned in a silken bob. She is the mother any girl would dream of: popular, beautiful, poised, as steady as the ship's tables bolted to the dining room floor. Before the trip is over, she sits me up on the bathroom stool and curls my hair by tying it with white ribbons. I become Shirley Temple and Elizabeth Taylor curled into one dizzily happy girl.

My memory's shutter is locked tight when it comes to meeting my father again. Not even two years of therapy will give me a glimmer. What I don't forget is place.

1949, Salzburg, my sixth stop in seven years. The house, the newly formed Italian Consulate, is gigantic to my child's eye. A mustard yellow with pine green shutters, looped by a white graveled driveway that once held carriages. In the back, a lawn for croquet and leisurely picnics. A thick wooded area waits to one side. Just inside the massive wrought-iron gates, a wooden bridge crosses over a stream filled with rainbow trout. I am looking at a castle, something out of one of the storybooks I am addicted to. It even has a name—Rupertihof. House of Rupert.

I am a migrating bird who has landed, where? In the right place? For how long? I slip off my shoes, my knee socks. I bear my weight on one foot and let the warmth of the wood climb up my leg and meld me to the spot on the bridge.

At the end of the summer Carolita goes back to the U.S. to begin college. She wears a white dress with red cherries. The dress recedes in my mind until it is a small white dot, the same white dot of her bathing cap, which grew large and luminous as it cut through the water to catch me. Except now I'm the one who wants to catch her.

Franca and I go to the American school set up for the children of American troops. I am in third grade. We now have an Austrian governess who insists on sending me to school in thick brown ribbed stockings. With my long, skinny legs, I look like Pinocchio and feel just as wooden. The American girls wear saddle shoes and bobby socks, and they stick together. My protests with the governess get me nowhere.

Or maybe they do. After a few weeks my father takes me out of the American school. It is expensive and I am still young enough to adapt, to learn a new language easily. As yet, I speak no German and have to be put back a year in the Austrian school, which sits on top of a hill. There is no room in the girls' section of second grade. I end up the only girl in an all boys' class. It occurs to no one that I might be lost in this new arrangement.

What possessed my father, I still ask myself. Maybe he assumed a strength I didn't have, or maybe he didn't give it that much thought. What is a child's comfort compared to what the world had just been through? Even though the people I met seemed full of good spirits, the memories of the devastation still had to be sharp and the future not yet determined. Nearby, Vienna, where my father worked two or three days a week, was a tense, *The Third Man* place. The city, divided into four zones by the conquering troops, allows no one to travel from one zone to the other without showing a passport at each roadblock. Rumors abound about mysterious killings, about the black market in American goods, mostly about Russians with shaved heads and dirty faces. Already the bad guys, they are seen entering the other zones in black limousines and kidnapping people off the street in broad daylight.

Salzburg, on the other hand, seems an idyllic, pine-covered oasis. Many people visit us. They smoke, drink, and go on and on about the music festival. *Otello* with Del Monaco and Tebaldi. Tannhauser. Jederman. My father takes them to Berchtesgarten in West Germany, to the Berghof, Hitler's retreat in the mountains, which is now an empty shell with breathtaking views. He walks his guests around the many lakes of Austria, through woods to gather strawberries and blueberries the size of rosary beads. At night our father gives dinner parties where the first course is always rainbow trout from our stream, covered in pale yellow mayonnaise he teaches me to make. I elect to be the trout decorator. The fish arrive at the table covered with scales of pimento and petals of slivered black olives. A Romanian woman with dark red nails and hennaed hair appears for week-long stays. She speaks seven languages and brings us presents. Franca hates her. I like the presents and am glad, when we go for walks, that there are four of us: a man, a woman, and two children. It doesn't occur to me that maybe Franca and I are in our father's way. He did not ask for us. We are a weighty package that our grandparents sent.

The Salzburg school is only a couple of miles away and I walk there as long as the weather allows. The teacher is a tall, red-haired man who limps and wears lederhosen even when the temperature outside is below zero. His knees are the color of his hair. He calls on me often to stand by his desk and read out loud to the class. German comes easily although I never take to Gothic script. Those double *sss* standing for ß seem a useless complication. I pick up the Salzburg dialect from my classmates. After my father's guests have eaten trout, game, and strudel, I curl down under the table and entertain them by talking with Lisle. She is an invention of my mind, the perfect friend, trustworthy, available whenever I need her. She is a Salzburg native and we speak in her dialect, a dialect that singles us out in my house. Our father and the housekeeper are Italian, the governess is German, Franca and I speak English to each other. The Salzburg dialect becomes the language of the heart, of secrets.

When Lisle and I aren't performing for my father's guests, we lock ourselves in the bathroom. I tell her how much I hate school. How red-headed men make me sick. How my teacher's skin reminds me of boiled-over milk. I tell her in a whisper that while I stand in front of the class, reading out loud, the teacher slips his hand in my underpants. How I squeeze my thighs shut and make sure not to miss a single letter of that Gothic script while that hand travels around my buttocks.

To my father I confess only that the teacher ties my left hand to the chair so that I will learn to write with my right hand. My father intervenes. By the end of the week, I may write with whatever hand I choose. The teacher still calls on me to read.

In the summer Salzburg becomes idyllic once again. We form a gang of pirates with the children of the new consulate. Our ships are the Oak and the Chestnut. Our target for plunder is the neighboring orchard, rich with apricots and plums. There are four of us. Mario, the oldest, is head pirate. A slick of dark brown hair keeps falling over his eyes. The handsomest boy I've ever seen. Franca, fearless at climbing trees, is named second in charge. Mario's sister Edda, a doughy girl covered in freckles, comes next. Scullery maid is the position I choose; I get to stay low on the ground to clean the fruit the others steal.

Under one of the pines behind the stream I sit on Mario's lap and receive my first kiss. As a gang we ride bikes through woods, gather pine cones, blueberries, and the prickly burrs of chestnut trees and sell them as souvenirs to my father's guests. Mario and I kiss some more until a new governess (this one is American and pines for her absent husband) tells my father.

My brother Paolo comes to visit. He decides I need disciplining and makes me copy pages and pages from the book, *Bambi*. I hate him for it, but maybe it is now, while struggling to write all those words, that I first fall in love with the act of stringing one word after another and discovering the cumulative power of that effort. A few years later, when I am most lost, I will come up with my own words to copy.

Salzburg has many colors in my memory—the yellow of Rupertihof, the pale yellow of my father's homemade mayonnaise, the blue of plums and blueberries, the boiled white skin of my teacher's hand, the red nails of my father's Romanian girlfriend. It has the smell of hot apricot dumplings shining with sugar, the lemon scent of my father's just-shaved cheek, the wet-dog smell of Artucello, my father's boxer. The sound of the crunch of bicycles racing around the gravel drive. Franca's misaligned notes on the piano. Louisa's violin playing. Cow bells in the fields as I walk to school. Yodeling. The tick of the teacher's pen against his desk as he scans the class to pick his next reader. Most of all I hear the wooden bridge by the gate of Rupertihof crack under the weight of my father's car as he leaves for and comes back from Vienna—a metronome keeping the rhythm of parental presence.

One winter flanked by two summers is the length of our Austrian stay. Rome is next. We live in a dark, rented apartment near the Via Veneto and are sent to the Overseas School of Rome. We discover global nomads like ourselves, brats of diplomats, the military, businessmen. I forget German, the Salzburg accent. Lisle has stayed behind in Salzburg with our pirate gang and my father's dog. I make new friends: Ann, who is English and sucks on garlic cloves in class. Babs, whose father is an American journalist. The ballerina Sonia, whose mother is both French and Russian. I belong among these nomads, I should feel at home, and yet the core of me stays on the edge of the carpet. A strategic position that offers the safest view.

No letters cross the Atlantic in either direction. The only reminder I have of my mother is a five-by-seven photograph in a creamy white cardboard frame on my bedside table. Carolita and Paolo sit in several leather-framed photos in the living room. Palmira enters our life—a housekeeper with Betty Grable hair and pillow cheeks. She wears ruffles and has a boyfriend who sports an inch-long nail on his little finger to better pick his nose and count the pink sheets of lire Palmira hands over every payday. Palmira smiles a lot, teaches me to iron, and beats up eggs and sugar into a frothy zabaglione each morning to fatten me up. The Romanian lady now lives in Rome.

We have cats who howl when in heat and get poisoned by the neighbors for their passion.

Clare Boothe Luce—American Ambassador to Rome—awards me a poetry book for the best grades at the end of fourth grade. She is a gawky stork in her pale long dress and silly white hat. I am proud of the book. I will reread the poems often and choose "La

Belle Dame Sans Merci" as my favorite. Yet I know that this prize is undeserved. I repeated second grade; I am a year older than my classmates.

The school lets me skip fifth grade to catch up. In sixth grade I refuse to learn the Gettysburg Address and I cheat on an exam. My new teacher, Mrs. Kramer, who has thick hair and lips, is forgiving. By the end of the year I become a class leader. I am also conceited, sarcastic, a know-it-all. I tell dirty jokes that scandalize one mother. My father reprimands me with a twinkle in his eye. I learned the jokes from him.

In 1954, my father accepts the post of Consul General in New Orleans. Now we will be closer to Carolita and Paolo. And to my mother.

At the New York docks, we wait forever for my father's car—a new Jaguar—to come out of the ship's hold. With his suave Italian accent, he protests to a dock worker, "I'm the Italian Consul General!"

The reply comes quickly, "You could be the King of England, you still have to wait like everyone else."

I have just learned an important American lesson.

On our drive down to New Orleans, we visit Paolo, now in boot camp. Everyone there calls him Paul. Carolita, who is Carol to everyone but me and our father, has just graduated from Wellesley and comes to live with us.

Franca goes to McGhee's, an all-girls private high school which has a reputation of being snotty. I get lucky. The School of the Sacred Heart has no room for me in the seventh grade. I end up at another private school—Isidore Newman. Richard, who will become a great friend, tells me on my second day that I don't look Italian because I'm not dark and greasy. To defend my country, I take to school a picture of the Italian ambassador. Manlio Brosio is blue-eyed, at least six feet tall, and reed-thin.

We need a dog, Carolita decides, convinced our lopsided household will gain an air of normality. For our father's birthday we get him a female cocker spaniel. He calls her Lollo after Gina Lollobrigida. He never gets attached to the dog—she is too sweet, too passive, she is a she. I am wary of Lollo for different reasons. How long will we keep her?

At school, I refuse anyone's attempt to call me Camy, Millie, Cams, Trink. I'm giving myself airs, some decide. I don't explain that there isn't much in my life that isn't changeable, fleeting. My name, every letter of it, has become as vital to me as my spinal chord. My classmates are curious. How many languages do I speak? Why don't I wear white socks or felt skirts with poodles stitched on them? Why did I try out for cheerleading in a tight skirt? (I didn't make the team.) They are most curious about my missing mother. I come up with the "Take me to Siberia" line. Sometimes I add, "You'd never make it." It shuts them up.

Looking back, I'd like to think my snootiness and sarcasm were another way of digging a protective moat around myself. "I can't be one of you, so look how different, special I am." I even try to distinguish myself from Franca who is sunny and sweet where I am dark and bossy. Maybe it's an errant gene that makes me so unpleasant. Today, a happy woman, I'm still rough around the edges.

In my first year in New Orleans I string my first words together—short melodramatic stories about unhappy people. My English teacher suggests I write what I know. But I know nothing. I'm just rolling along here. To know is to look back, to gather information, distill it, make sense of it. I want none of that. To encourage me, Mr. Akers gives me an "A" in content. Grammar is another matter. Grammar is locked in by rules I haven't mastered. I get a "D" in grammar.

There is much I have to learn besides the proper English use of the conditional. Walking down the street, a classmate is shocked when I try to hold her hand as I have always done with friends in Rome. "Only lesbians do that," she whispers. I don't know who lesbians are, but I keep my mouth shut. One morning on the way to school I sit in the back of the streetcar and am told by a tiny black woman that I am in the wrong place. I learn to jitterbug to Bill Haley and the Comets. I excel in French. I make pralines and cool them on the marble countertop next to the sink of the dark kitchen in the back of the Consulate, a grand white house on St.

Charles Avenue in the Garden District. The house has since been torn down and replaced by modern apartments. Always a parrot, I conquer the New Orleans drawl. I dream to Johnny Mathis and Sinatra. Elvis leaves me cold, but I get my hair cut in a ducktail. I slip pennies into my new loafers, but I refuse to wear white socks. I will always prefer a straight skirt. I am a teenager and filled with contradictions.

One year after our arrival Carolita gets married and leaves after a huge wedding, which my grandparents attend without my mother. I watch her drive off, elegant in her dark Italian-tailored suit, with her lumbering, heavy-voiced American husband. I will miss the way her blonde hair touches her jaw and the weight of her tall presence in the green painted breakfast room we use as a dining room. I will miss her curt efficiency in running the household. But, I tell myself, this time I don't mind her leaving. Not really. I'll take over her vast bedroom with the screened-in porch where I can watch the streetcar trundle through the live oak trees lining the avenue. I'll be able to thicken my eyelashes with blue mascara and watch all the television I want. My father is too busy with his work and his new friends to pay much attention. The new housekeeper, Giulietta, is too busy cooking and learning English. I'll be in control.

We stay five years in New Orleans. I visit with my mother every summer for a week. I feel no attachment. We share no history. She looks dirty. Her fingers are stained with nicotine, her nails are purple with the iodine she paints on them to keep them strong. We never touch. I'm ashamed of her. What she thinks of me I don't know.

My father is transferred to Boston while I'm in eleventh grade. Starting a new school in twelfth grade will be disastrous, the headmistress of Newman decides. Barnard College accepts me.

My father goes off to Boston in his new Mercedes, refusing to take our cocker spaniel with him. Friends of his take Lollo away. It doesn't occur to me to protest. Discarding friends, houses, dogs, is a given. I stay first with one friend, then another while I go through summer school to satisfy my requirements.

New Orleans becomes many shades of pink from the camellias in the back garden. The city is also the champagne color of Lollo curled up on Franca's bed, the shiny white of Carolita's wedding dress, the gray-blue of my father's Jaguar that we washed every weekend in Audubon Park. It is the sound of mosquitoes, the St. Charles streetcar bell outside my bedroom window, my Italian shoes beating a jitterbug rhythm for the first time. It is the smell of caramelizing sugar, the taste of my first forbidden Hurricane at Pat O'Brien's.

During my last Miami visit with my mother, she asks me what I want to do in my life. I've stopped writing by now. My mind has to stand still for too long. The theater, I think. To dress up in someone else's skin is easy for me, familiar. "I want to act," I tell her. "Follow your dreams," she says. I feel those words press against my back, pushing me forward to turn that somersault. Follow my dreams. It's a possibility I have never considered before. I look back at this woman with her unkempt hair and purple fingernails. I allow myself to recognize her.

My father is transferred to France my senior year at Barnard. I want to stay in America but my father says no. I join him in Toulouse for six months, then leave him to live with Franca in Rome. I stay in the Eternal City sixteen years, working in the film business. When my personal life collapses, Rome becomes just another bead to string. I pack up, sell my house just north of the city, and return to New York where I remember being happiest.

I start over. I grow a new skin. I meet a soft-spoken Virginian and get married. I begin writing again, but this time I add humor to my dramas. My books get published. Slowly I've started to reach inside to write what I've gathered in my travels. The images from the past, always snatched as if from a moving train, begin to stay with me. They are solidifying into a whole, becoming a story I want to read.

Last week I walked along the beach, barefoot. To one side of me was the Atlantic Ocean, on the other America. It was raining hard. Overnight the ocean waves had knocked the sand back into a high wall. A hurricane was wreaking havoc further south. I dug my feet into the wet sand and thought of how far I'd come from Prague, how many layers of skin I had shed along the way. There have been moments when I have screamed with loneliness, days when I have tried imagining one town, one whole family, one school, the same friends from kindergarten through high school. It's beyond me.

I am grateful, in the end, for what my global childhood has given me. Composure. Sophistication. Street smarts. A tough skin. The ability to glide through social gatherings, to listen, to watch, to constantly assess my surroundings. The strength to walk away from a bad life into a good one. After sixteen years in America I finally took the oath of allegiance. I am now a citizen.

When I finally left the beach to walk inland, I didn't put my shoes back on. The gravel on the road was sharp and pricked my feet. It felt great.

Pat Conroy, *whose unflinching gaze exposed the hypocrisy of the "perfect" military family, identifies military "brats" as forming a separate nation within the boundaries of the United States, an "unorganized tribe" united by their common nomadic experience. They are "strangers everywhere and nowhere." The son of a Marine Corps fighter pilot, he moved more than twenty times in his childhood, attending eleven schools in twelve years. Silence, invisibility, and easy adaptation were expected of him as unwritten rules of the road. He built his own protective shell from the materials his mother provided, the "excuse or rationalization" that kept them all going despite loss and pain. It permitted him to leave his best friend without regret, to "close the door and not look back."*

Conroy divulged both the "truth and cliché" of domestic violence in the military by revealing the beatings his family "unwitnessed" rather than compromise their mission. It was only after his father retired that Conroy drafted his searing best-seller, The Great Santini. *He wept as he wrote of "the ancient shame of a son who cannot protect his mother... a father who could love him only with his fists," a safety felt only when the country was at war with more distant enemies. For his courage, Conroy had to face the hostility of officers' wives who, like his mother until her divorce, were invested in the myth of the perfect family.*

Undiscovered Nation

Pat Conroy

I was born and raised on federal property. America itself paid all
the costs for my birth and my mother's long stay at the hospital.
I was a military brat—one of America's children in the profound-
est sense—and I was guaranteed free medical care and subsidized
food and housing until the day I finished college and had to turn
in the ID card that granted me these rights and privileges. The
sound of gunfire on rifle ranges strikes an authentic chord of home
in me even now. My father was a fighter pilot in the United States
Marine Corps and fought for his country in three wars. I grew up
invisibly in the aviator's house. We became quiet as bivalves at
his approach and our lives were desperate and sad. But when the
United States needed a fighter pilot, we did our best to provide one.
Our contribution to the country was small, but so were we most of
the time, and we gave all that we could.

I think being a military brat is one of the strangest and most
interesting ways to spend an American childhood. The military
brats of America are an invisible, unorganized tribe, a federation
of brothers and sisters bound by common experience, by our uniformed fathers, by the movement of families being rotated through
the American mainland and to military posts in foreign lands.
We are an undiscovered nation living invisibly in the body poli-
tic of this country. There are millions of us scattered throughout
America, but we have no special markings or passwords to iden-

tify each other when we move into a common field of vision. We grew up strangers to ourselves. We passed through our military childhoods unremembered. We were transients, billboards to be changed, body temperatures occupying school desks for a short time. We came and went like rented furniture, serviceable when you needed it, but unremarked upon after it was gone.

I was "drafted" into the Marine Corps on October 26, 1945, and I "served" the Corps faithfully and proudly for 21 years. I moved more than 20 times and I attended 11 schools in 12 years. My job was to be a stranger, to know no one's name on the first day of school, to be ignorant of all history and flow and that familial sense of relationship and proportion that makes a town safe for a child.

By necessity, I made my own private treaty with rootlessness and spent my whole life trying to fake or invent a sense of place. *Home* is a foreign word in my vocabulary and always will be. At each new base and fresh assignment, I suffered through long months of trying to catch up and learning the new steps required of those outsiders condemned to inhabit the airless margins of a child's world. None of my classmates would ever remember my name when it was time to rotate out the following summer. My family drifted in and out of that archipelago of Marine bases that begins with the Pentagon in Arlington, Virginia, and stretches down the coast to Parris Island in the South. I spent most of my childhood in North Carolina and not a single person in North Carolina knows that salient fact. I've been claimed as native son by more than a few southern states, but not by the one I spent the most time in as a child.

I've spent my life and my writing career thinking I was southern. That was only partly true and a tribute to my mother's fiery sense of belonging to the South. I know now that I'm something else entirely. I come from a country that has no name. No Carolinian, no Georgian, has ever been as close to me and what I am in my blood than those military brats who lived out their childhoods going from base to base.

My mother, the loveliest of Marine wives, always claimed to her seven children that we were in the middle of a wonderful, free-flowing life. Since it was the only life I'd ever lived, I had no choice but to believe her. She also provided me with the raw material for the protective shell I built for myself. As excuse or rationalization, it gave me comfort in the great solitude I was born into as a military brat. My mother explained that my loneliness was an act of patriotism. She knew how much the constant moving bothered me, but she convinced me that my country was somehow safer because my formidable, blue-eyed father practiced his deadly art at air stations around the South. We moved almost every year preparing for that existential moment (this is no drill, son) when my violent father would take to the air against enemies more fierce than his wife or children.

That was a darker part of my service to my country. I grew up thinking my father would one day kill me. I never remember a time when I was not afraid of my father's hands except for those bright, balmy years when Dad was waging war or serving in carrier-based squadrons overseas. I used to pray that America would go to war or for Dad to get overseas assignments that would take him to Asian cities I'd never heard of. Ironically, a time of war for the United States became both respite and separate peace for my family. When my father was off killing the enemy, his family slept securely, and not because he was making the world safe for democracy.

My mother would not let us tell anyone that Dad was knocking us around. My silence was simply another facet of my patriotism. My youth filled up with the ancient shame of a son who cannot protect his mother. It would begin with an argument and the Colonel's temper would rise (one did not argue with the Colonel or the Major or the Captain or the Lieutenant). He would backhand my mother, and her pitiful weeping would fill the room. Her seven children, quiet as Spartans, would lower their eyes and say nothing.

Later, my mother would recover and tell us that we had not seen what we had just seen. She turned us into unwitnesses of our own history. I breathed not a word of these troubling scenes to my teachers, coaches, relatives, or friends of the family. If asked, I think I'd have denied under torture that my father ever laid a hand on me. If the provost marshal had ever arrested my father for child abuse, his career in the Marine Corps would have ended at that moment. So my mother took her beatings and I took mine. My brothers and sisters, too, did their part for the Corps. We did not squeal and we earned our wings in our father's dark and high-geared squadron.

To this day, my father thinks I exaggerate the terror of my childhood. I exaggerate nothing. Mine was a forced march of blood and tears and I was always afraid in my father's house. But I did it because I had no choice and because I was a military brat conscripted at birth who had a strong and unshakeable sense of mission. I was in the middle of a long and honorable service to my country, and part of that service included letting my father practice the art of warfare against me and the rest of the family.

The military life marked me out as one of its own. I'm accustomed to order, to a chain of command, to a list of rules at poolside, a spit-shined guard at the gate, retreat at sunset, reveille at dawn, and everyone in my world must be on time. Being late was unimaginable in the world I grew up in, so I always arrive at appointments early and find it difficult to tolerate lateness in others. I always know what time it is even when I don't carry a watch.

I thought I was singular in all this; I later discovered that I speak in the multitongued, deep-throated voice of my tribe. I have a visa to an invisible city where I'm welcomed as a native son. I speak a language I was not even aware I spoke. Military brats of America are an indigenous subculture with our own customs, rites of passage, forms of communication, and folkways. When I wrote *The Great Santini,* I thought I'd lived a life like no other child in this country. I had no clue that with *The Great Santini,* I had accidentally broken into the heart of both the military brat's truth and cliché. This great family of military brats has had no voice because we've assimilated so well into the slipstreams of American life. We've only recently found ways of reaching out to each other, letting each other know we were around, that we endured and even

110

prospered in our trial by father and the permanent transiency of our sturdy breed. We are brothers and sisters who belong to a hidden, unpraised country.

This is my paradox. Because of the military life, I'm a stranger everywhere and a stranger nowhere. I can engage anyone in a conversation, become well-liked in a matter of seconds, yet there is a distance I can never recover, a slight shiver of alienation, of not belonging, and an eye on the nearest door. The word *goodbye* will always be a killing thing to me, but so is the word *hello*. I'm pathetic in my attempts to make friends with everyone I meet, from cabdrivers to bellhops to store clerks. As a child my heart used to sink at every new move or new set of orders. By necessity, I became an expert at spotting outsiders. All through my youth I was grateful for unpopular children. In their unhappiness, I saw my chance for rescue and I always leapt at it. When Mary [Wertsch] writes of military brats offering emotional blank checks to everyone in the world, she's writing the first line in my biography.

Yet I can walk away from best friends and rarely think of them again. I can close a door and not look back. There's something about my soul that's always ready to go, to break camp, to unfold the road map, to leave at night when the house inspection's done and the civilians are asleep and the open road is calling to the Marine and his family again. I left twenty towns at night singing the Marine Corps hymn and it's that hymn that sets my blood on fire each time I hear it, and takes me back to my ruined and magnificent childhood.

I brought so few gifts to the task of being a military brat. You learn who you are by testing and measuring yourself against the friends you grow up with. The military brat lacks those young, fixed critics who form opinions about your character over long, unhurried years or who pass judgment on your behavior as your personality waxes and wanes during the insoluble dilemma that is childhood. But I do know the raw artlessness of being an outsider.

Each year I began my life all over again. I grew up knowing no one well, least of all myself, and I think it damaged me. I grew up not knowing if I was smart or stupid, handsome or ugly, interesting or insipid. I was too busy reacting to the changing landscapes and climates of my life to get any clear picture of myself. I was always leaving behind what I was just about ready to become. I could never catch up to the boy I might have been if I'd grown up in one place.

In 1972, my book *The Water Is Wide* came out when I was living in Beaufort, South Carolina. It was not the most popular book in South Carolina during that season, but it was extremely popular at the Beaufort Air Station, where the Marines and their wives looked to me as a living affirmation of the military way of life. I accepted an invitation to speak to the Marine Corps officers' wives' club with the deep sense that some circle was being closed. Seven years earlier my mother had been an officer in the same club and she'd produced the first racially integrated program in the club's history. Neither of us knew that my speech would mark a turning point in both our lives.

Instead of talking about my new book and my experiences teaching on Daufuskie Island, I spoke of some things I wanted to say about the Marine Corps family. I was the son of a fighter pilot, as were a lot of their kids, and I had some things to tell them. I was the first military brat who'd ever spoken to the club—I was a native son. I could hear the inheld breath of these women as I approached the taboo subject of the kind of husbands and fathers I thought Marines made. For the first time in my life I was hanging the laundry of my childhood out to dry. I told those women of the Corps that I'd met many good soldiers in my life, but precious few good fathers. I also told them of my unbounded admiration for my mother and other military wives I'd met during my career as a brat. But I told those women directly that they shouldn't let their Marines beat them or their children.

I thought I was giving a speech, but something astonishing was unleashed in that room that day. Some of the women present that day hated me, but some liked me very much. The response was electric, passionate, immediate. Some of the women approached me in tears, others in rage. But that talk to the officers' wives was the catalyst that first made me sit down and start writing the outline of *The Great Santini*.

A year later, the day after my father's retirement parade, my mother left my father after thirty-three years of marriage. Their divorce was ferocious and bitter, but it contained, miraculously, the seeds of my father's redemption. Alone and without the Corps, he realized that his children were his enemies and that all seven of us thought he hated our guts. The American soldier is not taught to love his enemy or anyone else. Love did not come easily to my father, but he started trying to learn the steps after my mother left him. It was way too late for her, but his kids were ready for it. We'd been waiting all our lives for our Dad to love us.

I had already begun the first chapters of *The Great Santini*. I wrote about a seventeen-year-old boy, a military brat who'd spent his whole life smiling and pretending that he was the happiest part of a perfect, indivisible American family. I had no experience in writing down the graffiti left along the margins of a boy's ruined heart. Because I was born a male, I had never wept for the boy who'd once withstood the slaps and blows of one of the Corps' strongest aviators. I'd never wept for my brothers or sisters or my beautiful and loyal mother, yet I'd witnessed those brutal seasons of their fear and hurt and sadness. Because I was born to be a novelist, I remembered every scene, every beating, every drop of blood shed by my sweet and innocent family for America.

As I wrote, the child of the military in me began to fall apart. I came apart at the seams. For the one thing a military brat is not allowed to do is commit an act of treason. I learned the hard way that truth is a capital offense and so did my family. I created a boy named Ben Meecham and I gave him my story. His loneliness, his unbearable solitude almost killed me as I wrote about him. Everything about the boy hurt me, but I kept writing the book because I didn't know how to stop. My marriage would fall apart and I'd spend several years trying to figure out how not to be crazy because the deep sadness of Ben Meecham and his family touched me with a pity I could not bear. His father could love him only with his fists and I found myself inconsolable as I wrote this. I would

113

stare at pictures of myself taken in high school and could not imagine why any father would want to hit that boy's face. I wrote *The Great Santini* through tears, hating everything my father stood for and sickened by his behavior toward his family.

But in the acknowledgment of this hatred, I also found myself composing a love song to my father and to the military way of life. Once, when I read *Look Homeward, Angel* in high school, I'd lamented the fact that my father didn't have an interesting, artistic profession like Thomas Wolfe's stonecutter father. But in writing *Santini,* I realized that Thomas Wolfe's father never landed jets on aircraft carriers at night, wiped out a battalion of North Korean regulars crossing the Naktong River, or flew to Cuba with his squadron with the mission to clear the Cuban skies of MIGs if the flag went up.

In writing *The Great Santini* I had to consider the fact of my father's heroism. His job was extraordinarily dangerous and I never knew it. He never once complained about the perils of his vocation. He was one of those men who make the men of other nations pause before attacking America. I learned that I would not want to be an enemy soldier or tank when Don Conroy passed overhead. My father had made orphans out of many boys and girls in Asia during those years I prayed for God to make an orphan out of me. His job was to kill people when his nation asked him to, pure and simple. And the loving of his kids was never written into his job description.

When my mother left my father she found, to her great distress, that she was leaving the protective embrace of the Corps that she'd served for more than thirty years. She was shaken and disbelieving when a divorce court granted her $500 a month in child support, but informed her she was not entitled to a dime of his retirement pay. The court affirmed that it was the Colonel who had served his country so valiantly, not she. But she'd been an exemplary wife of a Marine officer and it was a career she had carried with rare grace and distinction. Peg Conroy made the whole Marine Corps a better place to be, but her career had a value of nothing when judged in a court of law. My mother died thinking that the Marine Corps had not done right by her. She had always considered herself and her children to be part of the grand design of the military, part of the mission.

There are no ceremonies to mark the end of our career as military brats, either. We simply walk out into our destinies, into the dead center of our lives, and try to make the most of it. After my own career as a military child ended in 1967, I received not a single medal of good conduct, no silver chevrons or leaves, no letter of commendation or retirement parade. I simply walked out of one life and into another. My father cut up my ID card in front of me and told me he'd kill me if he ever caught me trying to buy liquor on base. I had the rest of my life to think about the coming of age of a military child.

I imagined that all of us could meet on some impeccably manicured field, all the military brats, in a gathering so vast that it would be like the assembling of some vivid and undauntable army. We could come together on this parade ground at dusk, million voiced and articulating our secret anthems of hurt and joy. We could praise each other in voices that understand both the magnificence and pain of our transient lives. Our greatest tragedy is that we don't know each other. Our stories could help us to see and understand what it is we all have lived through and endured.

At the end of our assembly, we could pass in review in a parade of unutterable beauty. As brats, we've watched a thousand parades on a thousand weekends. We've shined shoes and polished brass and gotten every bedroom we ever slept in ready for Saturday morning inspection. A parade would be a piece of cake for the military brats of the world.

I would put all of our fathers in the reviewing stand, and require that they come in full dress uniform and in the prime of life. I want our fathers handsome and strong and feared by all the armies of the world the day they attend our parade.

To the ancient beat of drums we could pass by those erect and silent rows of fathers. What a fearful word *father* is to so many of us, but not on this day, when the marchers keep perfect step and the command for "eyes right" roars through our disciplined ranks and we turn to face our fathers in that crowd of warriors.

In this parade, these men would understand the nature and the value of their children's sacrifice for the first time. Our fathers would stand at rigid attention. Then they would begin to salute us, one by one, and in that salute, that one sign of recognition, of acknowledgment, they would thank us for the first time. They would be thanking their own children for their fortitude and courage and generosity and long suffering, for enduring a military childhood.

But most of all the salute would be for something no military man in this country has ever acknowledged. The gathering of fighting men would be thanking their children, their fine and resourceful children, who were strangers in every town they entered, thanking them for their extraordinary service to their country, for the sacrifices they made over and over again to the United States of America, to its ideals of freedom, to its preservation, and to its everlasting honor.

Military brats, my lost tribe, spent their entire youth in service to this country and no one even knew we were there. I wrote *The Great Santini* because in many ways the book was the only way I could take to the skies in the dark-winged jets, move through those competitive ranks of aviators and become, at last, my father's wingman.

Mary Edwards Wertsch *discovered at age four that the letters of her name also spelled "army," the larger identity she was born into. She is author of the 1991 landmark study,* Military Brats: Legacies of Childhood Inside the Fortress, *an examination of the long-term effects on American military children of being raised in the "warrior society."*

Military brats may think of themselves as nomads, but in reality, she writes, they do not move in community and have no "kinship networks." She recognizes a legacy of "psychological diaspora" and the need to grieve over not belonging. Delayed maturity and problems with commitment may follow if brats can't adapt. Though she enjoys the ambiguity of "standing both inside and outside two cultures," those of the military and the world at large, she cautions brats against "perpetuating marginality" by making choices that keep them on the outside.

In this excerpt, she responds to a learned rhythm as she gives up a job out of the sheer need to move again, "the best and worst of rootlessness." She takes to the road, exhilarated at reclaiming her identity, yet without direction or prospects. Bravado and survival instinct drive her from Virginia to the Pacific, where she arrives with few resources other than her portability. "I had put myself in limbo, awaiting circumstances themselves to make my choices for me." She finally recognizes that such freedom is fatalism.

Wertsch married a rooted Midwestern scholar and lives in St. Louis with him and her two sons.

Outside Looking In

Mary Edwards Wertsch

When asked by civilians if it was really all that different to grow up in the military, we children of the Fortress sometimes draw a blank. In our gut we know it was different. Very different. But how to explain? It's possible, of course, to point out that it's all the difference between living under an authoritarian regime and living in a democracy, but that doesn't go far enough. It might supply a bird's-eye view of structure and form, but it leaves out the heart, the flavor, the drama.

And drama is the key. Growing up inside the Fortress is like being drafted into a gigantic theater company. The role of the warrior society, even in peacetime, is to exist in a state of perpetual "readiness": one continuous dress rehearsal for war. The principal actors are immaculately costumed, carefully scripted, and supplied with a vast array of props. They practice elaborate large-scale stage movements—land, air, and sea exercises simulating attacks and defenses. But even apart from such massive stagings, the minutiae of form in each costumed actor are carefully shaped to the last detail. No liberties may be taken with the way a warrior-actor stands, walks, salutes, speaks; this is not a theater of improvisation.

And then there is the supporting cast: the wives—who may lack costumes but whose lines and movements are crafted every bit as carefully—and the children, the understudies.

But the thing about the drama of the military is that it is not confined, as movies would have it, to the most spectacular scenes of families parting and reuniting, of actual combat, of military funerals. Drama is the very medium of life inside the Fortress, its color and texture, a quality that so thoroughly imbues even the most ordinary moments that it cannot be subtracted. Shopping at the commissary, riding home on a bike, sitting in a movie theater— even the most trivial actions can have a staged, rehearsed feeling to them that is largely alien to the civilian world.

...Certainly by the time a military child is five years old, the values and rules of military life have been thoroughly internalized, the military identity well forged, and the child has already assumed an active stage presence as an understudy of the Fortress theater company. In my own case, the year I was five is the first year I can remember clearly thinking of myself as a child of the military. At that time we were living at Fort Myer, Virginia, and my father, an Army colonel, was working at the Pentagon.

Summer, 1957. I had been learning how to read and write in preparation for first grade. One day I wandered into my sixteen-year-old brother's bedroom and, to my delight, found that I could actually read the single word emblazoned in big gold letters on the black pennant above his bed.

"Mary!" I exclaimed with joy. I had not realized I meant so much to my big brother, whom I held in fearful awe. To my consternation, my brother instantly doubled over laughing.

"Not 'Mary,'" he finally gasped. "Army!"

I was disappointed, to say the least, but the incident nevertheless left me with an enduring attachment to that shining word on the pennant. The similarity to my own name was a fact I could not overlook; to me it constituted proof of something I already felt. I was an extension of it, and it of me. No one could have convinced me otherwise....

About 7:15 one morning, my father set off as usual for his job at the Pentagon. I followed him out back, marveling at his rigid bearing, barrel chest, and that wondrous uniform with bright ribbon, shiny buttons, and neat silver birds on the shoulder. His uniform awed me. It was more than the buttons and birds and shiny trim on his hat. There were perfect creases down his pants. Not a spot on the smooth expanse of khaki. Not a smudge of dirt on his shiny black shoes, in which I could almost see my face. I felt unworthy in his immaculate presence.

Then, suddenly, one of the sparrows up in our oak tree scored a direct hit on his hat. I screamed with laughter as my father stomped and cursed. I was sure I'd never seen anything so funny in my whole life. The Colonel was furious, and from the sound of his curses it was hard to tell who had committed the greater outrage, sparrow or his five-year-old daughter....

Christmas, 1957. My big present that year was a portable mono record player. I couldn't believe my good fortune. And along with the record player came my first very own record. It was wrapped in bright paper and tied with a ribbon, but I could clearly see it was a 45 rpm. Could it possibly be my current favorite, "Wake Up, Little Suzie"? Or even "You Ain't Nothin' but a Hound Dog"? I snatched the paper off.

But no. It was "The Pledge of Allegiance," sung by the U.S. Marine Corps Band. Even then, enough was enough. I've never played it, though I have it still....

Dinner, en famille. It must have been 5:30 sharp. My father, still in uniform minus the jacket, was at the head of the table. Mom was holding down the other end, ready to scoot to the kitchen should anything be wanted. My brother, sixteen and sullen, was across from me. The atmosphere was grave. My brother said nothing. My mother said nothing. It must have been one of those times when no subject was safe. And Dad just sat there, ramrod straight, glowering at his food and chewing critically.

Finally, secure in my role as the little Electra of the household, I turned to my father and said, in my best casual imitation of my mother, "Pass the tomatoes, Dave." No "please," no "sir." And to top it off, I'd called him Dave.

The entire family exploded in laughter at this brazen impertinence. Even The Colonel. His face turned red. Tears ran down his cheeks. He laughed so hard his voice went up two octaves into a high-pitched, breathless "hee hee hee." My brother and mother, weak with laughter at the sacrilege, were hanging on to the table for support. It looked like the revolution had triumphed, and I was the heroine of the hour.

Five minutes later, after we had mostly recovered and the general atmosphere had calmed to reminiscent chuckles, I decided to try it again. Fatal mistake. My father roared out scorching rage. "That's enough of *that!* You will *not* call me Dave! And when you speak to me you will say *please* and follow it with *sir!* Is that *clear?*"

Yes, sir, it was. In the exacting theatrical world of the Fortress, such were the consequences of ad-libbing one's lines.

For six weeks in October and November of 1978 I was a supremely happy young woman. With the sole exceptions of my wedding and the births of my children, all which occurred long afterward, I still rank that time as the most ecstatic of my life. But virtually no one I knew then understood that.

It was not hard to see why. I was drained from my parents' bitter divorce after thirty-four years of marriage. My own love relationship had recently ended. There had been an exhausting union battle at work. About the only really good thing in my life right then was the newspaper job I dearly loved—and to everyone's shock, I had just quit. There was no new job lined up, and I had very little money. On the face of it, my actions were inexplicable, my attitude surreal.

But I had been seized by a need to move on that was so overwhelming it eclipsed any sensible notions of sticking out the usual cycle of job queries. More than anything else in the world I wanted to get out of Virginia and feel the freedom of the open road. I wasn't worried about jobs; I figured I had enough experience to get me in the door someplace. I also had a head full of freelance ideas and a book I wanted to write.

I packed my yellow Honda Civic with the few things I considered really important: clothes, dictionary, camera, a portable typewriter, a box full of my newspaper clips. Then I hit the road, headed north under clear blue autumn skies, a stack of maps beside me and no particular destination in mind.

Ah, the exhilaration of it! The past was literally behind me, the future literally down the road. I could turn the car—and my life—in any direction I chose. Every road sign signified a new opportunity, a whole new world of choices and decisions, all of which I would make myself. As I drove along, happily pondering whether I should make my new life in Philadelphia, New York, Chicago, L.A., or any point in between, I had no worries. Things would work out—I was convinced of that—and I would become who I wanted to be in the place of my own choice. And if they didn't? Well, I was master of my own fate, I told myself. I'd learn what I could from a bad experience, then pull up stakes and start over someplace else. God knows I knew how to do that. Whatever happened was going to be for the best. Even if I bombed out, I could always write about it. For a writer, I figured, there is no wasted experience.

By the time I reached the Pacific in mid-November, I had fifty bucks to my name. I was worried, but still sure I could pull it off; I had always known I could survive anywhere, make the best of it. That was a truth I'd learned so long ago it was as much a part of me as blood and bone.

Only much later did I realize just how classically military brat that was, and how my odyssey revealed both the best and the worst of rootlessness.

As an Army brat, I was so used to moving, to breaking camp one place, setting up in another, it had become the natural rhythm of my existence. In Virginia I had stayed so long—more than three years in one job—that I chafed and yearned for life on the move. My cross-country adventure was the joyful reclaiming of my identity.

Happy? Yes, I was happy—I was going home. And home for me was the comfortable familiarity of constant change and an uncharted future. For me, a modern American Bedouin, life on the open road, destination unknown, was as delicious as a long drink of cool water in the searing desert. It was freedom.

Or was it? For there was another side to it that was not free at all: a fatalistic side in which my wanderings were not so much an exercise in autonomy as an offering up of my life on the altar of fate. It may have looked as though I had taken control of my life, but in effect I had put myself in limbo, awaiting circumstances themselves to make my choices for me—a striking re-creation of my life as a military brat. How long could I keep driving—until I got sick or injured? Until I was sidelined by an accident or breakdown? Until I ran out of money, as I ultimately did? I drove for six weeks, bouncing from city to city in my glorious dance of delusion, about as autonomous and free as the ball in a pinball machine.

The end point turned out to be legendary San Francisco. There I set up camp, ready to pursue my *dreams* as so many had before me. And things did not work out.

I survived, all right—even made a living from writing. My dream was derailed by something altogether unexpected. Within weeks I found an intense dislike for the city growing within me. A dislike so strong it could not be ignored. A dislike that, ironically enough, centered on rootlessness.

I saw San Francisco as a city cut off from its past, heedless of its future, enveloped almost obscenely in its celebration of the moment. A city where, to borrow the words of someone I met there, "everyone you meet seems to have run away from home." Loudly and self-righteously, I declaimed against it. What I failed to see, of course, was that I had projected my own plight onto an entire city. The mirror image was exact. What I condemned outwardly was the very thing I was loath to face within; inevitably, the image became unbearable. Within seven months I was gone.

This time I chose Chicago—a city I came to love deeply, in no small part because its down-to-earth, see-life-for-what-it-is philosophy helped me finally take a good long look at the legacies of my rootlessness.

And what I found was both good and bad.

There are two questions one can pose that reveal rootlessness as instantly as a litmus test.

The first: *Where are you from?* Military brats do not relish the "where from" question and go through life vainly trying to parry it. Some answer "Nowhere." Others, "Everywhere." There are many versions: citing the last place they've been, or the one they liked most, or launching into a full-blown explanation that reveals far more than the questioner intended. One military son told me, "When people asked me where I was from, it used to be painful, a dilemma. So I had to just sit down and decide something to say and stick to, so people wouldn't think I was lying. Before that, it depended on my mood: *This month I'm from California.*"

The fact is, there is no way to answer the question that is not awkward. The moment it is asked, it sets up a barrier between the military brat and the civilian questioner. A civilian asks the question to get a handle on the person; but no answer the military brat can possibly give will satisfy. The let's-get-acquainted convention has begun badly, underscoring the gap between our world and theirs.

The second litmus test is a question rarely asked in social situations, but one I posed to every interviewee: *Where do you want to be buried?* A person with roots always knows the answer; he or she probably hasn't given it much thought, but hasn't had to—it's the kind of thing that's answered just by who one is. The response of a person without roots is quite different. "Wherever I am when I finish up," said one military brat. "I have no firm attachment to any geographic location." Another answered, "Buried? Never. I want to be cremated and my ashes scattered. I don't care where."

We think of ourselves as nomads. The term has a nice, definitive sound to it, and suggests, somewhat reassuringly, that our experience fits neatly into a known category. But the term is less a description of us and our lives than an indictment of the language, which has yet to reflect the realities of life inside the Fortress.

Nomads in the true sense are groups of people—Inuit, Bedouin, Masai—who move at will in search of hunting grounds, pastureland, water. Like us, they have no permanent home and they move constantly. But true nomads move in entire communities; the social fabric of their lives is kept intact. Nomad children grow up knowing their grandparents, aunts, uncles, cousins. They have lifelong friends. One can speculate that if a nomad were asked "Where are you from?" he would answer, "From my tribe, the such-and-such." And if asked "Where will you be buried?" the answer, too, might be something on the order of "With my tribe." Whatever the answer, it would imply deep rootedness. For while movement is an important ingredient in the lives of true nomads, the most basic reality of all—the sense of identity in community—is as rock solid as it is possible to be.

American military children, by contrast, do not have kinship networks to anchor them. The constant change is not balanced by social stability. For the military brat, each time the family moves, the world dissolves and is swept away.

We are not really nomads. There is no easy label for us.

When I lived in Chicago, I worked in the Loop. Every day I would catch the El downtown and join the great river of urban workers pouring through the streets. The observers of this twice-daily deluge were the street bums and bag ladies huddled immobile in doorways or sprawled along the edge of Grant Park. The curious thing—and I now realize this is a very curious thing, though it seemed quite natural at the time—is that I didn't identify with the thousands of office workers around me. I identified with the street bums.

The thought would come to me as I walked, quietly inserting itself into whatever I had been thinking. *The only difference between me and that bag lady is our position on the pavement.* It was not a dismaying thought or even a striking one—just the registering of an observation I recognized as true in some fundamental way. It never occurred to me to repeat it to anyone else; in the first place, it was just a mental notation, not meant to be voiced. In the second place, the idea would certainly have lacked credibility for anyone who knew me—for in appearance, manner, and lifestyle, I was a long way from a street bum. But there the thought would be, as much a part of my daily life as the packed underground platform at Washington and Randolph.

Occasionally I'd try to figure out how it was I saw truth in it. I never had a clue—until the first interview I did with a military brat, when somehow I happened to mention it. Suddenly I understood. Why shouldn't I identify with street bums? Like me, they're very portable people. They're resourceful. They don't *belong* anywhere. They're physically in the community but emotionally outside of it. And they know that the only thing they really have is inside their skins.

I did not envy them their poverty, their literal homelessness, the emotional barrenness of their lives. There were real differences between them and me. But in some sense, too, there was a kindred spirit.

The first legacy of military childhood transience is what might be called the psychological diaspora. As adults most of us manage to slow or stop the moving—and yet still we find ourselves caught up in a strange migration. It is a migration of the soul, all the more mysterious to us because it has no clear origin and no certain goal.

There is only one antidote to the angst of the diaspora. Belonging. It is not easy for a military brat to learn what that even means, much less to find it. Yet belonging is the single greatest quest of our lives, a quest that lives in many of us as a powerful unnamed yearning.

My feeling is that it is crucial for military brats to put the right name to this yearning, face our unrequited need to belong, and address it as best we can. Because if we do not, the yearning, like anything imprisoned in the unconscious, will play havoc with our lives.

Those of us born into the psychological diaspora must find our way out of it, or suffer the consequences.

We must find our own answers to the unresolved question of belonging. And we do find belonging, partially—although the nature of belonging, for those not born to it, is that it must be found over and over again.

Another corollary seems to be that for military brats, a pre-requisite to belonging is grieving over not belonging and repeated loss. That stands to reason: It is necessary to break down the old immunity to attachment before one can become attached to something new. And belonging, more than anything else, is about attachment.

With concerted effort it is possible in adulthood for military brats to hugely resolve the dilemma of the diaspora. And that holds true for two other difficult legacies of our childhood wanderings as well: delayed maturity and problems with commitment.

One of the most intense outsider experiences lived out by military brats comes when their families are stationed overseas. Iran, Thailand, Bavaria, South Korea, Ethiopia, France, Japan, Italy, the Philippines, Spain, to mention a few...all represent worlds of adventure to families sampling the foreign culture.

But if for many the overseas experience is an exercise in unrelieved outsideness with regard to the foreign culture, it is also an intense dose of *insideness* in the American warrior community. Most American military people live on bases or in homing areas that are walled off from the indigenous population. It is an oddly isolated life, one in which it is possible to delude oneself that one is still on American soil, just relegated to a particularly boring Fortress island out of sight of the mainland....

Perhaps all pettiness in life is the result of standing outside of someone else's experience, unwilling or unable to bridge the gulf. Military people are not immune to this, and may even be particularly vulnerable. Outsiders—especially those who cannot help that status and do not like it—sometimes feel they have to compensate for their uncomfortable outsideness with a false sense of superiority.

So it is that some military people, children included, come to objectify the foreign nationals they live around, imprisoning them in stereotypes....

My father was stationed in France from 1961–64. The first year there, when I was ten, I was sent to an American dependent school, and I saw the French only from a distance. It was easy to view them as alien with habits I couldn't understand and didn't care for. The political situation of the time was tense as well, which exacerbated our sense of being outsiders; it was a liability to be an American. The Algerian revolution was raging, and although President John F. Kennedy and his wife were personally very popular with the French, his early sympathies with Algerian desires for independence rankled terribly. An extreme right-wing terrorist group, the OAS [Organisation de l'Armèe Secrète] fanned anti-American sentiment. That first year we lived in a small French town, and the American car we had foolishly brought with us was repeatedly vandalized. "Yankee Go Home" and "OAS" were scratched into the paint, and the antenna and locks were frequently broken....

Then my parents made a decision for which I will always be grateful: They sent me to a French school for the next two years. It was a difficult outsider experience, one could even say a trial by fire. But after I learned the language and began to make French friends, my perspective inevitably changed. I still felt like an outsider, but now the channels were wide open. I fell in love with the French language, the French culture, the French people. I felt totally challenged and stimulated by that culture, and found myself living on a plane of heightened awareness in which even the smallest, most mundane details of life in the French context seemed exciting. It was immensely rewarding: The more I responded to the culture, the more it seemed to respond to me.

I was nearly thirteen when my father received orders to go back to the States, and the parting from the country I had come to love was almost unbearable. We left from Le Havre, on an ocean liner that pulled away from the docks one June evening at twilight. I remember standing on the deck for a long, long time watching the lights of Le Havre, trying not to blink so I could fill my eyes with as much of France as possible before the horizon would draw the curtain and I would have to turn away, begin my grieving. In France I had found a midway point between outsider and insider, which suited me perfectly. I'd learned French and French ways well enough to lose some of my outsideness in that culture, but I also knew I was too American to ever be a true insider there. That didn't matter. I loved the feeling of ambiguity, of standing both inside and outside of two cultures.

In fact I mourned the loss of that delicious ambiguity for years and years, until I was finally old enough to plan my return. And still, after a quarter of a century, I feel a kinship to France, and the sweet sorrow of an old and unrequited yearning.

But the effects of living overseas are very long-term, and continue to be a part of the military brats who have been [abroad]. Perhaps there are military brats who have lived in other countries and then put the experience totally behind them, in a sealed compartment of their past, but I have yet to meet one. In some way all [of us] appeared to be permanently changed and enriched. Some spoke of a longing for another country such as I had for France, and they often call it, paradoxically, "homesickness."

The overall effect of all these experiences is that military brats spend a great deal more of their childhoods on the outside looking in than on the inside looking out. Although military brats have a natural sense of insideness with one another, it is never given a chance to develop because of the highly transient lifestyle of the warrior society. Standing on the sidelines observing other people's in-groups becomes a way of life—and the outsider way of life that was forced by circumstance during childhood is then perpetuated into adulthood by military brats who know no other way to be. Even when they perceive it as a problem, they do not see a way out....

While it is hard to perpetually live the outsider role, it is harder still to abandon it. The outsider role is the central paradox of a military brat's life. A sense of belonging is our single greatest need and our single greatest quest—yet many military brats perpetuate their own marginality by making choices that are guaranteed to *keep* them on the outside.

This has been at work in my own life in at least two major ways. First, I so longed to return to France that I tried twice to expatriate myself. The first time a family crisis brought me home;

the second time, I was defeated by my own refusal to work illegally. I could have stayed and survived as an illegal alien, but I was too much of a by-the-book military brat to reconcile myself to that. Near the end of that second stay, a delightful, elderly museum guard with whom I had struck up a conversation proposed a very French solution to my dilemma: advertise in a newspaper's personals column to marry a French airline pilot. That way, he pointed out, I could have dual citizenship *and* reduced air fare—a brilliant suggestion which I somehow failed to pursue.

The second way I was affected by the outsider syndrome was much more serious. Although from early adulthood I wanted to find the right man and settle down, secure in the stable emotional base I badly needed, I spent a decade dating only foreign men, and only those who were in the United States temporarily. The relationships were not without their rewards, but the long-term unworkability of it was always there, and always more apparent to them than it was to me. None of the foreign men wanted to settle down in the United States. For my part, I was perfectly willing—I thought—to go and live in an alien culture for the rest of my life; it didn't seem all that different from what I'd always done. But the reality was that the best I could have hoped for in a foreign culture was an endless marginality without any hope of gaining true insideness. It works for many people, but permanent marginality happened to be the opposite of what I needed in my own life. I believe now that those many decisions to connect with foreign men rather than Americans—I could not even seem to bring American men into focus during that period—were manifestations of a bad case of the outsider syndrome. What I wanted was *belonging*—yet I went out of my way to make sure it would not become a reality in my life.

Finally, I am happy to say, my own case of the outsider syndrome played itself out. I'm not quite sure how it happened, but the end of my last foreign relationship had a wonderfully clarifying effect on my thinking. It suddenly became obvious that I had been exhausting myself in a long, futile exercise. Not long after that, I met the man who was to become my husband: the son of a close-knit Midwestern farm family who, despite living in a big city as a scholar and intellectual, took care to maintain his roots. The first firm step on my own road to belonging was to find a mate who was comfortable with his own roots, and with whom I shared enough cultural commonality for us to communicate easily and well. It has been a happy choice.

The daughter of Canadian Mennonite missionaries, **Faith Eidse** *understood at an early age that she must share her parents with the needy people around them in Congo. Her father translated the Bible into Chokwe, her mother trained midwives and clinicians at a tropical medicine clinic, leprosarium, and tuberculosis ward.*

 Eidse felt she had inherited their calling and helped bathe patients, but that knowledge did not satisfy her desire for attention. As she grew older, she felt orphaned by her parents' mission, isolated from their roots, detached from their work, and unable to commit to a calling of her own. Sent away to boarding school from the village she loved at age eight, she faced danger when revolution broke out, bringing chaos, bloodshed, and suffering. Danger ruled, too, at the mission dorm, where children were falsely accused, beaten, and subjected to punitive prayers. Silenced, they numbed their feelings and learned the victim's desire to please. She carried inside both an incessant longing to belong and a fear of attachment. In writing, she discovered the ability to create emotional bonds denied by a fragmented home life, travel between continents, her outsider status, and her boarding school years.

Embers

Faith Eidse

Say yes and I'll tell you a story.

Back when my father was the Canadian linguist in an African village, I used to wait behind Chokwe hunters to have my dreams told. Dreams are sleek civet cats, small and slippery, and just when you think you're staring them right in the eye, they glide through your fingers and are gone. By the time I reached my father, my dream had vanished—purling shoulders to ringed tail. All I remembered was a sense of weightlessness and drift.

The hunter was a monolith of pure culture and language. I was a fluid mix—striped copper, black, tan—part Canadian prairie, part African soil, part American School of Kinshasa student. I could not hope to hold my father's attention, to be the voice he recorded, his microphone trained on the purest sounds of Chokwe and Lunda, tapes big as dinner plates twirling.

I found my mother at the clinic dressing burns and dispensing drugs to women coughing blood, babies sneezing intestinal worms. These people in their wretchedness perfectly deserved my mother's care. She bowed with them, freckled hand on spongy curls, offered up a prayer for healing. She was their guardian, called away from family—days, nights, weekends. If only I could do something to earn her touch....

During grass fire season, when the orphans burned the front lawn of the mission orphanage, I lined up with the brashest of them to run through live embers. Blue-orange flame defined the edges of the burn, orange hot spots glowed, white ash wafted into a black night. Cicadas called and responded.

"It doesn't hurt if you call on good spirits," said one orphan.

"I can walk through slowly, see?" said a boy who'd been at the mission orphanage all his life.

Across the road Mom and Dad sat in chiffon lantern light, reading language books, medical journals. I dared my parents to look up and stop me as I raced across sharp, scorching grass spears, pain drilling my spine, echoing off my eardrums.

"Aiyee, kachia!"—hot—I cried, jumping up and down in the cool white sand on the moonlit road. I sat under reflected light and examined my singed feet. I had raised blisters, but no good excuse for them. Too embarrassed to show Mom, I crept past her on screaming feet, chased cockroaches from the bathroom sink, and filled it from the rain barrel. Carefully, tenderly, I soaped and rinsed my own feet, swaddled them dry in bath towels, and slipped into bed.

Because I could not distract my parents from their missionary service, I shadowed them. Their work became mine; their calling so big it dwarfed any puny need of my own. I understood when my father left the dinner table to greet this teacher or that pastor that I would have to share my parents. I cringe at my continuing need to feel significant to them, my need to earn degrees, win prizes and contracts. Sometimes I feel obsessed, as though I possess a deep well that requires constant filling with attention. Even as an adult, on a rare visit to my retired parents in Canada, I'm jealous when my father leaves our conversation and rushes to the door to greet my theology-student cousin. I'm jealous even though I deliberately rejected theology or nursing and gave myself to writing.

By age eight, I had shuttled between the Belgian Congo, Canada, and several U.S. cities, where Dad earned graduate degrees. The day we returned to the Congo in June 1963, I followed the village *mamans* to the river like a hatchling. Infected by the rhythm of the village, I sang the new revolutionary songs, filled chitinous gourds from underground springs bubbling through white sand. I learned to wrap a wiregrass head pad and carry water on my head —no hands, swaying with the slosh—a mile uphill.

In January 1964, despite rumors of war, I begged to go to school with my friend at another mission. My parents relented. Within two weeks of my arrival at Mukedi, the Simba revolution broke out around us. Three Belgian priests were hacked to pieces eight kilometers from my school, their hands taken as trophies. It was a brutality learned from colonizing soldiers.

Rescue planes arrived over a burning countryside, the airstrip surrounded by angry men with guns and spears. The village chief held off the revolutionaries, pacing between us and them, shielding us from their vengeance, while we squeezed nine into a four-passenger plane. A Congo National Army plane circled, with helmeted soldiers peering from portholes. It tried to land. Bullets pinged against its taut belly. It rose, circled, and tried to land again. A missionary father jumped into a pickup truck and raced crazily into its path. With its landing gear inches from the cab, it pulled up and flew away. Our single-engine Cessna lumbered down the airstrip and lifted off, barely clearing brush fires and deep ravines. Above the engine hum, my head crooked against the ceiling, I wondered if my parents and sisters were safe. Stiff-necked, unmoored, disjointed, I climbed out of the plane and we drove through Kikwit, numb and mute. When we reached the Mennonite Brethren guesthouse, my sister Hope came running across the yard, arms wide. "You're alive!" she said.

Sometimes, in our isolated lives, all we had was each other. Sometimes all we didn't have was each other. We hardly quarreled or argued in our perfect family. Where would we go if a serious rift opened? There were no safety valves, no relatives, few permanent friends to run to.

For months we were thrown together in a UN refugee camp in the airless Congo basin. To steel myself against having nothing, I squandered hours in real time, pretending I was someone else—the guard in paratrooper boots at the gate, Claudia at the American school, who had twenty-four colors of Crayolas. I wanted just five—flaming orange, magenta, lilac, indigo and black—to paint the evening sky.

That fall, after we'd returned to Kamayala and found patients and orphans safe, Hope and I were sent to the mission dorm, five hundred miles away, with no telephone or bus lines connecting us. Our letters were censored by dorm parents for spelling and complaints. We stopped writing our true feelings. We stopped knowing them. Instead we learned to submit to shameful accusations, angry fists, and prayers we were required to repeat, indicting ourselves. We learned the victim's desire to please.

At the mission dorm our lives were regulated by rising and dinner bells. The hands that beat us also fed us, and the parents who loved us completely were far away. Dad said we could erase the miles with letters and prayer; at bedtime, my parents were often the gods I prayed to.

Dad said we could even erase the Atlantic Ocean and surround ourselves with grandmas and cousins. On one level, it was futile to summon our family in this way. On another, letters winged back and forth. The illusion wove Canada into Africa and gave us a sense of connection, though the real soil I dug my toes into was African.

At home, during school vacations, I carried a basin with soap and water and washed the rat-chewed feet of Mom's patients with Hansen's disease (leprosy). One woman slept in her hut on a bare bamboo bed with a stout stick at her side, but she could not feel the rats chewing her feet until their teeth sank into live nerves, good flesh. Then she flailed her stick with numb claw-hands, her fingers receding, her body reabsorbing knuckle bones.

It was this woman's feet I was washing when Mom noticed the dirty water pouring into leaky rubber gloves, into an open sore on my hand. She rushed me to the clinic and anointed my hands with hydrogen peroxide. She put me on a secret leprosy cure and made me promise not to tell. "People are still prejudiced about leprosy," she said. I wasn't permitted to mention the thumb-sized Dapsone tablet I choke-swallowed for six months every Sunday night. I never did, not even to my sisters. There was something familiar in hiding who I was, something reminiscent about being an outsider looking on, an observer trying to blend in.

I proposed a biology paper on Hansen's disease that permitted me to visit *L'hopital de la rive*, where patients sat on railroad ties above the Congo River and wove baskets as physical therapy. Sometimes their fingers were already so numb, they used their teeth to tighten the raffia strips. I visited the leprology surgeon in Kimpese who restored finger tendons, hammer toes, and sunken profiles so patients could walk openly in the market again.

During my first eighteen years, I had moved eighteen times, crisscrossing the Atlantic, the dream always on the other side. Not raised under one flag, unfamiliar with moving in one direction, not schooled with students who proceeded as a class, toward college and graduate school, I grew up not knowing what I would be. I felt the pressure to fit in, to find meaning in my parents' work, but there was a constant tearing inside, a sense of having given enough already, of detachment, of not belonging. I was gradually rejecting a life of service, seeing it alternately as exhausting or imperial: Mom snipped off a man's gangrenous toe at the leprosarium and I saw the plea in his eyes. She hadn't asked him if he wanted to live without his toe.

Only once as an adult did I experience what my parents might term "a call to service." It was a moment of false clarity during a bus trip through the Alleghenies in 1973. Behind a Greyhound depot, the sunset flashing through an apple orchard, I saw myself in a white lab coat, adjusting a microscope lens, watching bacilli squirm. "I'm going to discover a cure for leprosy," I told a woman on the bus. The moment and the call passed. Without committal.

I know from experience that the least satisfying farewells are the ones denied. Melancholia builds up over unresolved grief, over losses we failed to, or cannot, mourn. "Let's not say good-bye," several well-meaning friends said on graduation night in Congo, and I understood their sense of the impossible. To cope with parting, I intellectualized my emotions and submerged my grief. Weeks later, in another city, on another continent, I'd get memory jags that paralyzed me for hours: I'd be playing soccer again on the field at school, a tropical storm at my back as I dribbled the ball up left field. I would look for Peanut at right forward. But my teammates vanished just as I passed the ball. They were insubstantial, gone. Peanut and I would reunite in Boston again twenty years later and find our lives amazingly parallel. Our eldest sons were both three, and our time in Boston was limited as our husbands finished doctorates and postdoctorates. The four of us, mothers and sons, were constant playmates for three surreal years. We healed scars we'd barely admitted having as we reminisced about our lives in Congo. When we had to part again, it was a different kind of letting go. Our good-byes came from a place of better knowing; we promised ourselves a closer distance.

My parents buy airline tickets and come to visit us at our overgrown cottage under Florida pines. When I meet them at the airport, my silver-haired Dad limps on numb feet behind my mother's wheelchair. She cants to the right, favoring her unparalyzed side, but she greets me in full voice. Dad was crippled years before by the electric generator in Congo, a vertebra nearly severed as he cranked it up so we could go on reading after dark. Mom had had a stroke. Her blood pressure has always been high after the kidney infection that nearly killed her during our first term in Congo. The tropical heat was always a trial; her feet overflowed her shoes. She never complained, but only in Canada did her ankles shrink back to their normal size.

I don't interpret dreams; I have no healing touch. Yet my parents need me.

In a moment of vulnerability, after settling Mom in bed, Dad tells me of his disappointments and I want to put my arms around him. But we have avoided emotional closeness because of physical distance, because of God's will. We have been separated too many years by too many miles to risk it. Ever since I buckled myself into the single-prop plane to fly to boarding school, we have protected ourselves so that the rip-tear of takeoff won't sting so badly. We have avoided touch for more than thirty years.

My Australian shepherd nuzzles between Dad and me, and I

bury my fingers in his thick scruff, absorbing the same soft comfort I did from guard dogs at the dorm. The dogs in my life, expert sensors of emotion, have always been better at being touched than Dad or I will ever be. We didn't demand closeness of each other. We couldn't without betraying our pledge to put God first, others second, ourselves last.

When next I visit Mom in Canada, she says, "That's the last time I'm coming to Florida." She has stopped traveling and that can mean only one thing. I have to move closer to this woman I have known so distantly all my life. I want to accommodate a relationship I've held too lightly, a woman I've known too fleetingly. If there's anything my nomadic life has taught me, it's that, in the end, some people are more significant than others.

I search and apply for jobs in icebound Winnipeg, admitting my need for nearness but also hesitating. I'm afraid I'll get too close, that I'll have to express and resolve conflicts we've avoided for decades. I'm afraid I'll have to tell Mom about the senseless blisters on a child's feet. I'm afraid she'll see my tears, or I'll see hers. Manitoba threatens to stifle and contain me. It's a fixed place that augurs conversations I'd rather not start. It presents the tension between found self in achievement and lost self in community. The freedom of the nomad is the loneliness of disconnection.

On a recent trip to Manitoba, where I failed to get the job, I made this journal entry:

> *The community is puffed and tentacled against the*
> *individual and will engulf you, suck you dry, leave you no*
> *energy for reading, no time for thinking on your own. It*
> *exhausts you with its demands, truncates your dreams until*
> *they seem stubby, mangled, impossible. You cave in to the*
> *needs of others, unable to complete the projects you start, to*
> *realize the dreams and waking visions you guard.*

I'm afraid of losing myself in community; I have become deaf to the sacrificial code of yielded freedom and achievement. The nomadic me recognizes that I'm afraid of sending roots too deeply into sandy Florida soil, soil that doesn't hold the weight of relationships as do the rich harrow rows of Manitoba. Yet the prairie furrows might hold me too fast, stifle the outsider that I guard so gingerly within. Letting go of freedom would be yet another loss to mourn.

My husband, sons, and I end up rejecting another offer from the north and stay on in Florida, where I take a job writing for an environmental agency. I find myself mirroring my father's actions, carrying a tape recorder to remote villages along the Apalachicola River; gathering stories of swamp dwellers who've lived entire lifetimes in one ecosystem. I, too, am sending roots deeper than I'd ever dreamed possible.

At Christmas the four of us camp in the Everglades and I find myself grasping for identity totems. We wander a hardwood hammock, a coastal forest that has floated from the West Indies or the Yucatan Peninsula. I am amazed when I touch a traveling tree, an immigrant gumbo-limbo. West Indians have named it a "tourist tree," after its red and peeling trunk. What appeals to me is its solidity despite its long journey.

We walk further into the woods, engulfed by a pungent skunk tree, riveted by a clutch of bromeliads, rooted on air. We are stopped dead in our tracks by a resurrection tree. Its roots ripped out of the moist Everglades soil by a hurricane, the resilient tree sends one spiky root straight up through the forest canopy, where it branches and sprouts abundant leaves, and the other right back into the rich earth. Such possibility despite drift, hurricane, uprooting, and depression buoys me.

Perhaps I have not rooted long enough to ache or weep with people, to feel trauma or pain. I have not felt their need close enough to me, or mine close enough to them. I write to create emotional bonds I've denied myself. I yearn for thick gumbo-limbo roots but recognize myself as the mangrove, whose vine and root are one. I simultaneously branch and root as I go, more devoted to freedom than to permanence.

Ruth Van Reken *was sent to boarding school from her parents' mission in Nigeria during her formative years. Like many missionary children, she was torn from family, yet chided for her tears. She learned to silence her needs, to sacrifice for a higher cause, and to pretend all was well. She built a wall of "good judgment" around her true feelings and became a captive within, increasingly sullen, detached from her emotions and from her parents, lest she feel the pain of separation. By high school she asks, "Do we know each other anymore?" The family's mission is set directly against their emotional needs for each other.*

It wasn't until Van Reken was a young adult that she came to terms with the pain of multiple separations. In this excerpt from her 1988 epistolary memoir, Letters Never Sent, *Van Reken relives the anguish she suffered as a child by writing the letters she couldn't write then. Her willingness to reexamine her childhood emotions helped her understand why she had become an often depressed, angry, and critical adult. When she reached the end of her 171-letter journey, covering thirty-three years of family separations, she realized that emotions can't be denied or repressed without consequences. By accepting as authentic those suppressed feelings, she experienced resolution to a lengthy sorrow. News of her book spread among adult missionary kids and became a watershed for many troubled families.*

Van Reken is also coauthor with David Pollock of Third Culture Kids: The Experience of Growing Up Among Worlds. *Their book maps bold clear lines of what happens to children raised outside their parents' home country, or even those raised on native soil under a foreign power, as it explores the effects of such a childhood on maturing, developing identity, and adjusting to the passport country. Van Reken lives and writes in Indianapolis, Indiana.*

Letters Never Sent

Ruth Van Reken

*My story begins in Nigeria in 1951. Going to boarding school was a
rite of passage for missionary kids—a sign that we were growing up.
Personally, I was eager for the adventure to begin.*

But right from the start, things were harder than I expected.

September 1951

Dear Mom and Dad,

I feel awful. Something inside is squeezing me so bad I can
hardly breathe.

You said it would be fun to get on the plane and go to boarding
school, but so far it isn't. I couldn't stop crying on the airplane, but
I didn't want the other kids to know. I kept my face to the window,
so they might think I liked watching the clouds.

When I got to school this afternoon, I was still crying and I just
couldn't stop. The missionary "aunties" who met us said I should
be more like Mae Beth. "Try to be big and brave like your sister,"
they said. "She's not crying."

They don't know that Mae Beth never cries, not even when
Spotty got run over by the car or our pet bird died. How can I be
like her?

And how can I live without my mommy and daddy? It feels like my heart got pulled out of me today.

Love,
Ruth Ellen

Dear Mom and Dad,

The days aren't so bad now. After school my friends and I play Red Rover and Annie, Annie, Over. We also play jacks and skip rope lots of different ways. On Saturdays we go swimming in the dam and have a picnic in the evening. I can really swing high on the swings now, too.

But I hate the nights.

Every night I still cry myself to sleep. If my roommates hear me, they call me a crybaby. Other times they call the auntie on duty. She tries hard to cheer me up by telling me how much fun we're going to have at the picnic Saturday or on the walk Sunday.

I just keep wondering what's wrong with me. Why can't I get over missing you the way the other kids seem to do? Maybe I'm the weirdest person ever made, but I miss my house, my bed, my brothers, my parents, and my African friends at home.

I've learned to cry more quietly. But I've got awful snotty corners on my sheets, where I blow my nose at night.

Love,
Ruth Ellen

As I watched the other children apparently coping well, I concluded that the problem must be mine. But whom could I talk to? I was praised for my bravery and independence. If people liked my brave side, I reasoned, they obviously wouldn't like my frightened, lonely side. So the wall of "good adjustment" began to grow around my true feelings, and soon I was a captive within those walls.

Dear Mom and Dad,

I'm trying very hard to be good. I know everyone wants me to be happy here, and it seems like I should be.

Aunt Gert tries real hard to be kind and do special things for us. Lots of evenings we go into her living room, and it's a real cozy feeling while she reads us a bedtime story. I like to play with Tessa, the school dog. I have lots of friends, and there are lots of fun things to do here. When I'm doing them, I feel okay and I think that outside I look pretty happy. But way deep inside, there's some kind of sadness that won't go away.

There's no way I can write you about everything that goes on. For one thing, I can't spell too well, and some things take pretty big words to tell. Another thing is that it's hard to explain what I'm feeling.

The teachers try to help us write you by letting us copy a letter off the board on Sundays.

> *Dear Mom and Dad,*
> *How are you? I am fine. This week we went (swimming, hiking, picnicking). It was lots of fun.*
>
> > *Love,*
> > *Name*

It's better than nothing, but if I were home, I could tell you so much more. Printing takes a long time. Sometimes I see that the teachers write extra notes on our letters to you. They always say we're doing fine.

I suppose it's true, but I wonder how they know. Nobody can know another person's insides, can she?

Love,

Ruth Ellen

Dear Mom and Dad,

I don't cry at bedtime so much anymore. The teachers think I'm better adjusted—they don't know I've just given up.

Saturday nights are still really hard because I think of you all going to the open-air meeting in town. I always loved that so much, and when I picture you there without me, I start to cry.

When I have to cry now, I just find some place alone. The others don't like to see me looking unhappy. I know they try real hard to make this school nice for us, but nothing is like your own mommy and daddy and home.

Love,
Ruth Ellen

January 1952

Dear Mom and Dad,

Thanks for a nice Christmas vacation. It was wonderful to see you again. There was so much I had waited to tell you, but when you asked me how school was, all I could say was "Fine." Why did I say that?

Maybe it was because I just wanted to forget about school while I was with you.

Maybe it was because I knew I didn't have a choice about going back, so there wasn't any point in telling you the truth.

Maybe I didn't want you to feel bad, since I know this is how we're serving Jesus as a family.

Maybe I was afraid you'd take the teacher's side and tell me why I shouldn't feel the way I do.

Or maybe it would take so long to tell you all that's inside of me that I don't know where to start.

I can't explain it. All I know is that the only thing I could ever say was "Fine." God knows it was a lie.

Love,
Ruth Ellen

March 1952

Dear Mom and Dad,

I'm excited that you're coming to spend your vacation near the school. I wish you could come more often, but I know it's far. And the teachers say it's not good for parents to come too much; they say it just gets the kids upset.

I guess I see what they mean. By now, most of us don't cry as much as we used to. Everybody feels better about that. Maybe when you leave, it will hurt like before and I'll cry again.

Actually, I'm scared about your coming. When I close my eyes, I can't remember what you look like. What if I've changed so much that you don't recognize me? Will I know you when you walk by? What if we can't find each other?

I'm worrying about it a lot, but probably Aunt Gert knows you. If I ask her, she'll show me who you are.

I'm scared...but I'm counting the days.

Love,
Ruth Ellen

April 1952

Dear Mom and Dad,

Thanks for coming one day early to surprise us! Aunt Gert called us out of story time, saying there was someone waiting outside. She wouldn't say who it was. I didn't dare hope—but there you were with Chuck and Tom, and I knew you! You hadn't changed after all!

And you knew us, too. It's so great to be living together as a family for a while. I love coming home after school instead of going to the dorm. Now there aren't as many rules to keep. I'm still scared I'll forget one of them and do something bad without even meaning to.

Right now it feels like I have more room inside.

Love,
Ruth Ellen

May 1952

Dear Mom and Dad,

I'm sorry your vacation lasted only a month. I was sad to see you go. At least summer vacation is coming soon.

I'm waiting to hear the schedule for the airplane rides home. Last time we were in the last group to leave. I wish they had enough planes to take us all on the first day. But if they send me home last, I hope they won't forget to send me *back* last, too.

I can't wait for the next few days to pass. Three whole months with you sounds like forever.

Love,
Ruth Ellen

The Second Year

I couldn't understand the way I acted when I was with my parents that summer. I couldn't wait to get home for vacation, and at first I forgot all about school. Three months would never pass, so why worry about it? I loved being with my family again.

But about halfway through the summer all the kids started thinking about the good things at school. They said they couldn't wait to get back again, and pretty soon that was all they talked about.

I saw the grown-ups smile at each other and shrug their shoulders. "See how much they like it?" they all said. "They don't even miss us." They sounded relieved. I could tell they liked it better for us to say we liked school, rather than to say we missed home.

A few times I said, "I'd rather stay home than go back to school." But there was always some nice grownup around who would say, "Of course you wouldn't. School is so much fun. I'm sure you'd rather go back, wouldn't you?"

So pretty soon I joined the others in saying, "I can't wait to go back." But when the moment came to leave, all I wanted was

150

to run back into my parents' arms. Why did I say it, when I knew i t wasn't true? It was part of the wall, growing thicker all the time, that I was building around my feelings. I couldn't let myself get too close, when I knew I'd be leaving. It would only make the pain worse.

September 1952

Dear Mom and Dad,

I'm in Room 16 this year, in the new wing. It's neat, and it's right next to the bathroom, too. Sometimes I sneak there during rest hour.

I like having Barbie in the room across the hall. It's sort of like we're still neighbors from home. I think it's hard for her to be away for the first time, like it was for me. She looks real sad.

I still cry but not as much as last year. Maybe I'm more used to it—or I know it doesn't do any good.

Love,
Ruth Ellen

Dear Mom and Dad,

I have the mumps. I'm in the second group to get them, and we have to stay inside this one room so we won't spread them. They even bring us our food here. I feel like a prisoner.

Today Mae Beth came to the window to see how I was. She thought I was lucky to miss so much school. We decided that it would be fun if she had to join me, so I told her to come close to the window and I'd kiss her through the screen. We laughed and thought it was funny, but somebody reported us.

Later Aunt Gert came in and said we would just spread it through the school that way. That's why they're keeping us separate in the first place. I guess it wasn't such a smart thing to do.

I feel extra lonesome when I'm sick away from you. Nobody can take care of me like you do, Mom.

Love,
Ruth Ellen

November 1952

Dear Mom and Dad,

Barbie is dead. I can't believe it. Why would Jesus take the nicest little girl here?

When she got sick a few days ago, we didn't think too much about it. Mumps are still going around. Then they took her to the hospital in Jos, and they told us all to pray. We did, but she still died.

At first I didn't feel too bad, because I knew God would bring her back to life. They keep teaching us about how Jesus did bring a girl back to life, and if you have faith, a whole mountain will move. (I've been trying to move Mt. Sanderson behind the school that way, but so far I haven't seen any change.) Anyway, I really thought I had faith. I just knew God would raise Barbie. I prayed and prayed, and all through the funeral I waited for her to come out of the box. I wanted to run to her parents and tell them not to cry so hard, because everything was going to be all right. I kept thinking she was going to come back, even when they put the dirt over her. And back at school I kept watching for her, because I knew she'd be back soon.

The Bible says you can ask for anything if you believe, and it will happen. I can't believe that God didn't keep His word, but so far I don't think He did. Because I *really* believed.

Love,
Ruth Ellen

December 1952

Dear Mom and Dad,

I got your letter today, Mom, saying you hoped I'd act better during Christmas vacation than I did last summer.

I know I was too grouchy. Each time I come home, it feels harder to let you hug me or hug you back. When I stay mad at everyone, it doesn't hurt so much to think about going back to school.

I'll try to do better this vacation, but I can't promise. I really do love you.

Love,
Ruth Ellen

January 1953

Dear Mom and Dad,

I tried real hard to behave this last vacation. How did I do? I found out that instead of getting angry and quiet all the time, I can pretend I don't care by being funny. When I joke about things at school or home, I can hide the hurt from you. I think you liked me better that way.

But either way, when the time came to leave, I felt as though I'd lost something. I'm glad we're going to America next year. Maybe I can tell you more then.

Love,
Ruth Ellen

April 1953

Dear Mom and Dad,

Mail comes about three times a week here. The other kids are kind of jealous because Mae Beth and I always get a letter.

Today Uncle Quentin kept calling the names on the envelopes, and kids went up to get their letters as usual. I began to get worried because our names weren't called and weren't called. I could feel all the other kids hoping that, just this once, we wouldn't get mail. Finally he got to the end.

"Well, that's it," he said. Everyone started to tease us, and then Uncle Quentin said, "Oops, I see one more." The other kids groaned, because they all knew it was for us. Uncle Quentin had just been holding it for fun.

I know everyone's parents can't send mail as often as you can, but I was so proud going up to get that letter. The whole school could see how much my parents love me! Thanks for that. I'm glad you're my mom and dad. And I love you, too.

Love,
Ruth Ellen

High School, United States

September 1959

Dear Mom and Dad,

My first day of high school. They've put me in the accelerated classes, so at least my strange education in Africa hasn't held me back in that way.

I'm hoping that starting over in a new school, with 400 kids in the class instead of twenty, will give me a chance. When kids ask where I'm from, I say Chicago. If only the kids who know me from eighth grade won't spoil it by telling others I'm from Africa, it will be okay.

Love,
Ruth Ellen

As the time for my parents' return to Africa drew nearer, I began to withdraw from them again. My anger grew and then gave way to the familiar pain, so great there were no other emotions left under which to hide it. But when I tried to express that pain, I always bumped into the reasons for the pending separation, and that locked me up. It was God's will that my parents return to Africa and how could I argue with God?

I sensed that my parents were hurting, too, more than they dared to show. Our private pains seemed to make it impossible for us to bear each other's.

December 1959

Dear Mom and Dad,

Knowing that nothing can change your being gone or my being alone, I have to shut you out of my life. It's as if I have to consider you dead. There aren't phones we can use to keep in touch. Letters take too much time. I have to face life as it has to be lived now.

When the ache comes, I push it back down. In the past few days I've cried enough tears for all four years, and I refuse to cry anymore if I can help it. And the only way I can do that is to try not to think of you at all. If I start wondering where you are or what you're doing, I immediately push the thought away. Africa is a different world. I will not meditate on it or you again.

Love,
Ruth Ellen

My method for keeping the lid on the pot of my family's separation seemed to work. Occasionally, if I wasn't careful, the pain bubbled up and raised the lid enough to let some seep out. But I quickly pushed it down and piled lots of activities and studies on top to keep it closed.

Thinking about my parents stirred up the pot, bringing it perilously close to boiling over, so I tried not to do that. I didn't want to get burned.

Grandma and Aunt Mae let us stay on with them, so we attended high school in Chicago. By anyone's standards, I had a very successful high school career. I worked hard at being a normal kid. I joined Bible Club and lots of extracurricular activities at school. I even got braces to straighten my teeth!

I made National Honor Society and was ranked ninth out of 365 kids in my class. I was voted "Girl Most Likely to Succeed" by my classmates, and I received three scholarships for college. High school was a good, even wonderful, time in my life. But I still missed my mom and dad.

June 1963

Dear Mom and Dad,

Tonight I graduated from high school. You weren't there to hear me make my speech as class vice president. I almost felt bad about that, but I got my emotions under control pretty quickly. No, it doesn't bother me. I'm used to it.

Living with Grandma and Aunt Mae made all the difference in the world. They faithfully represented you every time a parent should have been there. They were at my graduation tonight. They've always let me bring my friends home, just as you would have. I've grown spiritually and physically.

But sometimes I wonder about *our* relationship. When friends fuss about their parents, I feel smug in my heart. *My parents would never do that,* I think. But would you? You write how proud you are of me—but would you like me as much if you had to handle my rebelling against curfew hours or turning down my radio?

I worked hard to keep you proud of me, and you haven't had to come home on my account. But do we know each other anymore? Your letters have been as faithful as they were in my boarding school years. You always tell me what you do, and I tell you what I do—but we rarely talk about what we feel.

I tried a few times, writing about my first crushes that weren't reciprocated, or how some boy liked me but I didn't like him back. I appreciated your good letters in response, but when they came a month later, I hardly remembered what you were writing about. After a while, it didn't seem worth it to write about that sort of thing.

I'm not worried about recognizing you physically, as I was in first grade. But my question is really still the same: Will I know you?

Love,
Ruth Ellen

November 1963

Dear Mom and Dad,

Thanks for including us in your discussion about whether to return for another term. It felt good to know that our needs and feelings still matter to you.

Outwardly the conversation was calm and matter-of-fact. We named all the perfectly logical, absolutely true reasons why it's probably God's will for you to go back to Africa. We acknowledged His provisions for us: Mae Beth and I have had a home, we've done well in school, we've stayed on track spiritually. We're now away from home, anyway.

But everything inside me was screaming, "No, no, no! It isn't fair, God. Our family has already given you twenty years. You've taken and taken from us; can't you let us quit now? We'll serve You in the States."

But I couldn't—or wouldn't—tell you what I was feeling so deeply. I was afraid if I told you, you'd think I was saying you can't go back. I do understand your call. I even agree with it—that's what makes me feel that I shouldn't mind it so much. If I love God, as I think I do, and this is His will, then shouldn't I be feeling happy?

When I came to God later with my anger and my pain, He showed me these verses from Matthew 10: "He that loveth father or mother more than me is not worthy of me: and he that loveth son or daughter more than me is not worthy of me. And he that taketh not his cross, and followeth after me, is not worthy of me. He that findeth his life shall lose it: and he that loseth his life for my sake shall find it" (vv. 37-39).

What could I say? There are times when God requires us to give up our rights to family for His Kingdom's sake. But he also says that He will then supply our needs a hundredfold in *this* life as well as the life to come.

I guess He's kept that promise. He's provided a close, extended family to care for me, friends in abundance, a warm home. If you must go back again, I must trust God to continue to be faithful.

But I wish someone would acknowledge the pain of what He is asking. Just once, I wish someone would give me a hug and say, "I understand. It's okay to say that the right thing to do hurts. Go ahead and cry."

If only I could find just one person who would understand my tears. I don't want anyone to judge you badly for leaving me, or to think I'm unspiritual or unwilling to let you go. I just want someone to let me cry without trying to cheer me up or explain all about everything I already know.

Love,
Ruth Ellen

Dear Mom and Dad,

I'm realizing that my unacknowledged anger has been what has bred my spirit of resentment. And that resentful spirit will destroy me faster than any of the actual situations I've ever been through. As I think about where all this anger of mine came from, the most obvious source is all our separations—leaving me with mixed feelings about your return to the States again next week. Having finally recognized my feelings, what am I supposed to do about them?

I think the key may have something to do with forgiveness. I heard a woman say she'd had to learn to forgive many people in her life just for being who and what they were.

I have to go back and do a good bit of forgiving, especially in the areas where I felt pain even when it was never intended by those who caused it. The kids who laughed at my hairstyle; you, for sending me away because it seemed the best thing for me at that time; and all those who locked me up with pat answers or quick words of encouragement, when what I needed was understanding and a hug.

The verse comes to me, "Forgive us our trespasses, as we forgive those who trespass against us." I'm sure I've also hurt many others unintentionally, and sometimes intentionally, by my words and actions. I need *your* forgiveness.

In spite of the turmoil I've felt these last few years, I do love you, and I know you love me, too. I've asked God to let me *feel* your love once again, instead of only knowing it. I can't imagine how He will do it, but I know I need it for my healing.

Love,
Ruth

Children burdened with outsider status by their parents' choice to live abroad may succeed in deeply connecting with the surrounding culture. Easily recognized as a foreigner in Lobito, Angola, where her parents were missionaries, **Nancy Henderson-James** dove in and attempted to absorb "home" by learning the several languages spoken around her. She also poured her young energy into caring for an orphaned Angolan baby when she was only fourteen years old; it was her effort to create love and family when she felt emotionally detached from her own family, after spending three years living independently at boarding school.

More than that, she wanted to absorb culture through love of baby Tez. Angola would be home and identity, despite her "exotic status" as an estrangeira, which she recognized as both protecting and isolating her. Tez responded and bonded to Henderson-James but also challenged her schedule-conscious North American child-rearing approach, so different from the more relaxed African child-rearing practiced around her. She was discouraged, overcome with melancholy, yet unable to talk about her feelings in a family where "relentless cheer" was the norm. Caring for Tez both generated suicidal thoughts and mitigated them. Yet Henderson-James wouldn't permit herself to grieve when she had to hand Tez out a train window to relatives, as the country descended into a forty-year war. In the end, despite decades of war and disconnection, Henderson-James embraces her immersion in Angolan language and child rearing as engraved identity.

Diving In

Nancy Henderson-James

Cachimbo, the misty cool season, was upon us when we arrived home in Lobito in the summer of 1958. The chilly weather didn't keep me from plunging into the bay for a swim. I stroked out into the clear deep, enveloped by the water that seeped into every pore, and looked down at the rippling sandy bottom. I floated, effortless, one with the water. Later on the beach, the salt dried around each little hair on my arm, making it rise up prickly. Though I would soon wash off the salt, I could never shed the belief that this was home. Thank goodness my parents had turned down an offer from a swim-coach friend to keep me in America to train for the 1960 Olympics. I wasn't sure if the offer was serious or a joke, but I was glad they didn't consider it. I was ready to dive back, now a teenager, into my Angolan life.

My sister and I had outgrown our Dondi school and were to spend the next year and a half at home studying by correspondence, now called "home school," and learning French at a local Portuguese school, waiting to journey to Rhodesia for high school. After zooming through my eighth-grade course, I used my extra time to learn a little Umbundu, the language of the Ovimbundu people, and plunged into full-time care of an Angolan orphan baby for five months.

I had spent three years away from home in Dondi, but now, for the second year in a row, I was living with my family. The years in

Dondi had prepared me for teenage independence by teaching me that I was, at least emotionally, on my own. I no longer expected deep family attachments, nor in crisis did it occur to me to ask for help. On furlough in Hartford the year before, I was absorbed by the question of how I was related to America and the wider world and where I belonged in it. Now, in my fourteenth year, I gathered family for myself through language and baby.

I grew up knowing deep within, in a way that was imperceptible, that language mattered. Portuguese found me when I was two, at the same time I was learning the mysteries of speaking English. My parents had moved us to Lisbon for a year to learn Portuguese, as preparation for living in Angola, at that time a Portuguese colony. While they attended classes all day, my sister and I were tended by our nursemaid Vitelina, who spoke only Portuguese to us, thus preparing us to go to the João de Deus nursery school. The Portuguese tongue is rich in melodic rhythm. I loved reproducing the lilt of the language, exaggerating each syllable, drawing out the vowels. *Ó pa, vá t'embora. Ai minha filha, dá me urn beijinho, ai que riqueza.* I loved rolling my *R*s, letting my tongue vibrate against the roof of my mouth. Some *R*s were guttural, requiring me to rasp out the words. The shape of the language burned deep into my brain so that even now, though I hardly ever speak Portuguese, on the rare occasions when I travel in Portugal I am given the strangest looks. I don't physically resemble a Portuguese person. My skin and hair are light; I dress in casual style. But the words that come out sound so authentic I am a puzzle to them.

Portuguese was the language at home in Lobito. Within the family, of course, we spoke English, but even on those days when we had no guests, we shared the house with servants who spoke Umbundu and Portuguese. I chatted in Portuguese with our laundry lady, cook, houseman, and gardener. The language cemented my connection to the small city of Lobito. It was an expression of my inner knowledge as I grew older that yes, this was my town, this was where I belonged. The shouts of the kids in the schoolyard up the street, the fishermen yelling *garopa, garopa* as they rowed by, Dona Isaura's shrill voice calling to her houseboy, formed the background of my life. Though my looks identified me as an *estrangeira*, I felt exquisitely at home riding the bus downtown or transacting my business with the storekeeper.

My first attempt to prove myself Angolan, oddly enough, was to take French lessons in a Portuguese school. We supplemented our regular correspondence lessons in English by walking five blocks to the small private *Colégio Luis de Camões* to learn French. On the walk home, we recited aloud our new conjugations. "*Je suis, tu es, il est, nous sommes, vous êtes, ils sont. Je finirai, tu finiras, il finira, nous finirons, vous finirez, ils finiront.*"

The indicative, the conditional, the subjunctive modes. Imperfects, present perfects, pluperfects. Present participles and past participles. Infinitives and imperatives. French had such structure, such regularity, and such irregularity. All of a sudden I realized that language was organized. I'd never imagined that English and Portuguese were more than sounds with meaning, that they had grammar and structure. French helped make sense of all languages.

Padre Alberto, our teacher and a Catholic priest, was a short, tubby martinet of a man. Even so, he was intimidated by these two *estrangeiras* in his class. My sister and I were older than the rest of our classmates by several years, since Portuguese schools typically start French, German, and English lessons in elementary school. Not only did he have to deal with our being Americans; even more exotic, we were Protestant. He had no idea that Protestants as well as Catholics were Christians.

"You're excused from the Christmas lesson in the textbook," he told Kathy and me.

Like most Portuguese teachers, he believed the ruler was the best enforcer of instruction. If our classmates messed up reciting the lesson of the day, they were called to the front, one by one, for a heavy crack or two of the ruler on the open palm. The ruler, a wide, heavy piece of wood with holes drilled in it, sucked up the skin with each whack. We sat up front in the narrow, cramped class-room, within a couple of feet of Padre Alberto, and we watched him raise his meaty arm and bring it down hard on the little boys' hands. With each smack of the ruler, they quivered, whimpered, and tried not to cry out. And when Padre Alberto finished disciplining them, they pranced back to their seats, full of macho swagger. I was quite sure that Padre Alberto wouldn't hit me, but to make certain, I studied diligently until the conjugations rippled off my tongue. Even if I hadn't been so studious, though, my exotic status protected and isolated me. I had returned to Angola glad to be home, knowing that I wasn't American, but Padre Alberto reminded me, in the way he gingerly trod around Kathy and me, that I wasn't Portuguese, either.

If French brought me closer to the outside world (after all, right next door in the Congo they spoke French), learning Umbundu seemed like a lifeline, anchoring me to the cultural pool of home. I had always envied my upcountry friends who spoke Umbundu fluently. To me at thirteen, learning Umbundu was a good time-filler after I'd whizzed through my eighth grade Calvert course. But I'm certain that it was also a latent political act, proving my allegiance to the good guys, the Angolans, against the evil colonial Portuguese. With it, I'd be able to forge a link with Mãe, who didn't speak Portuguese very well but who had allowed me to hang around her laundry tubs or ironing board when I was a little kid.

I made a trade with my Ovimbundu friend Rebeca Valentim. I would help her with English conversation, one of the trio of European languages besides Portuguese that she was expected to learn in school, and she would teach me her native tongue. Rebeca, a couple of years older than me and the middle child of six or seven, came from an educated family. Her father was a nurse at the railway hospital and he had worked hard to gain the status of *assimilado*, an officially and legally recognized Portuguese citizen. Like me, Rebeca straddled several cultures.

We sat at a table on the upper verandah overlooking the bay on her weekly visits. She brought her English text from school. My mother had unearthed the Umbundu lessons she and my father had once studied for me to use. I thought I would pick up Umbundu as easily as I had French. I was accustomed to hearing it spoken around me and could follow the gist of conversations. In the *sanzala*, after church or with my mother on an errand, I could make out what she and Dona Emilia were talking about. The language was easy to pronounce, none of those wacky spellings and unarticulated letters of French. But the grammar wasn't anything like French or Portuguese or English. Umbundu was tonal and had six classes of nouns. I had difficulty distinguishing one set of nouns from another and remembering how the adjectives agreed with the nouns.

Learning Umbundu was hard, but Rebeca was fun. I could see her striding up the driveway from the bus stop in front of our house. I'd run downstairs to gather juice and cookies for our afternoon labors. If our mostly reliable kerosene-driven refrigerator were working, I'd clink some ice cubes into tall aluminum glasses to chill down the juice. Rebeca, hot from the cross-town ride, mopped her face and traced patterns with her fingers in the condensation dripping down the glass, delighted by the icy intrusion on our tropical day.

"So what happened with Padre Alberto this week?" she asked in Portuguese.

"One of the little boys pulled away his hand just as Padre Alberto swung down the ruler. He lost his balance, pranced forward on one foot and almost fell over! I could hardly keep from laughing. But then Padre Alberto grabbed the boy by his ear and whapped him around the head. He went crying back to his seat and I was glad I hadn't laughed out loud."

With Rebeca eager to hear the latest Padre Alberto story, I could poke fun at his silly self, even when being in his classroom could feel scary.

I'm not sure how long Rebeca and I labored over Umbundu and English. I could tell that weekly meetings and my slack internal drive couldn't bring me to even a basic level of fluency. Still, as I look back, the time Rebeca and I talked, in any of the three languages, laughing and discovering each other, was as important to me as learning her language.

Before catching the bus home, Rebeca sometimes suggested in her basic English, "We shall walk in the garden or on the beach?"

The beach, my home away from home, was nature's gift. Day after day, the water lapped the sand, sand dollars washed to shore, starfish were stranded on the beach at low tide, sea anemones anchored to the bottom waved their tendrils, independent of me. But I was part creator of our garden and had a proprietary interest there. I puttered without consulting my mother or our gardener. I pinched off sprigs of the edging plant and pushed them into the sandy soil so that over time all the beds sprouted a low creeping border. I loved to show Rebeca the garden, the elephant ears, the huge poinsettia bush, the yellow and red canna lilies, and the multi-colored hedge along the driveway that looked as if we had spattered it with red, yellow, white, and green paint. Sometimes we spotted the chameleon making his slow, deliberate way up the branch of the custard apple tree, swiveling his eyes nervously at us.

Our language lessons were cut short by the arrival of the orphan baby.

Technically, Tezinha wasn't an orphan. When her mother died, her family, unable to supply her with the milk she needed to survive, took her to the mission orphanage at Dondi, expecting to reclaim her when she was older. Despite regular feedings and loving care by the nurses, Tez, stunted in her newborn state, failed to thrive.

I knew several missionary families who were raising orphan children. Children in Angolan culture tackled adult responsibilities every day, lugging water from the well, taking charge of their younger siblings. My mother listened seriously to my earnest desire, my daily badgering to "have an orphan," and arranged for Maria Teresa to live with us temporarily. She was tiny, an eight-pound infant, whom we immediately renamed Teresinha, little Teresa, which soon shortened into Tezinha or simply Tez. She was as delicate as a newborn, unable to turn over or hold her head up. But she was seven months old.

The day she arrived, my mother drove me to the train station. We stood together on the hard-packed dirt between the station and the tracks, my heart beating so hard I could see the bodice of my shirtwaist jump. I carefully folded my arms, to contain any unseemly excitement. We looked up the track into the distance, listening for the whistle to tell us that the train would soon arrive. Right on time, the train chuffed and squealed to a halt, doors were flung open, and passengers disgorged. My mother pushed ahead through the crowd and I raced to keep up, a slight girl with golden brown hair a few days past my fourteenth birthday.

We spied Dona Clara walking toward us, cradling a tiny parcel. She shifted it into my arms. I drew away the blanket to look at the baby and she winced against the bright light, crinkling her eyes and turning her face into my chest. Like any new mother, I unfurled her fragile fist to count her fingers and let the baby grab my index finger. I couldn't tear my eyes from her. I took in every detail from her tiny toes and fingers to her dark brown eyes, from her satin skin to her tightly coiled soft hair. I wanted to squeeze her, to meld her Angolan self to me. We drove her home to introduce her to her new family.

I was ready for this project. I had no doubts about my ability to care for and love this child. Had I not babysat three children under the age of four when I was twelve years old? Had I not borrowed babies to jiggle on my knee and volunteered to work in the crèche at church on Sundays while the parents were attending the service? Had I not changed my baby brother's diapers when I was eight and carried him around on my hip?

I still had five months to fill before embarking on the long journey to my new high school in Rhodesia. My sister plowed ahead with her taxing ninth-grade course. David, my eight-year-old brother, would soon be returning to Dondi, leaving only Mark, my five-year-old brother, at home. Dad's attention was directed at administering the mission churches, schools, and clinics along the coast where we lived. Mom ran our house as a hostel for missionaries in transit, organized women's literacy and sewing groups, and occasionally checked on our studies. I longed to cuddle a baby.

If I couldn't ingest Umbundu and make it part of me, maybe I could absorb Ovimbundu-ness through Tez, skin to skin. Maybe bathing her slippery brown body, dressing her in clothes that I washed in the bathtub, and feeding her formula I mixed by hand would entitle me to enter the Ovimbundu world of love. Angolan mothers carried their babies on their backs until age two or three, rocking them to sleep there, and bringing them around front to suckle when they awoke, in a natural rhythm of body connection. I'd never seen mothers impatient or angry with their small children. For me, Tez would fill the niche my pets and dolls had filled. Through her, I would create the family connections my dolls mutely provided—qualities I observed in abundance among Ovimbundu families. Through this live baby I hoped I would gain a family of my own.

Tez was ravenous. Day and night she sucked down the bottles of milk I mixed for her. As predictably as the tide moved in and out of the bay in front of our house, Tez cried for milk. Before I went to sleep I fed her, and midway through the night I stumbled across the room to her crib to feed her. At church I heard the ladies whisper to my mother in Portuguese, "Nancy has circles under her eyes like a new mother."

I paid no attention to my exhaustion. I was exhilarated by the miracle of Tez plumping up. Her skin turned a glossy brown as ounces added up to pounds on the scale. Even more exciting, she smiled. The little line of worry between her eyebrows smoothed out. She chortled. She held up her head without a waver. She reached out for the rattle I held and flipped herself over in amazement. I laughed and clapped at her great feat. She was nine months old. At ten months she sat by herself and at eleven months grasped the slats in the crib and pulled herself up, compressing her infancy into a few short weeks, like the chicks I used to feed. She crowed with delight.

I was glad for the infant-care book, published in the 1940s, that my mother gave me when Tezinha arrived, because I wanted to bring her up correctly. I carefully read the instructions on how to put baby on a schedule, what to feed her, and how to potty train her. Its rigid approach to caring for infants, though, clashed so radically with the relaxed Ovimbundu style that I was confused about which way to proceed. Should I follow the intuitive ways evident in the culture all around me or should I adhere to the categorical how-to approach of this authoritative book? Without an Angolan mentor to show me the way, I chose the way of the book. After all, it sounded so sure of itself. When I read its suggestion for placing the baby on a potty starting at age four months, I was afraid I had delayed too long with Tezinha. I was afraid she'd fallen way behind schedule and that she'd never be properly trained. So while I knelt over the tub, scrubbing her diapers and clothes, she sat beside me on her potty until she pooped, chirping and playing, patient with me.

The book also mandated a rigid sleeping and eating schedule and advocated placing her in a playpen when she was awake, feeding my nascent moralism. Tezinha, I felt, should follow her schedule. Tezinha and I had our first clash when I insisted it was time for her nap and she was equally insistent that she wanted to stay awake. Why, I wondered, would she refuse to lie down? Why did she pop upright when I tried to put her down? She knew she was supposed to go to sleep. I rapped her once, twice, three times on her knuckles to force her to let go of the crib railing and lie down. With a great wail, she plunked down in bed but within seconds she pulled herself up again. I rapped her knuckles again, harder. Sobbing, she lay down. Suddenly, I became aware that Mãe, our laundry lady, stood in the door to my room. My room was just above her laundry area and Tez's screams must have been easy to hear. Crying babies in her culture were tended to immediately. Ashamed of my cruelty and embarrassed to have been found out, I froze in place. Mãe looked worriedly at Tez, who continued to cry, until she could stand it no longer. She rushed over to Tez, scooped her up, and comforted her.

The mission of bringing up Tez, the thrilling job I had pleaded with my mother for, was rattling me. I no longer knew what was right. The book from my mother laid out in detail exactly the schedule baby should follow, and I reasoned that this would also be my mother's advice. Mãe was showing me a different path, but one I couldn't intuit. The older Tez got, the more feisty her opinions, the less I knew how to cope. I sank into a discouraged gloom that I thought was shameful. Tez was here because I had insisted my mother find me an orphan, but now I was failing and I had no right to ask Mom for help. I had learned from my mother's relentless cheer to keep bad news from her. I plodded through my chores and caretaking, wondering how I could continue. Slowly, as I made Tez's milk and washed her diapers, walked with her on the beach and bathed her, the worm of melancholy burrowed in and made me question my very life. Yes, I thought, if I'm no longer here my mother and father will miss me and they will finally understand how hard it's been taking care of a baby. I wasn't taking good care of Tez. What use was I?

I brooded especially during the repetitive task of mixing milk in an empty kitchen. I suppose I chose those times when Tomas was not there so as not to disturb him at his work, but in the still, unoccupied space my despair had free rein, unhampered by the need to keep a good face on. I dipped cooled boiled water out of the pot on the stove. *I wish someone would help me.* I didn't know, I just didn't know, how hard this would be. I measured the powdered milk and sugar. Would Kathy notice I was gone, she in her own private world? What would happen to the family if I weren't here? I mixed the milk and sugar with water, stirring them to a smooth paste. I dipped my finger in the mixture and tasted the sweetness. *I'm sure Mom and Dad will be sorry when I'm gone.* I pictured them stricken on the verandah, my mother clinging to my father, my father draped over my mother. I could almost hear their sobs from the kitchen where I lurked, invisible and ghostly. I thinned the paste and poured the milk into Tez's bottles. I sterilized the nipples and sealed the milk in. I was surely a failure.

The notion that I could bring my despair to my mother never entered my mind. She was always busy. Dramatic, attention-calling action, thankfully, also was foreign to me, and I had time to mull over my best course of action. I loved Tez fiercely and protectively, even as she baffled me. If I weren't here to care for her, who would? My sister loved Tez, I knew that, but she was too busy with school to help. My parents were occupied with their work, my brothers were too young, and Mãe and our cook and gardener had their hands full. In the end, it was Tezinha who kept me anchored in life. Leaving Tez alone seemed worse than the relief I imagined from dying. I stayed alive for her.

Early in January of 1960, just as Tezinha was on the verge of walking, she, my mother, sister, and I boarded the train. Kathy and I were on our way to our new high school in Rhodesia, and Tezinha was returning to her family up-country. As I look back on that time, the notion that we could simply hand Tez out the window of the train as we whistle-stopped in Bela Vista is absurd. But that is what we did, with little sense of the impact on her psyche or on ours.

During the overnight train ride, Tez slept with me snug on the inner side of my bunk. I recalled the scrawny bundle I'd been given at the train station in Lobito, how fragile she had been five months earlier. Proudly I stroked the robust child beside me now, almost ready to walk with her rounded, muscled legs. Under my care, she had grown to a bouncy toddler, greedily eating her way out of infancy. I put my arm around her silky body protectively, even jealously. I had no idea what her family was like and was sure they could not love her as much as I. But if they didn't, what would become of her? She had seared herself into my emotions and I wondered if I could let her go, if I could undo the chemistry in the few hours I had until morning.

After we stopped briefly in Vila Nova, I started counting down the minutes until we would arrive in Bela Vista. Thirty, twenty-nine, twenty-eight...Tezinha's bag of diapers, clothes, and toys sat on the seat beside me, ready to be handed out the window. Tez stood gripping the sooty windowsill, watching the grasslands go by, not suspecting that she too would be passed through the window into another life. We were quiet in the cabin. What could we say? I kept my hand on Tez to steady her from the rocking and lurching of the train. And then I felt the train slowing down. I heard the squeal of the brakes and the whistle warning us that Bela Vista lay just ahead. I pushed up the window to look out at the familiar red dirt of nearby Dondi. I could see the back of Fadário's general store a block away on the main street, where we used to stock up on gum on Saturdays. We stopped with a hiss in front of the brick station with its red-tile roof. The crowd awaiting the train surged forward, anxious to get on in the brief moments before the train chugged on to Chinguar.

"Mom, who's coming to get Tezinha?" I asked.

"Probably Aunt Lillian," she answered.

Aunt Lillian saw us just as we spied her, a large woman, with short dark brown hair and a plump, smiling face. Her white nurse's dress reassured me about Tezinha's immediate fate. When I saw Aunt Lillian's familiar face, I smothered my fears about Tez's spectral family.

I picked up Tez for a last touch. Her soft hair tickled my nose when I nuzzled the top of her head and nibbled my way down her wide forehead to her nose. She grinned at me and grabbed my neck in an impulsive wet baby kiss, as if she wanted to eat me. I wanted to hug her back, to squeeze the breath out of her, but Mom said we had to let her go because the conductor was already yelling *partida* (all aboard). I passed Tez and her bags of clothes and toys out the window into Aunt Lillian's outstretched arms. The train whistled, lurched, and moved on. I waved until I was simply waving at the African savannah, until Tez's kiss dried on my cheek.

"Well, on to Rhodesia," said my mother.

I sank back into the seat. But I still had Tez on my mind, where she has stayed for the last forty years. I saw her rolling over for the first time on a blanket spread out on the verandah; wearing the pink calico dress I had made her, with a matching bow around the braid on top of her head; sitting in the grass and pushing away the kitten climbing up her front; cocking her head and waving her backhanded goodbye.

I stashed Tez inside with all my tenderness and guilt and attachment and loss, and I carried on.

About a year after I handed her out the window, war broke out in Angola, a war that would last until the present. It started as an anticolonial conflict. In 1975, after fourteen years of fighting to preserve their colonies, the Portuguese suddenly gave them independence, handing Angola over to the socialist revolutionary government allied with the Soviet Union. In the ensuing chaos, the war for independence evolved into a decades-long, grueling civil war, a war that split me off from my childhood and Tezinha. I never saw her again.

Still, forty years later, all those afternoons learning Umbundu with Rebeca and those months of nurturing Tezinha count for something. I know now I could never be fully Ovimbundu or Portuguese, but my Umbundu lessons took on new meaning recently when I unexpectedly received a letter from Rebeca. She wrote in Portuguese that she intended to break the long silence between us. She reminisced about the good times we'd had at the Casa Missionária, as we sipped our cold juice, walked in the garden, and swam on the beach so close to the house. She remembered my stories about Padre Alberto. Finally she listed her seven children and their considerable accomplishments: Silvia is a doctor specializing in cardiology, Alvaro is a vet, Alda is in medical school, and her two youngest, Afonso and Felisimina, are in tenth and eleventh grades. But her notes about her middle sons, Valentim and Gilberto, who are well past high school age but are both in twelfth grade, reminded me of the reason for the years of silence: the terrible war that engulfed Rebeca's family, drove me from Angola, and has continued unabated for forty years.

I have little hope that Tezinha's life after 1960 will ever be revealed to me. From the time she was two, Angola was at war. I don't know if she and her family were spared disruption, hunger, or even death, as hundreds of Angolans fled to neighboring countries and more were killed and maimed by land mines. Through all the unknowns, though, she has remained a part of the child-mother in me, a profound connection with my Angolan childhood. When my own two sons were babies, the lessons I learned from her encouraged me not to go by the book but to trust myself.

As I stand on the American side of the Atlantic Ocean, I conjure up the bay in front of my Angolan childhood home. I remember countless hours of building cities in the sand, diving off our tilting raft to touch the gently swaying tentacles of the anemones, collecting sand dollars to skip across the flat water, watching the ships steam by. I see Rebeca and me strolling along the beach and Tez crawling full tilt into the salty water. In my fourteenth year, I dove into their Ovimbundu culture. Forty years later, I find that my attachments to Rebeca and Tez, unlike the saltiness of the ocean, cannot be washed off.

Section III
Rootlessness

Where are you from?

Like a haunting refrain, the question echoes through the lives of unrooted children, as if the answer could solve the riddle of the child's identity. But unrooted children often cannot easily answer the question. They have no permanent home; they aren't from anywhere. Beneath the surface, they struggle with a much more fundamental question: Who are you?

All children must figure out who they are and where they belong. Rooted children can take their clues from history, from their environment, from the traditions they are born into. But mobile children, raised in a world of changing backdrops, are expected to be cultural chameleons, turning themselves emerald in the Amazon forest, tawny on dry Arabian sands. To successfully adapt to the transitions in their lives, they must flow in and out of cultures, taking on the colors of one, slipping from the bonds of another. Some embrace the many influences they are exposed to, while others are more selective, adopting only those aspects of a culture they choose to retain. They are able to immerse themselves in new cultures, keeping pieces of themselves hidden and adapting well with frequent moves.

But what of their interior selves? Some children deal with transition by managing superficial changes with ease, seemingly conforming to the new host culture but camouflaging their inner lives. They learn new languages, wear the proper clothing, play the part like the seasoned performers they have become. Yet others suffer great difficulty in dislocation and cannot make themselves entirely comfortable anywhere. Without the supportive structures of a place they can call home, they flounder in new environments, unable to conform or blend in with their surroundings. Theirs is not the exhilaration of freedom but the loneliness of isolation. Awkward outsiders, they always feel out of place. A gnawing restlessness shadows their lives and prevents them, even in adulthood, from establishing permanent roots. They search for home in the rhythms of breath and time and in attempts to absorb rootedness through ritual and personal connection. Family, religion, language, memories carried within, become the home these children are able to return to, a home not defined by geography.

For Nina Sichel, brought up by an American mother and a German father in the international community of Caracas, Venezuela, home is "a shifting definition." Raised to consider herself American, she nevertheless suffers culture shock her freshman year in a U.S. college, when she finds herself immersed in a place and tradition that feel foreign. Traveling back and forth, she realizes that she cannot be defined by place. "I learned that I never really was part of any one culture, but that there are bits and pieces of me that belong everywhere, and just as many that belong nowhere," she writes. It is only when she has children of her own that she understands that home, for her, is where her family is, regardless of geographical place.

Tara Bahrampour, whose family fled the Iranian revolution for a more tranquil life in the United States, also draws strength from her close family ties. At school, she feels isolated from the mainstream. "It scares me to think that I am the only one in my class… to whom Iran is real." Her classmates try to refashion her as a typical American teenager to help her fit in, but she feels silly and ashamed, as if she were betraying her Iranian side. "We had not fit into any mold; compared to Iranian kids in Iran or American kids in America, we had a sense of being untethered in the world," she writes.

Free-floating anxiety wakes Anora Egan from troubled sleep, and it is only when she centers herself through conscious breathing that she remembers who and where she is. A childhood of near-constant moving left her yearning for roots. "I felt I wanted a home but…I didn't know how to settle, only how to be a foreigner, moving from country to country." Desperate to be "invisible," she immerses herself in languages, philosophy, religion, even a foreign marriage, all in an attempt to "be someone with a clear identity."

Section III

She searches for home in metaphor, knowing she won't find it in place. Home is where her breath is, her roots float "in emptiness."

An ongoing feeling of separateness and an inability or reluctance to root mark all the writers in this section. "What it is that I am, fundamentally, is a matter of earnest agony to me," declares Clark Blaise in his memoir of border crossing. Every time his French-Canadian father failed in his salesman's job or was run out of town for fighting, young Blaise was packed into a car and driven north, to his mother's Winnipeg home. In contrast to the instability his father's impulsive nature forced upon them, his mother's family home was "a place where everything was intact." His uncle's house represented all of Canada to the young Blaise, with its air of permanence and collections of magazines dating back decades. The legacy of all those years on the road is an ongoing urge to travel. "The cardinal directions still move me; I dream restlessly of the eternal *setting out*, steering on a highway for what I know will be a long drive...".

The journey to self-discovery can be a protracted one for the unrooted child. The restlessness bred into these children because of their parents' mobility leads them to seek identity in something other than place. Roots are not portable; these children cannot secure themselves to an impermanent home. In developing an integrated identity, they must piece together selfhood in other ways. This is the great challenge for the rootless child.

*Children raised as foreigners are children made rootless. Born in the United States to an American mother and a German father, brought up in Venezuela but returning to New York each summer, **Nina Sichel** grew up feeling as disconnected from her host culture as from the place she was taught was her "true" home.*

"What is it I am looking for?" she asks in this meditation on roots and the meaning of home. Returning as an adult to Caracas to see her mother, who can no longer travel, she is pulled by nostalgia to revisit the important places of her youth. Searching for symbols and memories to anchor her, she finds instead a continued feeling of impermanence and a longing to move on. She realizes that although she feels no particular ties to the many places she has lived, her roots are found in her deep commitment to family. She currently resides in Tallahassee, Florida, with her husband and children but tries to reunite several times a year with a family still flung across two continents.

Going Home

Nina Sichel

I've come home to see my mother. I've come home after all these years because my mother cannot travel anymore, cannot even leave the apartment, and I want to be with her. Left behind are my husband and children, who did not grow up here and who only know this place superficially and who cannot possibly understand what I mean when I say, I'm going home. Because for them, home is a real place, and for me, it is a shifting definition.

I grew up in Venezuela. I was brought to Caracas as an infant in my mother's arms, and here I was raised, along with my brother and my sister. So were a host of citizens of foreign countries who came and went, according to their parents' positions with the embassies or the oil companies or the other international corporations that did business in Latin America. I've lost touch with most of them. They moved on, every two years or so, and we stayed. We stayed while my father built a career as the manager of a paint company, we stayed while the company—and my father—prospered, we stayed while my father became a nationalized citizen and my mother begged, "Don't bury me in this godforsaken place."

I come home to an onslaught of memories, a rush of emotion. I've lived away more than half my lifetime, and it's been years since I've felt drawn to this place, pulled back by nostalgia or reminiscence or bittersweet hopes for reunions that don't happen with friends who no longer live here. But something swells in me, excites me when I see the mountains sweeping down to the sea, highway lights tracing their beadwork up the sides to the tunnels. Something fills me with longing when I breathe deeply of the thick sea air as I step down the ladder that's been pushed to the door of the airplane. And there are the masses of people crowding around the conveyor belts waiting for luggage, and the eager men in uniform who are so quick to take it from you, hoping for a big tip, and there is my father, patiently standing among the crowds of welcomers waiting, just outside, to hug and kiss the new arrivals and block the exits. We climb the three thousand feet to the city in half an hour and the long, narrow valley stretches ahead of us, full of light and traffic and life, as we drive toward the east, toward the residential section my parents live in.

Someone has placed a splash of flowers in the living room to greet me, but my mother is asleep, and I don't wake her. I bend to kiss her, and she doesn't stir. Her sleep is deep and peaceful.

In the morning I rest on the terrace of my parents' apartment with a *cafecito* cooling nearby, and I take in the view. The apartment building sits high on the hill in one of the last areas where building is allowed. Above it, another one is being built, but above that is *zona verde*, the "green zone," where no more construction is permitted. These buildings weren't here when I was a child, and neither were the buildings I can see climbing up the hills across town, crowding the mountainside like tombstones in an old city cemetery.

I look out and see that much is the way I remember it. The tulip trees are in bloom, bursts of orange spattered among the rich green of the mangoes. Feathery pink mimosas explode from ferny leaves. There are many large and leafy spreading trees, spiked by the fan of palms, and parts of the valley of Caracas still look green. But the view from the terrace is slowly being eclipsed by towering new apartment buildings and by giant satellite dishes on the red-tiled roofs of the older homes. They squat, all facing the same direction, looking like skeletal sunflowers, bringing in television shows from the States, from Spain, from Brazil. They bring in advertising for U.S. products and create demands that never before existed. I go to the market with my father and find familiar items, made in the USA, sold for outrageous prices that rise almost daily, keeping pace with the soaring inflation. This, I suppose, is progress. This is modernization. Petrodollars have made Caracas part of the global village.

It rains every afternoon or evening during my visit here, great squalls of tropical rain sheeting down across the city in heavy downpours. In the morning slanted yellow sunlight on the *monte* behind the building makes the tall grass glow green and yellow, and the sky brightens to a rich blue. Fog, or smog, softens the contours of the city before it, too, lifts and the day sparkles. By midmorning clouds begin to form, by the early afternoon the sky is filled with them, the sky hazes, and then the rain begins to fall, first on one hill, then another, until the storms all come together as one enormous rainfall. The rain falls so thickly that I can't see the hills across town. There is a rhythm to the rainfall and a sharp, clean smell that soothed me as a child when illness forced me to stay in bed, and I hope my mother is lulled as she moves in and out of sleep.

At night when it is clear again the hills glitter with flickering lights, and the tourists who ride up to the city for an evening away from their Caribbean cruise ships are charmed by them. We who live here know that by day the lights are merely bare bulbs strung in front of hovels where impoverished dwellers live in destitution. Many of them moved here from the country, hoping for better fortune in the big city but finding only an overcrowded squalor. Their need was something that many of my schoolmates didn't see, or if they did, they dismissed it as something foreign, something Latin American, something backward. This overwhelming poverty and this easy dismissal upset me then, and they still anger me today, so many years later.

I tell my father I want to see my old elementary school, the first one I attended, the one I went back to as a teacher's aide one summer when I was home from college. I remember how surprised I'd been that time at the shock of recognition when, after fifteen years, I again entered the kindergarten room. There, in the same places, were the stacks of creamy drawing paper, buckets of crayons, pots of white paste that had the same minty smell. Even the dolls were the ones I'd played with, naked and pink. But the school no longer exists. It has been turned into a clinic, and my father is uncomfortable driving past it. He explains, "Not long ago there was a shoot-out there, hostages were taken, and people died—a horrible thing." He suggests, instead, that we visit the second school I went to, the one I attended from sixth through twelfth grades.

Academia La Castellana was a new school then, and there I was enrolled, along with an international group of about four hundred other students, children whose parents sent them to American schools so that they'd have some semblance of stability and educational continuity as they followed their fathers' job transfers around the world.

Our education in an international school based on the American system did not prepare us to enter university in Venezuela; it was always assumed that we would go to the States for college. To enter the Venezuelan university system would have required revalidating the entire high school curriculum and basically doing it over in a Venezuelan school. None of our friends—Americans, Dutch, English, Scandinavian, Japanese, not even the Venezuelans enrolled in our school—chose to revalidate, though some did return to Venezuela after college. And some chose never to leave.

For most of us, being raised as foreigners meant our stay in Venezuela was free of permanence. For some, a temporary stay meant a year or two; for others, time dragged on indefinitely, but always, always, the time would come to say goodbye. Our parents may have chosen to remain, but we would leave. We were raised to be different, we were raised knowing we wouldn't stay, knowing that as soon as we finished school we would leave and probably not come back. And for the children in my family, American citizens, the place we would go to would be the United States.

Academia La Castellana, site of adolescent rebellion, teenage romance, high school mischief, no longer exists, having merged with another American high school the year I graduated. But the buildings still stand, more or less intact. I can still find my way there. We drive through streets that look vaguely familiar. Some of the old homes and apartment buildings endure, but many have been torn down and replaced with something newer and more elegant. Other places on the way haven't changed at all: we pass through the *barrio,* where half-naked children run by a stream of untreated sewage, the way other children did thirty years ago. They look up from their play as we pass by. We circle the golf course of the country club, drive through a tunnel of bamboo, and then we are there, where Academia La Castellana once was.

A tall white wall, graffitied and topped with shards of glass, now surrounds it, and it has been reborn as a hotel. Friends have told me it is a hotel by the hour. I don't know if this is true. It doesn't matter. I remember with a smile the lecture on decadence when we girls defied the dress code and came to school in mini-skirts. The principal came around with a ruler and sent most of us home to change. And I remember walking into school another day to find that our lockers had been strafed with machine gun fire, bullets had drilled perfect circles into the metal doors. We had an assembly that day, an unscheduled one, and we were told that due to anti-American sentiment we were to behave especially well and not to draw undue attention to ourselves, either on campus or during the bus ride home. My father remembers my mother warning me, telling me to lie down on the floor of the car or bus if I heard any gunshots. I don't remember hearing any, and I don't remember her warning. I do remember protesting, "But I'm not a *gringa;* I've lived here all my life."

My mother missed the States terribly, and she idealized life there. She left in the mid-1950s, a good time to idealize. She was spared the various revolutions of the 1960s, though she faced dictatorship, student revolution, bombings of the American embassy in Caracas, and robbery at gunpoint one morning near the home of a friend. She never felt more alive than when she walked in the streets of New York. Her love of the city, and the joy she took in it, were palpable and contagious. She was proud of her American nationality, and just as proud when someone would compliment her by saying, "I would never guess you were North American." We were told not to speak English in the street; we were told there was no greater place than the USA.

My mother went home to birth all her babies, home to her mother and home to the States, making sure that our citizenship could never be questioned. Babies born of American mothers abroad assumed their mothers' citizenship, but my mother would take no chances. "It's the greatest country on earth," she told me. "Not like here."

Years ago, my mother came to visit me where I live now, in Tallahassee, a small and pretty town in northern Florida. I took her to my children's preschool and she looked around and smiled, and with her eyes shining, she said to me, "This is wonderful. I feel at home here." And I remembered all her longing, while I was growing up, for a house with a white picket fence in a small town in upstate New York and her sense of displacement in a big and busy city in the tropics where all around her were walled city homes.

My mother assembled jigsaw puzzles, and her favorites were always scenes of covered bridges, maple trees in fall colors, American primitives like those of Grandma Moses, whose farm was not far from my mother's home and whose book of paintings she kept in the living room. Immersed in an intensity of tropical light and color, she missed the quiet tones of the North and yearned for the Catskills, the Adirondacks, cold Lake George.

Every summer my mother went home to her family, and we, her children, went with her while my father stayed back in our Caracas home, working. We said goodbye to all our friends and all that was familiar and spent the summer in upstate New York, where the grass grew soft and smelled sweet and the ground beneath our bare feet sank like a damp cushion and where there were no lizards or palm trees or even bougainvillea, but there were maple trees we could climb and bent and crooked apple trees with hard little fruits to wonder at, and strange new worlds to discover. My mother sat in a thickly carpeted room with a bay window that didn't open, a room filled with old people who sprinkled their talk with words in Yiddish, and ate things like pickled herring and called it a treat. It was so different from all we knew. It was so foreign, but my mother was ecstatic.

To us, it was all very strange. In the States there was food that didn't exist in Venezuela, and it all came in bottles and jars, and you had to get it yourself from a supermarket, even the fruit, because there were no men who came every morning in converted pickup trucks to deliver fruit fresh from the farm to your doorstep, and there was no bread man arriving at dawn with a warm paper bag filled with crusty French rolls, and there was no maid who rose well before the rest of the household to squeeze juice from succulent oranges. In the States, we found a different way of being the same people and a different manner of sustenance. Here we opened plastic bags of spongy white bread that we bought in the supermarket and that was already sliced, and here was a jar of sweet heaven, Marshmallow Fluff, gooey, sticky, and eaten to excess between slices of bread thickly painted with peanut butter. Our cousins spoke English and begged us to teach them Spanish, and we did, starting with the dirty words. Their friends believed us when we told them of the famished tigers that prowled outside in our gardens at night, and we laughed at their gullibility, for we knew well that there were no tigers in all of South America, and that these gringos were fools. And then we thought, these are Americans. These are us.

By the end of the summer we'd had enough of this strangeness. We were wild with excitement to get back home, where we would eat our own food again and be with our own people and hear Spanish being spoken and breathe in the thick smell of coffee as it hissed from the espresso machine and open our windows at night to the cacophony of cicadas and hear our mother tell us that it wasn't safe to drink the water from the faucet even though other people did.

My children call me every night while I am away. "We're eat-
ing in front of the TV!" they shout over the long-distance wire.
"Daddy rented us a video. We went canoeing. School is boring.
When are you coming home?"

"Soon," I tell them. "Just a couple more days. I'll be home
soon."

Their pictures are on the walls of my parents' room. I've been
gone two days, and I miss them with an aching that is like a wail,
low and mournful and constant. They are hundreds of miles away,
past the mountains, past the sea, past the miles and miles of grassy
scrub that is most of the peninsula of Florida. They are only a
phone call away, but we are a world apart.

On a shelf in a closet are albums and albums of snapshots my
parents took of us as children, as adolescents, as adults. I take some
down and go into my mother's room. We look through the books
together. There are no dates, no names, only dozens of pictures of
people in various poses, doing different things. I recognize family members. There are pictures of my brother and my sister and
me as babies, pictures of my husband, of my own children, of my
grandparents. Some of the people in these books are strangers, and
I want to know who they are, why they were important enough to
be included here, in the family albums. We laugh over funny stories
the photos bring back. Yet I want more stories, more memories than
the ones I can summon. I was so busy rushing through my youth
that I didn't stop to memorize any of it. I knew my parents would
be there to tell me; they recorded it and I knew they'd remember.

But my mother's condition is eating up her memory. On some
days her recall is as sharp as the blue Adirondack air on a clear
autumn afternoon; on others, she is vague, unable to recollect even
what she had for lunch. Now, there is a distancing and forgetful-
ness and fatigue that sometimes infuriates me but more often
leaves me mourning the loss of her vibrancy, her excitability, even
her restlessness. I point to people in the pictures. She remembers
the names of some of them, but she sometimes confuses their relationships. She agrees with what I tell her of what I remember, and

she is happy to hear my recollections. But she can't tell me many stories of my past, and I want her to. I want her to remember more of it. I want her to help me define it.

The maid comes in with a tray. My mother is tired. It is time for lunch, and then my mother sleeps. The afternoon stretches before me.

My father comes home early from work; it is only midafternoon, and the air is hot and still. My mother naps in her room; the women who take care of her are busy in the kitchen. We go out to run errands.

There is no mail waiting at the post office. My father tells me it sometimes takes three weeks or more to get a letter from the States now. At the fruit stand, I see something I've never seen before, and the young boy who works there tells me it's called a kidney. I break it open, and the flesh inside is soft and sweet and tastes faintly of cinnamon. Guavas, pineapples, avocados big as U.S. papayas, papayas bigger than watermelons. Flies buzz, and the air is filled with the scent of sweet decay.

I buy roses from the Italian flower vendor across the street. He recognizes my father and asks after my mother; he tells me I look just like her. This is not true, but anyway I am touched. The roses are a deep, deep red, and their rich and musky perfume is like a balm. We go to the coffee shop to buy an espresso, the only kind of coffee made here, and we order two *negritos*. We stand as we drink them, and I ask my father about racism. I remember class snobbery, but I don't remember much racism, and I wonder if I was sheltered from it or if it just wasn't an issue. "There isn't much," he tells me. "Some, but not much." The people here are brown, their faces a mix of black, white, and Indian features. There are still pockets, far from the city, where native cultures survive, barely. But in the city, everyone is mixed, integrated—everyone except the foreigners, who maintain their own enclaves and send their children to American, British, German schools. The foreigners, who seldom plan to stay.

Caracas is the Cradle of the Liberator. This is the birthplace of
Simón Bolívar, revered as the greatest of Latin American heroes
and once the most powerful man on the whole continent. He
was the visionary who dreamed of a united Spanish America,
the man about whom I learned little in our international school,
where he was referred to in passing as the George Washington of
South America. What has happened to his vision? A statue or at
least a bust of the Liberator graces every plaza in every city, town,
and hamlet in the country. He was a tiny man, with an intent
and proud expression. But I was raised a U.S. citizen, and his life
had little to do with mine. Our heroes were men of the American
Revolution.

"You mean North American," my Venezuelan friends would
correct me. "This is America, too." And by the time I came to the
United States, I, too, felt insulted when it alone was referred to as
America.

I moved to the States to go to college, and I was sent to a
small school in the Northeast, to be close to my mother's family.
I brought my coffee, my cornmeal to make *arepas,* my Venezuelan
folk music. I brought my English books of poetry, my American-
made blue jeans, my poster of Bob Dylan. I was coming to the
country I'd been told was mine: the land of the free, the home of
the brave, the greatest society on earth.

In my freshman year at college, I met the man who would
become my husband, born and raised in the United States. I made
Venezuelan food for him; he brought me to rock concerts and introduced me to variations of jazz and blues that I'd never heard before.
I made other friends: white girls from Long Island, totally different
in outlook and attitude; a beautiful black girl called Celeste, who
braided cornrows in my hair; Queenie, from Africa, big and lonesome and with a sing-song to her voice. Once I met a boy from the
Andes, and we sang *Alma Llanera,* a Venezuelan folk song, at a gathering of international students, but it was the last time I went—I
couldn't fit in any group, not even an international one, and I isolated myself with just a few close friends.

One awful day, a girl from my dorm floor stormed into my room in a fit of misguided fury, hurling racial epithets at my roommate. The girl was black; my roommate was white; the misunderstanding had to do with the volume of music that was played late at night, but the fury had to do with something I'd never been exposed to—unresolved racial tension that exploded in strange corners of this country. I'd never heard anything like that, and I was terrified. I hadn't known Americans could be so different. I hadn't been taught these things in school, I hadn't been prepared. I didn't know what to do and felt afraid, anchorless. The situation was resolved in time, but I was unnerved.

Culture shock is a peculiar thing. It feels as if all your guideposts have been turned upside down, as though the words you read were unexpectedly printed backwards, as if the air you took for granted with every breath were suddenly scented in a strange and unfamiliar way. I looked around at the people I went to classes with: I looked like them; all of us wore jeans and T-shirts, we spoke the same language, though some of us had different accents. We had similar interests, similar callings. We were intelligent, we were young, we were finding our paths, defining our interests. Yet the very way the other students walked in the world, viewed their place in it, and approached others made me feel like a stranger, and there were times of intense longing for the familiarity of home.

Gorgeous autumn came, with its exuberant, fiery flush, and then stark winter, all browns and grays. For months there was no color, and little sign of life outside my frosted dormitory window. I had never felt cold so brutal, and I didn't like it. My glasses fogged when I entered buildings. I missed the explosion of tropical color and noise, I missed the fresh air and fruit. I gained a lot of weight on tasteless food. I learned to stand a certain distance from my friends or they would back away; I learned not to embrace them or the motion would be misunderstood. I learned that individuality here mattered more than family ties, and it mattered so much that all else mattered very little. And I wondered whether my attachment to my family was extreme, or whether it was one of the gifts I'd taken for granted as I blundered my way through adolescence.

"Where are you from?" I was asked, and I always answered, "I was born in the States, but raised in Venezuela." I wouldn't be defined by place; I was not from anywhere. My sense of family was extremely strong, but my sense of place was weak. Home was not a place, not a country. Patriotism didn't stir my soul.

For me, foreign-raised, the question became one of torn loyalties. Trying to belong here, belong there, belonging nowhere. For a time I felt I was constantly shifting allegiances, searching for connection in groups that inevitably excluded me for being different. I shuffled back and forth in identity the way I did in language: if the right definition didn't come one way, it would come another. Always a minority, I learned that I never really was part of any one culture, but that there are bits and pieces of me that belong everywhere, and just as many that belong nowhere, and sometimes I felt wonderfully flexible, and sometimes I just felt disconnected.

After college, I moved seven times in ten years as my husband developed his career, and I moved from job to job. There was a certain freedom in this rootlessness. I was pliant, easy to uproot, I made no great demands as I attempted over and over again to find work that was stimulating, interesting. Six months here, three years there, one year somewhere else. I knew there were always greener pastures somewhere else and we would find them. Yet I also wanted more stability so that I could develop something of my own that was worthwhile. Once during this time, I sat with my father and told him of my frustration with the constant change and my yearning for a place to settle down, a place that had everything I was looking for. "Live as if you were staying here forever," he told me, and I wondered at his advice. I took it to mean, then, to stop wishing for something other than what I had, to make do. I thought he felt my restlessness was perhaps a reflection of my mother's, and that he didn't want this restlessness to interfere with my husband's future.

My mother had always been restless, always interested in other places, other languages, other people. She was the first of her family to go away to college. When she graduated, she moved to New York City, where she met my father, a foreigner, born in Germany, raised in Uruguay, educated in California. They met, they married, and they lived abroad in two different places before settling in Venezuela. Then they had children. And their differences in background, in outlook as a European and an American, in temperament, and in habit became less important than the values that bound them together and that they attempted to instill in us, their children, values that stressed the priority of family interests and the primacy of deep commitment. The world could fall apart around you, but your family was always there. Family was your best friend, family was what you came back to.

And so I've come back to see them. Back to my parents, back to the city in which I was raised, back to what seems so familiar yet has changed so much. The apartment is quiet with the sound of people growing old. There are no more children here.

What is it, then, that I am looking for? Talismans, place markers, fragments of my past. Memories. I tear open closets, drawers, the armoires, in a confusion of excitement, of joy at the familiar, and I want to share this with someone, but I am there, alone, and crowding the room are fleeting, silent memories. I smell the damp and musty scent of old wood and spirits in the armoire that's used as a liquor cabinet. Cut crystal goblets glint from deep inside the other one. It's all there, the way it has always been, the way the portrait of my grandmother at four still gazes wide-eyed and innocent, from its place on the dining room wall, the way the clothes in my parents' closets are still folded, precisely.

When I was a girl, my mother filled the house with flowers. I treasure images of her returning from a trip to the flower stalls, arms loaded. She spread newspapers on the kitchen table and then began her artistry. Vases of battered silver, crystal, even a copper teapot were filled, then placed strategically where the fading light of the afternoon would catch them, glowing on the polished wood of an antique table.

My father brought me pink roses when I was a little girl, home sick with a sore throat. He presented them to me as I lay in my bed, and my mother went to get a vase. He was still in his tie and jacket from work, briefcase in his hand, as he tenderly handed me the roses.

There is a vase I do not recognize in the armoire. It is painted clay, blue and white, and my mother tells me it was a gift from one of her friends, long ago. I fill it with the tiny red roses I bought earlier in the afternoon and bring them to her. She smiles when she sees them, and I place them near her bed, where they will catch the last light of the day. She can see past them to the sunset, spreading its colors against a sky that grazes the tops of the mountains across town.

"I love it here," she tells me, "where everything is taken care of."

It is five in the morning and it is time for me to leave. The sky is still dark, and the lights of the city sparkle outside the window. I look down at my mother, asleep in her bed. She is home, she is cared for, she is content. I will not wake her. I bend to kiss her, and she doesn't stir. Her sleep is deep and peaceful.

I think of my children, warm and snug and curled in their beds. They will meet me at the airport when I arrive. They will rush to embrace me, arms outstretched; they will tell me how they missed me. My husband will smile and kiss me. I will fold my arms around them all like wings, and we will stand like that a moment, then turn and drive back through the grays and greens and browns of piney woods and live oak canopy. I'm going home.

Neither expatriate nor immigrant, **Tara Bahrampour** *is the daughter of an Iranian architect and an American singer. This excerpt from her memoir,* To See and See Again, *describes the cultural differences that exist between her two worlds. Watching her two nations at war on the nightly news from her refuge in the United States, she feels a divided loyalty between her mother's faddish California and her father's earnest homeland. She tries to blend into U.S. pop culture even as she longs to return to Iran. She worries about her brother's resistance and is dismayed at how far her friend Shahrzad goes in denying her heritage, even to the point of changing her name and claiming to be Italian Catholic.*

Bahrampour comes to realize that families who move often have to be close because they have only each other as reference points. Neighbors and friends are always changing. Without the closeness of her family, the evidence of her past in Iran, which anchors her, would float away. The one exception is Carla, an expatriate she played with in Iran and reunites with years later. After she returns to Iran as a young woman and reconnects with her father's family, she realizes she will always feel untethered in the world.

Witness and observer of two clashing cultures, Bahrampour has developed into a journalist and writer. She became the fourth generation of her family to attend University of California at Berkeley and then moved to New York City, where she graduated from Columbia University's School of Journalism. She has contributed to many U.S. periodicals.

To See and See Again

Tara Bahrampour

One day at recess [my friend] Jill asks what my school was like in Iran. I end up telling her about how they closed the school down because of the revolution, and by the end of my story a crowd of kids is standing around asking me to repeat the parts they missed. I tell it again, and from then on there is always someone asking me to tell my story because they haven't heard it yet.

Each time it is the same story, full of precise, disjointed details. "It was November 4," I start in a dramatic voice.... "We went to the park with our parents.... The next day...the streets were full of rioting and people yelling and starting fires, and our bus driver made us close the curtains and get down...." Everyone listens gravely, nodding at the right moments, reminding me when I leave something out. And then the next day they bring over another kid who hasn't heard it and say, "Tell him about the revolution," and I solemnly start from the beginning as if it were some holy legend.

It is. It scares me to think that I am the only one in my class to have seen these things, the only one to whom Iran is real. A whole country, a whole life of streets and shops and shopkeepers and bus routes that only I know. With my classmates gathered around, I search my mind for every shred of it that I can remember.... They ask for my story again and again, and I tell it gladly, desperate to save myself from forgetting.

Sitting in class, I notice that every single shoe has a long crest running down the side. "Yeah, they're Nikes," Jill says when I mention this coincidence. "You can get them at the Nike store at the Beaverton Mall."

"You'll have to think of a nickname and then get it ironed onto a baseball shirt at T-shirt Plus," Lori says. "Everyone has one."

"You can get these at the GAP," Julie says, fingering the heavy denim of her wide-leg jeans. "Ask for San Francisco Riding Gear."

"And you really should get your hair feathered," Lori adds. "It would look so good."

Mama takes me to the mall and buys me two pairs of San Francisco Riding Gear, a pair of brown Nikes, and a yellow baseball shirt with my new nickname, "Dandelion," ironed onto the front. When I tell Mama the part about my hair she asks me if I'm sure. "It took so long to grow out," she reminds me, and I stroke my long braids, remembering how happy I was the day they finally brushed the top of my jeans.

"Well, maybe just a little," I say, and I tell the hairdresser to just take a couple of inches off the bottom and sides. But at school I still look different from everyone else. "Go to Renee at Apropos," Julie instructs me, and the following week I come out of the hairdresser's with thick, fluffy layers, a new curling iron, and a metallic-blue spray can of AquaNet.

I skate out on the main rink now with everyone else, and I even stay on for girls' fast skate. Jill says she's never seen anyone learn to skate as quickly as I have, and I try not to smile too hard. With my new hair and my jeans with the thick creases down the front, I hardly stick out at all anymore.

Now I go to work on Ali.

"You really should get your hair feathered," I say, using my fingernail to carve a white part through the top of his hair. I walk him over to the bathroom mirror. "And why don't you get wide-leg jeans?" I add as he squints at himself.

"Because I don't want them," he says, and ducks out from under my hands.

Suddenly I feel silly. I look in the mirror at my own chopped-up hair. I don't regret cutting it, but I wonder what Ali thinks of me looking so different from when we left Iran. I hope he doesn't think I have changed. I haven't. I still play "primary school in Africa" with him and we still play our space games where we fly out to visit each other on different planets. Ali must know I haven't changed; he never notices hair or clothes anyway. He just shakes his hair out and goes back to the letter he is writing to a center forward of the Iranian soccer team who he has discovered is living in Tulsa, Oklahoma. He tells the soccer player about how last year we got up in the middle of the night to watch Iran play in the World Cup. The soccer player writes back, thanking Ali for remembering him and writing at the end, "God willing, we will all be back in Iran soon and I'll send you and your family tickets to see us play."

Shahrzad writes from California. "I am going to a new school in Simi Valley. I've changed my name. I'm telling people I'm a Catholic Italian now." She signs the letter "Love, Sherri," with a bubble dot over the i.

Catholic.

Italian.

My eyes run back and forth over the two words. I might be embarrassed by my relatives. I might not tell people at school that I am Iranian. But this letter is like a slap in the face. Shahrzad—my partner in a fifth-grade oral report on Iran's Khorasan province, the only friend who understood how much I missed Community School—has slipped from Iranian to Italian like the misreading of some alphabetical list. Why Catholic? I want to ask. Why Italian? How can you say you miss Iran if this is what you do? And who will remember it with me, if not you?

It is one thing to keep silent; it is another thing to lie. I want to fly down to California, find Shahrzad's school, tell everyone what she is and show her that she can't just cut away her Iranianness. Instead I tuck her letter into a drawer and stubbornly keep writing "Dear Shahrzad" in response to the letters she signs "Sherri."

And then at school I get a shock. Snaking through the noisy hall toward the cafeteria, I look up to see the freckled nose and dark hair of a boy named Frank McClaskey. When he sees me his face wrinkles into a scowl and he hisses, "Go home, Iranian."

I don't flinch. I don't let my eyes lock on to his for more than the second it takes for me to hear what he says. The other kids sweep me down the hall and I take my place in the lunch line, keeping my face blank, as if by refusing to react I can erase those three words. But inside I feel dizzy, as if suddenly, in the middle of a crowd, someone has punched me in the side.

Ali, who tells everyone about the revolution, would not have walked away. Ali would have said something back, something so smart that it would have left Frank McClaskey standing there with his tongue too big for his mouth. But what should I have said? *I was born here and I'm as American as you?* It's the truth; but it's not what Ali would have said. I should have just coolly said, *Maybe you should go to Iran yourself, Frank. Don't you have some hostages over there who need rescuing?* But I wouldn't want to sound like a barbarian or a fanatic. I can't figure out what Ali would have said, and I don't want to ask him. It would be too embarrassing to admit that someone said "Go home, Iranian" to me. It would be making a big deal out of it, which is just what Frank expects me to do.

And yet I also feel strangely gratified. I hardly know Frank McClaskey, and I know that what he said is idiotic. But he is a popular boy, and what he said means he has taken time to find out who I am. I begin to keep a nervous lookout for him, the way I would with a boy I had a crush on. No one says anything like that to me again, but whenever I see Frank now I feel a welling of anger mixed with an odd exhilaration over the fact that here, in a place where I am used to being ignored, someone with plenty of friends is aware of me. I am even a little proud to have been identified as an Iranian, to be sharing something with the worried-looking Americanized Iranians who were on the news earlier this month, sitting in the Washington, D.C., airport, their visas suddenly revoked.

Families who move a lot have to be close. Nobody else sticks around—no neighbors or school friend or even other relatives—the brothers and sisters and mother and father have only each other as reference points. Without those anchors, the evidence of their past is in danger of floating away. But Carla's family sang our song long after we ourselves had forgotten it, and when she sings the words now, I feel like I am hearing from a sister who disappeared long ago, carrying with her a little box of my life. She feels this too. "I can't believe you're real," we keep saying. "I can't believe you're sitting in front of me now, and that we like each other so much."

Later, I think back to the only comment Carla made that did not ring fully true for me. "Isn't it hard," she said, "to think about settling down here when you've grown up living the expat life?" I started to nod, but then I stopped. The expat life? After the last time I saw Carla, she moved on exotically, to Cairo and Rome, making friends with foreigners who sat together at swimming clubs and embassy parties and returned home with crates full of antiques. Carla continued this life long after I came to America; she was old—a senior in high school—when her family finally flew back to St. Louis for good.

Even if I had stayed in Iran [through high school] I don't think I would have called my life "expat." The word evokes aloof, wealthy outsiders; white-suited diplomats and archaeologists; people to whom the place they live in remains foreign no matter how long they stay. It is the opposite of "immigrant," which implies large families crammed into small apartments, perhaps not legal, hampered by their foreign accents and their dark skin (expat skin is simply pink and peeling from the sun). Immigrants miss their own country—maybe they didn't want to leave it in the first place; expats love the adventure of being away. "Expat" can always go home again. "Immigrant" is close to "refugee."

My life in Iran was, of course, adorned with some of the trappings of the expat life. Our Americanness—both my mother's background and my father's education—was a ticket into an elite made up of anyone who bore the stamp of the West. It was reflected

in our parents' choice of a plot in Shahrak, in our attending
Community School, in Mama's working at CBS—even in Baba's
job at the university, where a foreign education provided an extra
mark of distinction. But [Carla] illustrated my own expatness with
a story I hadn't remembered, an indication of how separate, at
the age of four, we already felt from those around us. One day we
begged to dress up like Iranian women, so Mama bought a length
of black cloth and made us two little chadors. We draped them
over our heads and squatted silently against a wall the way we had
seen Iranian women do in the street. We already knew we would
never wear chadors in our real lives; no matter how many dark,
draped women we passed on the sidewalk, we would end up in
minidresses and tights like our mothers. Ours was an expat game.
You don't see children of immigrants to America dressing up as
Americans for a day; they make sure to dress American every day.

But despite all this, my family were not expats in Iran. We were
growing up there, our relatives lived there; it was our home. When
we saw the red-painted letters that spelled "Yankee Go Home," we
did not turn the focus in on ourselves. Yankees were the apple-
cheeked American military fathers who wore pirate costumes
at the Iran-America Society Halloween parties; Yankees were
the widehipped midwestern mothers and the thin-lipped blond
California mothers who complained about how the Iranian-made
cornflakes just didn't taste as good as the real thing. When we saw
those dripping red letters telling them to go home we shrugged,
half agreeing that they should leave if they were that nervous, half
surprised that they left so fast and easily. Our school closed and
opened and closed again like an illness in remission, but we did not
take it personally.

And yet, when we finally left, we were not immigrants to
America either. Three of us had been born there; four of us spoke
perfect American English. Landing in America, we went straight
to Grandma and Grandpa's backyard swimming pool in the hills.
But as soon as we arrived I began to miss…the expat life. Abroad,
our lives had been unlike anyone else's. We had not fit into any
mold; compared to Iranian kids in Iran or American kids in

America, we had had a sense of being untethered in the world. We had traveled all our lives; we were seasoned experts on jet lag and layover and the toy shops at London Heathrow. Our futures too were uncharted. With no model to follow, we could imagine ourselves anywhere in the world.

Anora Egan *grew up moving every one to two years, living in half a dozen countries in the Middle East and Europe. "I have lived in so many places I cannot remember them all," she writes. She managed her frequent childhood changes by immersing herself in each new environment and by developing almost native language skills and genuine friendships with local people. She was a French student in Catholic schools for years, an American in public schools without an American upbringing.*

Her search for identity and community continued in her adult life. Egan immersed herself in Chinese culture, studied in China, and in time, married a Chinese man. After the marriage ended, yet another form of immersion awaited her—this time, a deep exploration of Tibetan Buddhism. Her essay explores the twin themes of rootlessness and immersion, stylistically mirroring a mobile life in short scenes that skip back and forth in time and place.

Breath Roots

Anora Egan

Dark. Black. Hot. Bewildered. Frightened. I cannot see.

Where am I? When is this? What form am I? Have I passed on? Am I being reborn? I need a time and place in which to be.

Pounding heart. Shallow breath. Quieting heart. Slowing breath. Quiet heart. Deepening breath. Easy girl. Easy. You are going to be okay. I'll find out where I am. I will know what to do.

I can see a little—the outline of the door, the walls. I know which way I am lying. I remember yesterday, last night. I know where I am. I have fixed myself in a place and time.

1981, in China. It is a winter night. Dim streetlights cast a dull light. Our coats are padded, our heads, scarved. Even gloved, our hands are cold. We are on the basketball courts of the Teachers University of Beijing. A movie is playing on the wall of the next building. There must be a hundred and fifty of us in the dark, in the cold. Soldiers. Cleaning women. Students. Professors. The movie is Indian. A woman is given into marriage. Her husband beats her; she has nowhere to turn. There are subtitles, in Roman letters, but the words spell no English and the sounds do not match the movements of the lips. The movie is dubbed in Mandarin with Pin Yin subtitles. I follow the story not only with the pictures but also the words. I look around. In the middle of the court, in the middle of strangers in this city, capital of China, I am the only

European American, the only white-skinned person in the crowd. In the dark, no one can see that I am a foreigner. In the dark, I belong. Invisible, I feel at home.

In China, during the day, the gray pall of coal dust fills the air and colors everything dull. I am dressed in navy blue like everyone else, but I am different. Everyone looks at me. It is not that I'm beautiful or that I'm blond; it is that I am white, my nose is long, and I am tall. I am a Westerner. The doors to China have only been open three years since the end of the Cultural Revolution. There are few enough of us in China that we stand out.

Sometimes soaking in the attention feels good, special. I feel I am someone because I am seen. But more often the looks do not nourish, do not reach out with a smile or a welcome. They are looks of curiosity, puzzlement, and distrust. These looks are like spotlights on a thief. I am a very visible intruder. In the light I do not belong. I yearn to be invisible.

In America, freshly back from overseas, I walk through airport customs in Hawaii, opening my suitcases, speaking effortlessly with the uniformed customs agents. The bathrooms are clean, have toilet paper and a delicate scent. All the signs are so easy to read, it is like drinking water after a day in the desert: no translation, no confusion. All the sounds have meaning. I understand everything, except the voices of foreigners. No one looks at me. I am invisible. I feel terrific, utterly free, unnoticed. This is my homecoming.

Later. I've been back a few months. I sit on a low wall at Harvard Square. No one looks at me. No one sees me. I blend right in. I do not know anyone, even in my America, even in my Cambridge. I have been away so many times, I never had time to know anyone in the town where I was born, in this town to which I returned year after year for short visits with my grandparents.

I watch the faces of the passersby, hoping, on some chance, that in this hub of the universe, I will run into one of the international travelers who has been a short-time friend this lifetime. All it will take is one such meeting, and I watch the faces. I want to find the ones I know. But the faces pass on with no recognition, no sign that I exist. I am so alone in this crowd. I blend in so completely, it is as if I've disappeared.

Airports. Passports. Tickets. Currency changes. A smooth amplified voice announces the next departing flight. Adrenaline moves through me like a storm. A rush. The fear. Excitement. A terror. A new place. Everything is strange.

Disorientation happens upon waking. Too many times of waking up in a whole new world. Different room, different bed, different sounds on the TV, different smells, different food, different people, different language, different buildings. Only my family was the same, and our personal things. Sometimes that was not enough. But that is how it was.

I grew up moving. I first traveled when I was three to London. And then at four, to Jordan. And when I was five, to Egypt. At six it was Saudi Arabia. Then to America. Then from America, this time to Lebanon. I was eight. Then there was a war. I was nine. We were evacuated, without Daddy. He had already moved to a new place. We flew to Greece and then to Italy and then to Israel. It was in Israel that we met up with Daddy again. And when eleven, to Italy and at twelve, to France. Then to America again. This time, to come home, for four years, to a place we had never lived before, Maryland. After that, it would pick up again. Off we'd go.

There were boat rides, train rides, bus rides, and jeep rides. Donkey rides, and cart rides, and even once a camel ride. Lots and lots of car rides, in a VW van around the Mediterranean, the way Americans travel around Europe. Yugoslavia, Turkey, Greece, Syria. Skirting Albania.

Moving, always moving, looking out the window as the world moves on by...with a quiet sad feeling that the rest of the world has a home and a life while I just pass by watching...with a relieved feeling that I am free, not stuck in a small place in the remote countryside, or a tiny apartment in a crowded city. I don't have a home. I don't have roots in a place. But I am free.

Roots. There are many kinds of roots. Deep central strong roots. Wide, shallow roots. Roots that crawl through roots. Roots that root on roots. Roots that need rock to root. Roots that need earth to root. Roots that root in water. Roots that root in air. Roots reach out wherever they need to go to find what they need to bring home.

It is 1981. We are international students in Beijing. It is a long weekend. We're in a van traveling to one of the emperor's palaces. Long hours riding on narrow roads through the countryside. I room with my Chinese teacher. She tells me she gets up in the middle of the night so I shouldn't be scared. She uses a word I would not find in the textbooks, one of the words children in families use. I feel close, getting closer. Almost family.

The long ride back, I am sitting next to the window, eyes on the passing countryside. On the side of a hill, a small home. Mud walls. Pink tiles on the roof. Windows. Red Chinese posters with Chinese characters hanging upside down on both sides of the door to bring good luck. Smoke coming out the chimney. Two bicycles against the walls. I want to go home there, to have a quiet, safe home in the country. I have no home anywhere. The van carries us back to the city, to the foreign student dormitories. That home remains the constant contrast to my life.

It is 1980. I felt I wanted a home, but as soon as I finished university in America and could have settled somewhere, anywhere, I got on an airplane for China. I didn't know how to settle, all I knew was how to be a foreigner, moving from country to country. I didn't know that at the time, I just did what I did—get a passport, get a visa, make plane reservations, and head out on a foreign excursion.

My American grandmother, Grandmere, grew plants in water. Ivy cuttings rooted in a crystal bowl on the dining room table. Other cuttings floated in vases on the windowsill. She would wash the glass weekly, clean the roots and put them in fresh, clear water again. We would watch the roots grow day by day, reaching out longer and farther to take in more nourishment to grow more leaves.

When the roots were developed enough, they were ready to survive in soil, soft soil so the roots could stretch and support the growth of more leaves to draw in more sunlight.

Sometimes in separating out the plants, we found that the roots were so intertwined that one plant would lose its roots to the tangle. That was the risk of rooting several plants in the same glass.

As a university student in Massachusetts in 1978, I am studying intensive Chinese. I have the chance to go overseas for the summer and a junior year abroad, to Taiwan. I am excited. I am scared. Each feeling pulls me in a different direction. I'm stalemated. I can't figure out what to do. Can I stand being so visible again? I'm checking it out. I go to Chinatown, in Boston.

I am in a Chinese bookstore. Everywhere there are Chinese faces, Chinese accents, Chinese voices. It is mostly Cantonese. My intensive Mandarin studies are no help. Not a bit. Might as well be Greek. I feel strange, out of place, very visible. I am the only Euro-American in the store. The only one born speaking English. I am overwhelmed by the looks, sounds, and smell. There is nothing familiar here. I am uncomfortable. It is clear. I will not go. I don't like to feel strange. It is somehow exhausting.

One man, wearing glasses and appearing educated, looks at me; really sees me, with a gaze that lets me know he is accepting but still curious about why I am there. There is something familiar about that look, something that makes me feel connected. I am an explorer. I cross cultures to learn. He sees me. Though I will never meet him beyond this moment, seeing his intelligent and understanding look bridges the gap for me, lets me know that there will be Chinese who can meet me where I am, even if it is only a handful.

In that moment I feel an awakening. I remember my breath. I have a breath that comes with me wherever I go. As long as I keep breathing I will feel okay. I can feel at home, rooted, in my breath. So I imagine it is okay to go. It is a turning point; my course is restored. I will go.

Three months later I am on a plane to Taiwan. Looking down over the island at night there are large spaces of black between spots of light, the cities. I can see the whole island as we head toward Taipei. I feel fear. There is only one person on the island I know. One woman who used to sit at the college library writing Chinese characters. One person in a whole island. I feel very alone. Seeing the darkness in which I have no familiarity scares me, and echoes the feeling I will have when I can understand but a few words of all the conversations happening. It will be like being deaf. Tonight it is like being blind. I wonder why I am in this plane, looking down on this foreign island. What am I doing so far from my English-speaking Massachusetts, the place I call home?

Looking back, years later, it isn't puzzling at all. I had spent my life flying to strange and faraway places. I knew how to do that. When in doubt, get on a plane and go somewhere. When there, try to learn everything you can about the place and try like anything to be one of them—operating instructions for a traveling human.

What I did not know how to do was to stay in one place, make friends that I would grow with, and become part of a community. Looking back, I wonder if I had a choice. This was all I knew.

I love spider plants. Their long stems reach out with little baby spider plants. Roots start to grow in air. They are still fed by their mother through the long stems, but they are ready to drop on their own at any time.

I collect them. I want to give each one of them its own little space. I put them one by one in little glass jars of their own. On my counter there are twenty little rooting spider plants. Every day their roots grow longer, they flourish. I study their roots, how they grow to draw in nourishment from the water; how their leaves grow to draw in nourishment from the sunlight. Seeing their process of growth, I feel I understand something about myself. It is clarifying. I identify with those little plants, with their little lives. All they need to grow and thrive is a little space of their own. It is as if in rooting them I am rooting myself.

I have lived in so many places I cannot remember them all—the houses, my rooms. So where are my roots? Did I root in each place and then forget because I was torn apart when I moved? Were my roots in the transient friends of the international expatriate community? Is that why my heart would tear every time one of us moved? Did I root more in relationships than in places? Or was I just hanging somewhere, rooted in air as we bounced around the world?

After the little spider plants grow and grow, it seems like they should get their own pot, their own little spot of earth in which to really root. So I plant them in dirt. But then it's not the same. The appeal is gone. I give away the potted ones. Is it because I cannot see their roots, that aspect of their being that is what I need to learn from? The potted plants are like people who do not move. Their roots are invisible. They don't need to be known. Or is it that they are known already because their roots are intact? But for me, as a mobile one, I have to be conscious about rooting.

My roots were torn from me repeatedly. We have to know how to root again, or we will not survive. I watch the plants root in water and see that I must have little strands of affection reaching out to people to exchange love to sustain my life. I see how the spider plants thrive in sunlight just as I need human eyelight to thrive.

I experienced so much that I could not understand. It has taken years of quieting down to slowly examine what I felt and saw, how I responded to the uprooting, over and over again. It is still so unclear, revealing itself like a craggy shoreline in the fog, oh so slowly.

I've needed to know who I was. Maybe something in the moving from country to country and language to language was confusing. Or maybe it was clear, and I did what any intelligent young girl would try to do. I don't know. I do know I was always wanting to be someone with a clear identity: American, French, Chinese, Tibetan.

Although I was born in Boston, I didn't feel I was a real American, probably because I spent so much time living outside of America. I held the passport, and America is where I came "home" to, but I didn't feel I fit in. Being American was more than just having the passport; I had to be able to talk the talk. I needed the right clothes. The right postures. The right expressions, and the right common experiences. I only had the passport. The passport was great overseas; in the early sixties it was still a good thing to be an American. With the black diplomatic passport we were waved through many borders, many airports. We were VIPs. But back in America with my American peers, I just didn't have "it." No one knew, or cared, about what I knew, and I didn't know what everyone else knew . Same age, same language, same accent, same neighborhood; worlds apart in experience.

I spent four years in French schools, but I could never be French either. They could grade me on the same scale. They could expect me to know which of the hundreds of nouns were randomly masculine or feminine. They could hold me to grammar that I had to learn from scratch. But I would never be French. The French were the aristocrats of Europe. They were the highest group for me. I tried with every ounce of my will to form the most precise French sounds my mouth and tongue could make. Once, only once, I was asked, "And are you French?" as a genuine question. Other times I knew the question meant, "Where are you from?" because clearly it was strange that I spoke French so well, but not perfectly. That was my last year in a French school.

I felt disheartened by the fast-moving modern world, wondering what knowledge and wisdom was left behind in the wake of our innovation. I got very interested in Buddhism, in awakening and enlightenment, in making the most of my life. I wanted to know what wisdom there was in the ancient Sanskrit language, if there was information there that had been lost in the industrial and scientific world I lived in. But I didn't find a suitable class to enroll in. As I met with teachers to see what direction I would take, I happened to talk with a teacher of Tibetan Buddhism. She noticed I held my hand on my chest and asked if I had a wound there. At the time I didn't know it was there; a pain that comes from not having any roots within myself. But I wouldn't know that

218

until much later. Again, there wasn't a class that fit my schedule, so I kept looking.

Chinese people seemed still connected to the wisdom of their ancient culture. I ended up taking Mandarin Chinese and left my interest in Buddhism behind. Once I started a language, I wanted to go all the way. Mastery meant getting to the point where people said you were native. Everyone knew the best way to do that was to live in that country and have a local boyfriend. That's the only way to achieve mastery. Even though mastery meant trying to be something that I was not, to get the accolades and admiration of my international peers was worth the effort. It was the major recognition available in that lifestyle.

The Chinese teachers gave me attention and compliments. "You do not seem American. You seem more Asian." "You have the sensibilities of the Chinese." "I normally wouldn't recommend Americans to study Chinese literature, they don't have the sensitivity for it. But I would recommend you." "Why have your grades fallen, you are so good at Chinese. Is something going wrong for you?" The human kindness they showed won my heart. I had wanted to study women's studies, the most modern studies of all history as I saw it, but I couldn't find a sponsor for my program and everyone was busy. The Chinese teachers had time for me. It was as simple as that. Maybe marrying a Chinese would be that way too. As simple as who made time for me.

I went to Taiwan during my junior year, did a post-graduate year in China, and a few years later, I married a Chinese man I had met my senior year at university. He was born and raised in Taiwan, and his parents were from northern China. His father wore the long robes of the Chinese men and did calligraphy in all its forms. His mother wore the long dresses of the Chinese women and cooked Chinese food in all its forms. This Chinese man I married was the real thing, except that he was interested in the West. And I appeared to be the real thing as an American, except that I was interested in the East. We crossed paths headed in opposite directions.

My Chinese marriage lasted a decade and gave us a beautiful son halfway through. When it was over, so was my interest in all things foreign. I had satisfied my desire to bridge cultures and the need to prove it was possible. I thought I was finished with trying to own some clear foreign identity. I was looking for meditation again, something I had explored before starting Chinese. I felt it was the answer to all my problems.

I thought I was finished with foreign excursions, but another one was ahead of me. I had tried finding community in the Unitarian church. I offered meditation at my house, but attendance was sparse and irregular. So I kept looking. I finally ventured to a strange and beautiful Tibetan Buddhist temple. I didn't want strange, and I didn't need beautiful. But I also found in the people a spirit of genuine openness and self-awareness that was compelling. I needed real human connection and I found that.

I slipped in like a foot into a soft, warm slipper. I ached from the world. I ached from failed loves. I ached and sought refuge. I didn't quite understand that I was once again seeking form and roots in something foreign that looked well defined, trying again to make myself into something known. Six months after I first visited the Buddhist center, I was chanting in Tibetan in my dreams, cutting my hair shorter, changing my clothes to the colors of the ordained, and asking to be a novice nun. In this community, many of the nuns were mothers, ordained after they had already had children, and I was welcomed. I could be a mother and a nun. At the time my son encouraged me. (Later he would feel differently.) Less than a year later I would request and get permission to be ordained in a Tibetan ordination ceremony.

I'm at the temple. It is ordination day. Our heads are shaved. The softest fuzz covers my head. Do not touch it. The top of my head, my crown, is sacred. That is where my spirit will leave my body upon death, if I prepare for it. And that is where it needs to leave my body for maximum awareness and compassion at death.

There are half a dozen of us. I am in a yellow handmade slip. I have a yellow sleeveless shirt. I feel bare. Poor. Humble. Scared.

What am I doing? But I also feel confident, grounded, strong. I know there is nothing more important than recognizing the central focus of being aware in this life, the central focus of helping end suffering. Nothing is more important. I am chilly. We are all waiting; the men in their underclothes and the women in theirs.

The doors to the prayer room are closed. The curtains hide us. The senior monks are in there, as is the teacher—the master, the powerful, unshakable one—and his head teacher, our teacher, the one who speaks English. The men are ordained first. The women wait. It is long for us. At last I am called in, first of the women. Is it because I wrote my petition in Tibetan and Chinese, copying lines from our prayer book? Because I am called in first, I will be the elder of the three of us. My pride, my focus on me, is intact, despite this act of profound humility. I could change my outer appearance suddenly, but my habits of mind would be much harder and slower to change.

The moments fly by. The monks. The teachers. The questions. The prayers. The prostrations. We emerge. We step into the next room. The monks dress us in our robes; in the sacred yellow robes. My heart shivers, and my breath pauses when I remember this. It was so sacred. We reenter the prayer room, and when it is over, I walk out carrying a bowl of fruit in front of my sisters, circling the temple three times, all of us chanting. We are ordained. Shaven, and in brilliant yellow robes that we will only wear on special occasions and for confession, we are as beautiful as yellow iris. Unabashedly exposed, we pose for pictures. Several people hug us and congratulate us. Others thank us for our sacrifice. It is a day of great joy.

I pull the *mala* (prayer beads) of 108 beads out of my bag and start to chant in words that are now as familiar as my own name. They are Tibetan. And they speak of things that are not of this world. I chant them as if they were the very sound of my breath. What have I become? Is it still me? What am I aiming for?

My compass had its true north, and I was following it, though the journey would look stranger yet before things quieted down.

For almost three years my life would be a whirlwind of activity trying to support myself, learn about and deepen as a nun, participate in the community, and find the middle way as an American in Tibetan robes. Interesting? You bet. Crazy? That too. Valuable? Of course. But very, very difficult. Before three years were up, it would be completely clear to me that I needed to return to lay life, offer back the robes, and resign from any responsibilities.

The transition back into lay life, though it meant no change in job or living situation, was gradual. Already, in three short years many deep changes were shaping in my psyche, and it was only slowly that I could reenter and start over as a woman.

Was this seeking of foreign identities like grafting, attaching a branch onto another plant's roots? Since I had no roots in the earth, was I growing roots in relationships—drawing nourishment from friendships? Was I growing roots in the cultures I connected with? Did I have to do this because my roots were frequently severed? Why did it happen this way for me?

Grafting works with plants. In a way it worked for me. But it looks strange. And as a person, it feels strange. But if you're used to feeling strange, because you kept being strange by going to strange places, then feeling strange feels normal, familiar. I was used to feeling strange. That's what felt normal for me.

For a while, trying to be like the people of the cultures I admired gave me a place among peers. I rooted on their roots. I adopted their families and friends. I drew from their cultures, from their spirit. And I tried to learn ways to attract their attention, to catch the eyelight that they gave. It was simple adaptation.

Twenty years before I had had a momentary realization that with my breath I could go anywhere and feel rooted everywhere. I had discovered the principle of the breath root, though the practice would remain elusive, as I kept putting myself in scary situations that would halt my breath. But there was much more to tap into than just my breath; there was consciousness, compassion and wisdom, that which is our soul, the lasting part of us, that part of us that is Great Spirit. This is what we need from eyelight.

Seeing roots grow in the transparent medium of water is amazing. Seeing roots grow in air is inspiring: it is like the most powerful rooting of all, the rooting in emptiness.

Clark Blaise *was born in the United States of Canadian parents who came from vastly different backgrounds. His mother was from upright Anglo-Canadian stock, settlers who helped build Winnipeg. His father hailed from a small French-Canadian town south of Quebec and made his living in boxing circles and as a traveling salesman south of the border. He was continually running out of work or being run out of town. Theirs was a volatile union, tested over and over by the many moves they were forced to make. Crisscrossing the U.S.-Canadian border, moving from state to state, feeling "invaded" by geography, Clark Blaise remembers his childhood as "alternating threat with nightmare."*

Yet he loved being on the road. "Travel excited me: in the bullet of a bus, the cab of a car, the world is concentrated, all perspectives converge." And though he ultimately claims a Canadian identity, based in part on the stability he associates with his mother's home, Blaise lives in the United States, where for many years he directed the International Writer's Workshop at the University of Iowa before moving to Berkeley, California.

Memories of Unhousement

Clark Blaise

I was born in Fargo, North Dakota, in 1940, along with Roger Maris and William Gass and Larry Woiwode. In that *Ragtime* spirit that haunts us all, I sometimes think of my mother pushing the pram, of Mrs. Woiwode pushing hers, of little Roger Maris, then six, dashing past us, bat on shoulder. Billy Gass, a bifocular teen-ager, squints a moment at these figures of life, then returns to the ice castle of his imagination, "The Pedersen Kid" crystallizing even then. *Beyond the Bedroom Wall* gurgles in his stroller. Babe Ruth's assassin takes a few mean cuts.

I am the only Canadian writer born in Fargo, North Dakota.

There is nothing obscure, really, about Fargo. In 1977, at a party in New Delhi, India, where my India-born wife, Bharati, was serving that year as a quasi-diplomat for a Canadian educational exchange, I found myself talking to an agreeable, white-haired American with a professorial manner, the U.S. agricultural atta-ché. I was merely a spouse, conscious of a peripheral role.

"I consider myself half a Canadian, really," he said.

"I'm more than half American myself," I replied. What it is that I am, fundamentally, is a matter of earnest agony to me. We shared a smile, wondering which of us would be the first to break. One-time Canadians in America have no problem; erstwhile Americans in Canada will always feel a little guilty. "I was born in

North Dakota," I confessed. Then, covering my tracks, "My parents had just come down from Winnipeg."

"I was about to say the same thing. Where in North Dakota?"

"Fargo."

"Amazing."

He was the first North Dakotan I had ever met.

"What year would that have been," he asked. "Forty, forty-one?"

"April 1940."

"I was just finishing my MA at North Dakota State that spring. My wife was an O.B. nurse."

Parallel lives were beginning to converge. As though a collision course plotted by children on separate planets had suddenly become inevitable, we said together, "St. John's Hospital?"

I added, "Dr. Hanna?"

He called his wife over. As she put her drink down and turned to join us, he said, "How would you like to meet the person who delivered you?"

Before the Interstate system obliterated the old America, you used to come across them at country crossroads: clusters of white arrows tipped in black, pointing in every direction. Somewhere on the plains you would see them, stop, and be thrilled: "Denver 885," it would say, or "New Orleans 1045," or, better yet, "Los Angeles 2000." Who decided on the city and the mileage, I'll never know. Perhaps they had taken over from the whitewashed rocks, the dabs of tar left by earlier waves of impatient travelers, when twenty or thirty miles a day was more than fair measure. Nowadays, the green, mirror-studded billboards conspire to keep our minds on the effortlessly attainable, the inevitable. No more than two destinations, they seem to say; don't tease us with prospects greater than our immediate ambition.

We are deprived of that special thrill when our destination, our crazy, private destination, made its first appearance in one of those black-tipped clusters. No reason at all that on a road between Chicago and Madison, just outside Beloit, Wisconsin, "Winnipeg" should miraculously appear. Yet in 1949, when I was nine and guiding my father on our longest trip home, it did. Nine hundred miles in a '47 Chevy with its split windshield, high fenders, and curved chrome bars over the dashboard radio was a typical fifteen-hour-long haul for my salesman father.

How, I think now, he must have wanted to delay it. He, who delayed nothing in his life, a man lacking all patience. For old times' sake, he said, we'd spend the night in Detroit Lakes, Minnesota. That's where they'd honeymooned. Up there in the headwaters of the Mississippi is where I was conceived.

We always returned to Winnipeg whenever my father ran out of work, or was run out of work, or town. We had left Fargo in 1941, Cincinnati in '43, Pittsburgh in '45, and—a week before—Leesburg, Florida. Every time we left, we headed back to Winnipeg, my mother's city.

My father was from the village of Lac Mégantic, a few mountain ridges north of Maine, directly south of Quebec City. Winnipeg must have been a torture to him. I remember him, slicing luncheon meats in an upstairs bedroom next to a leaking window in my grandmother's house, sipping forbidden beer and smoking Canadian cigarettes—their aroma so much nuttier than his American Tareytons—though Canadian corktips inflamed his lips.

He never spoke of his dislikes, he merely acted on them, without warning. He was probably not entirely sane.

My father possessed—or rather it possessed him—a murderous temper. He had pounded out twenty victories in three weight divisions in two countries under various names that served him like flags of convenience, before getting knocked out—and quitting, he said, though my mother came to doubt it, years later—by Bat Battalino, an eventual champion. The kindest interpretation my mother could put on his behavior in later life was brain damage: "All that pounding he took." To this day, I love boxing, and I realize that somewhere around the radios and under the porch lights of my childhood in two dozen cities, I absorbed the pointers of boxing. My father's friends, if it could be said he had friends and not just cronies, had often been boxers. The violence of boxing, of his language, of his friends, of American life in general, drove my mother indoors.

Boxing credentials were good for one thing in Montreal in the 1920s. The career path took him to Canada's most successful export industry, helping assure, through bribery and intimidation, the delivery of Montreal's finest whisky to Prohibition-dry New York.

The first return to Canada that I remember was 1945, following an assault charge against my father in Pittsburgh. We crossed into Canada that midnight at Niagara Falls and were in Winnipeg three days later. Canada was still at war, the same war (I'm told) that had sent us to North Dakota six years earlier. Canada, part of Britain's war effort, would be the front lines, everyone thought, as soon as the Luftwaffe finished mopping up. Lindbergh assured us it wouldn't take long. German U-boats already controlled the Gulf of St. Lawrence. The French-owned islands of St. Pierre and Miquelon, off the coast of the British colony of Newfoundland, were rebelling against the Vichy regime; no one knew how long that would last, a fogbound Casablanca. Once Britain fell, Newfoundland and Labrador would of course be ceded to the Nazis, just like the Channel Islands. The Frenchies in Quebec refused to fight an English war anyway; Adrien Arcand and his Brownshirts were poised for a coup whenever Hitler ordered it. All of which had left Ontario, in 1939 and '40, feeling itself in the probable front line of combat. Even the *bunds* of Buffalo and Detroit were stirring up border hate. The Ottowa River would become America's Marne. And so my parents fled. I would be born in isolationist, accommodationist America. My father could be whatever he wanted to be, not just a dirty Frog in English Canada.

This is my first memory of Canada: the soldiers at Canadian customs, their jaunty berets. The smell of a different tobacco in the air. My Winnipeg uncle in his colonel's rough khaki, deep lines and dark skin, bushy eyebrows and salt-and-pepper hair, his thick moustache and his short, stocky body, reminding me years later of a Sandhurst-trained Israeli. One summer morning, when

I was five, he had taken me and my cousins out on the lawn—he in his full uniform, the rows of First World War medals on his chest—and smoked glass for us. The scientists of the Free World had gathered in Winnipeg in 1945 for a spectacular view of a solar eclipse. I remember my twin cousins, limber girls of eight, doing backward flips all around my grandmother's house.

My first long exposure to Canada took place five years later, following one of my father's failures in central Florida. We'd driven up from Leesburg, those clustered signposts serving us well: Atlanta 600, Chicago 1000. Yankee place names frightened me. I was a southerner, I drawled inexcusably (I was soon to learn, in Winnipeg schools), I was as ignorant as a mudfish of history and mathematics. Yet travel excited me; in the bullet of a bus, the cab of a car, the world is concentrated, all perspectives converge. We tore around America, rolling double sixes on that old Monopoly board of two-lane blacktop. One day for Florida, another for the pine flats of Georgia. Then they came fast: Tennessee, Kentucky, Indiana, Illinois and, before the half-week was out, that sign in Beloit: Winnipeg 945. We were in the green and watery states now, the Land o' Lakes and Sky Blue Waters in the lee of Canada—I expected moose, bear. We were in Fargo for an afternoon, and I wandered down the main street of my absurdly obscure home-town. We drove past the house we'd lived in that spring of 1940: Fifth Street S.E. My mother pointed out where Hinckle had lived, the man who took all my baby pictures.

Many years later, when my first book of stories was published, I got a letter from a nursing home in Minneapolis. Mrs. Hinckle had read the review in the *Star*. There couldn't be two Clark Blaises, not born in Fargo of Canadian parents, she said. I had to be the sweetest little baby she'd ever seen, the one my mother had worried over, the one her late husband had adored.

How like my mother, I think now, to have found another woman, in Fargo, who would remember names, who would read books and reviews, even in a nursing home. My mother's friends; my father's friends.

Of all the distinctions I have invented in my life and come to believe in with the force of myth, the difference between Canada and the United States—so frail in reality, so inconsequential in the consciousness of America or the world or even most Canadians—is still my last, my most important illusion. It matters to me, or it mattered until very recently, that a border exists. That people so similar should be formed in such different ways. That because I inherited those differences, I should have something special to say on both sides of the border.

I was *invaded* by geography the way other self-conscious youngsters are invaded by God, by music, by poetry, or a butterfly's wing. Through my childhood and adolescence and well into my adulthood and the ragged fringes of middle age, the faith in a Canada being of a different order of history, experience, and humanity granted me an identity. It was never easy to claim it, but I never doubted it was there and that I belonged to it. Canada was always the large, locked attic of my sensibility, something I would never *know*, but be obliged to invent; it cultivated a part of me that America never touched. The significant blob of otherness in my life has always been Canada; it sits like a helmet over the United States, but I seemed to be the only person who felt its weight.

North, North, North: that glorious direction, and the provincial bison shield of Manitoba, the narrow highway that cut through the wheat fields to the West and the French-speaking hamlets along the Red River to the east, their lone church steeples gleaming (to my mother's disgust) higher than the bluffs that hid the rest of the town, rising even taller than the wheat elevators that stretched westward, each of them announcing a calloused, sun-reddened Protestant or Ukrainian town. And then, the highway divided, trolley tracks appeared and we were in Winnipeg.

I think often of the compass points. Like the arrow clusters at cramped country crossroads, the cardinal directions still move me; I dream restlessly of the eternal *setting out*, steering on a highway for what I know will be a long drive and reading that first, firm challenge to the continent. *East.* And I see fishing boats and a pounding Winslow Homer rocky surf and the great cities, and

I think, *yes*, that's the direction for me. Culture, history, people, excitement, sophistication. But then, on my drives to the Pacific, I thrill to those days of unbroken signposts, the barren miles of low hills and bluffs and promotional museums of forgivable, fake-historical tackiness, and I think, *West, West,* let me ride to the ridge, let me be free. Well, this time it was *North*: this was just about as far north as anyone from Florida could think of going. This was the western end of the Canadian Shield; east of here and the town names turn French and the faces along the highway are unmistakably Indian. West of here, golden fields of the world's hardest wheat.

I know the South—*South*—too well. It's the only compass point that fails to conjure a dreamlike essence. When I think of the Florida I knew, I remember only walls of leggy pine with slash marks on their trunks, hung with resin buckets, and I remember the Coke machines in country gas stations where for a nickel I could lift a heavy metal lid (I can remember the first whiff of that cold, moist air; I remember the pleasure of trailing my fingers in the dark, iced water), of spotting a bottle cap in one of the metal tracks and gliding it along to the spring catch my nickel had released. And I can remember draining those stubby little Coke bottles with their raised, roughened letters on the side, always checking the bottom to see where it had been bottled, how far it had come, though nearly all were good ol' bottles from Plant City and Orlando. Well, all I remember of *South* is sand and heat and thirst and skies the colour of sweaty undershirts. I remember the years of childhood, alternating threat with nightmare.

On Wolesley Avenue in Winnipeg, on the banks of the Assiniboine, my grandparents had their house. Three houses away, my aunt and uncle had an even larger home, with a garage full of canoes and kayaks and a basement full of hunting rifles and decoys and a special room for a billiard table. Since my uncle was in those days a writer and commercial artist as well as president of the Wheat Pool and Ducks Unlimited—and was soon to become Winnipeg's best-known television personality—and my aunt was a broadcaster, they had studios and libraries on the second floor. The third floor held guest rooms and an attic full of bundled magazines going back to the beginnings of *National Geographic* and *Reader's Digest,* as well as the splashy American weeklies like *Life* and *Collier's* and *The Saturday Evening Post.* They kept the hunting and fishing magazines and everything Canadian, particularly everything relating to the prairies and especially the Assiniboia region of Manitoba. My uncle…had been a Homesteader, one of Manitoba's founders. Nothing important had ever been thrown out. The house was virtually a computer, although means of retrieval were still a little primitive.

That house, and their lives, represented something to me called Canada, that was more than merely attractive; it was compelling. In the various towns of my first ten years, we had always lived in small apartments carved out of old servants' quarters, on the fringes of other people's families, and we always seemed to be sharing some vital function of other people's lives. Kitchens, bathrooms, entrances, hallways, washing facilities, and later, when we moved back to the States in the early fifties, televisions. Whatever the reasons, Canada, by virtue of its cool, English houses and its politeness and its streetcars and its formalities and its formidable understanding of the world outside—as brought to us every day by the BBC noon news—was a more comprehensible and interesting place to live than America. Not that America was ever excluded. It's just that Canadians, like long-suffering spouses, would be forced to know everything about America, while America knew nothing, cared nothing, for them.

My parents had moved back to Canada at a time when its differences from the United States were unforced but unequivocal. Canada was like a heavy novel that others found dull and difficult but that I found accessible from the beginning, thanks to my accidental placement inside an emblematically Canadian family. I visited my aunt and uncle every day and shot pool in the basement by myself or with my cousin. My parents and I were staying in the second-floor bedroom and study at my grandmother's. Between the houses and school, I became a Canadian.

My grandmother was a classic of the grandmother type; too old to have a life of her own, but young enough to manage the lives of several others. She was small but sturdy, she had wit and a dead-pan delivery that could "really get me going," as she put it. She had taken up driving and a wee bit of smoking and brandy drinking (the sign of an amateur in these matters; she kept her cigarettes loose in an old sugar bowl in the kitchen cupboard), and she would smoke only at predictable times in the morning and evening, when the dough was rising after a good punch-down.

My grandfather, when awake, was the focus of our awareness, though not of our attention. While he was up, we all kept an eye on him. He was classically senile; a bald, tall, stooped old patri-arch, a one-time doctor, a breeder of flowers and fruit trees, and an importer of draft horses, the consolidator of an insurance group, now the largest in Canada—a man of great substance in Western Canada. Up on the second floor, in the room occupied by my par-ents and me, I would read the volumes of *Who's Who in Western Canada* that told my grandfather's tale ("The Luther Burbank of Canada" with the names of his prize-winning Clydesdales), and I never tired of reading the biographies of him in the Canadian *Reader's Digest*, and all the profiles in the medical and insurance journals. I learned to feel a touch of family pride whenever we passed an office of the Wawanesa Mutual, the insurance company he'd built. *Everyone* in Winnipeg seemed to be rich and famous and confident; all of my relatives had power and recognition; casual visitors to my uncle and aunt's house turned out to be cabinet ministers, American governors, authors. When I walked down the street with my aunt or uncle, people stopped and often turned around to watch us. After the bruised, violent, anonymous lives we'd lived in those mildewed southern towns, Winnipeg was a jolt of pure, cold oxygen, the only place left in the world that con-formed to the notions of reality, and of a happy childhood, that I'd gotten from reading, or my own intense imagining.

At the age of seventy-five, my grandfather was merely a dis-turbing presence. He was strong and stern, and he kept himself busy through a ten-hour workday in his old study and sometimes in the living room, underlining every sentence in every book and magazine in the house. He did not know his name, or that of his wife and daughters (he'd had nine daughters, one son, and all five of the survivors visited regularly, except the son in Toronto and my mother, the eldest). His memory had deserted him rapidly while he was still in his sixties, and as a doctor he'd recognized it—it had been his father's fate as well—and had gotten out of medicine and cut back on the insurance. He'd retired, physically exhausted after paying back hundreds of thousands of dollars of Depression debts (always explained to me as the failure of American farmers to pay him for the Clydesdales he'd imported), but the insurance company had treated him generously. His faculties continued to fail. He was apparently alert enough in 1940, however, when my mother brought me up from Fargo for my first visit, to feel the bumps on my head and declare, "Don't worry, Annie, this boy will never be a fighter." So far as I can determine, he never spoke to me, or of me, again. His heart repaired itself under the protective seal of a worry-free dementia, and he still had his work, the underlining of every word in the daily *Free Press,* and all those stacks of magazines upstairs. That was my Canada, and that was my grandfather's house; a place where everything was intact and even madness could be quietly accommodated. There was, in fact, only one thing that could not be housed, because he was not organically a part of it, and that was my father.

"See what *he* wants," my grandmother would ask, not unkindly. She was as afraid of giving offense as my father was; therefore they worked out elaborate systems of mutual avoidance. He rarely came downstairs. When he did, an aroma of tobacco preceded him by at least half a minute, and my grandfather would lay his pencil down, carefully marking his place in the work still before him, stand, and—high, quivering voice fierce with outrage—order him out. "How dare you, sir, walk across my carpet with your dirty boots? Out, out, I say!" My father, in Winnipeg, never went outside in the winter, and was always in slippers. My grandfather was furious, muttering, "The cheek, the gall! I will report this, don't think I won't!" That would be a sign for my mother, first, to interpose herself. "It's all right, Daddy, he's Leo, your son-in-law."

Now my grandfather was in a proper Victorian rage—what was
this middle-aged woman *doing* in his house, insulting him with
familiar names and sluttish behaviour? He threw my mother aside.
"I don't know why you're shielding him, Lillie, but I'm getting to
the bottom of this. I won't rest"—by which time my father had
sneaked back up the stairs, cursing to himself, and my grandfather
would be left standing, hands clenched, undecided over the next
challenge, having already forgotten the source of the rage, remembering only that he was enraged and had to act it. All the women
in his life now were "Lillie," my grandmother's name, except my
grandmother, who was usually just "mother." After he died, at the
age of eighty-two, my grandmother had her own few bad years,
heaping invectives on her husband, not for those last twenty inglo-
rious years, but for the years of his magnificent achievement, the
Who's Who years. Who or what to believe? Even as I write this, my
own mother is enacting the dramas of her parents, and as I reach
back into these events of thirty or more years ago, I'm aware that
truth is simply a matter of framing and reframing. I've chosen to
believe certain versions; I've rejected others. I too was blessed with
a gifted memory, and I've worn it down by now to something dull
and ordinary, and I write this in the terror that the family disease
awaits me. When my grandfather's fists clenched, he'd go back to
the chair and begin the assault on a new column of print.

The winter of 1949–50 was one of the snowiest in Winnipeg
history. It would lead to a spring flood that is still remembered,
to sandbags in my aunt's and grandmother's backyards, to those
canoes and kayaks pushing off directly from the driveway and
bringing relief a few blocks downstream. And, as the head of the
Red Cross, it would be my aunt's finest hour: in the pictures we
were sent (by that time we too had pushed off; they caught up with
us in Cleveland, in a rooming house on Euclid Avenue), my aunt
and uncle would be bundled in their parkas against the slanting
sleet, under helmets with the red cross painted on the sides, and
it would remind me of British air-raid wardens. The pictures were
grainy, black and white, some of them smeared from rainwater on
the lenses (a beautiful, accidental effect; what would its equivalent

in language be?), as millions of dollars of property and boulders of ice, houses, and trucks hurtled past their houses, borne on the fury of a horizontal Niagara.

That would be the spring. Right now, it is still a hard, Siberian winter day. Winnipeg should not exist, except as an urban planner's act of defiance, an experiment on the heartless Russian model. Yet it does exist, like Edmonton exists, like Montreal exists, and the effects of that anomaly—the intense communalism, the isolation, the pride, the shame and absurdity of carrying on normal life at forty below zero—create a population of stubborn, sceptical survivalists hungry for recognition and certification, a people born with the ache of anonymity and the conviction that they'll always have something to prove. All of which leads to that bone-proud prairie loneliness, the suspicion of anyone who's had it easier—east, west, or south. In my mother's family, self-reliance was a creed; bottled-up and bitten-back, no grief was exposed, no help asked for, though none was refused. There seemed to be a fear of softness, a numb acceptance of fate, a determination bordering on mission to make do with the cards that were dealt, to curse no one but oneself, and then only silently, or after sanity departed.

In my mother's family they constantly headed deeper north, as though to test themselves, as though Winnipeg itself were not test enough. My cousins began their kayaking at ten or so, portaging between rivers and lakes right to the shores of Hudson Bay. They had a farm a few miles west where they grew flax and ran traplines; and in the fall I went with them—Florida child that I was, accent and all—and learned to shoot at an early enough age to avoid the usual reservations of an urban academic.

I have seen most of the northern hemisphere's major cities by now, but Portage Avenue in the early fifties remains for me something special, like a Russian movie, molded on a scale of epic tedium that nevertheless achieves a certain impressive weight. If we could rid our minds of notions of charm and beauty and still be receptive to urban grandeur, then Portage Avenue, the east-west axis of Winnipeg and half the province of Manitoba would stand as a model. It was conceived on a scale of spaciousness in keeping with the open fields and possibly in revenge for the two thousand miles of crabbed forest at its back. It was wide, straight and flat, and down its middle in its own *maidan* rolled the endless herd of rumbling streetcars. Standing at our corner, Stiles and Portage, I could look a couple of miles to the west, the buildings showing not a single variation in height and not a single uniformity of design, and spot, in embryo as it were, the line of streetcars that would be passing me in the next half hour. Since no one could stand outside for more than ten minutes anyway, it was most compassionate of the transport commission to flood the rails with more cars than any city had a right to expect. That was my Winnipeg; a city of prompt and endless convenience.

Up on the second floor in the bedroom we had converted to a small apartment, with a hot plate for my father's coffee and a small skillet for my mother's eggs—the smoke-filled haven of my father—a small drama was being enacted that would alter all our lives. My mother had reactivated her old teacher's permit and was, by now, substituting on a near-daily basis in various parts of the city. I was in school, struggling to overcome the deficiencies of a rural southern background. Thanks to family connections, I was not routinely demoted two grades, as were other American transfers, and was managing, with after-school tutoring, to make a successful transition to the world of ink and nibs, formulae and long compositions. I was singing British folk songs instead of the U.S Military Academy hymns. No one sang "God Save the King" or "O Canada" louder than I every morning in the hall. And for the first time, I was enjoying my classmates. In Florida, students were to be tolerated or avoided while pursuing the fugitive pleasures of the text. Here, there was no school yard fighting, despite the tempting foreign target I must have offered. The captains of the various team sports—most of them imposing Icelandic boys with names like Thorlaksen—would often choose me first, simply because I was American. They took the time to teach me the unfamiliar games British Bulldog and broom hockey, and would even stop the action if they saw I was too hopelessly out of place. When ice hockey started, I was permitted to sit inside.

No one could have been more displaced than my father. He'd ask me when it was safe to go downstairs and to slip outside (this necessitated checking on my grandfather and enduring his scolding for having sneaked into the house "from the stables" and for having walked on the rugs). My father, Leo Romeo Blais, had been going across the river to French St. Boniface and to the furniture stores of the borax North End, the parts of town rich in contacts for the salesman's life he knew. Like my mother, he had a transferable skill. He worked a few days and decided things were too slow, too old-fashioned. He didn't know the Canadian furniture scene any more, and the American brands, when carried, were far too expensive. Of course he didn't mention anything to us about working or where the search was taking him. That wouldn't be his style.

One day after school I went upstairs to read old magazines and the *Who's Who*. I had a phenomenal memory (the incarnation of my grandfather according to the family); I was committing those rows of fine print to memory. My father was there at his place by the window looking out on the snowy roof, up Stiles Street to Portage, in the distance. On his knees was a letter. On the window ledge were some notebook pages he must have taken from me. When he saw me, he folded the letter back in the envelope. I tried to show I wasn't interested, but a small suitcase on the bed was packed.

I went over to my cousin's to shoot pool. My grandfather was sleeping; my father would have no trouble sneaking out. I couldn't imagine where we'd be going next, but *West*, I remember, excited me. I felt ready for it now; West was the only direction we hadn't explored.

I played pool till the phone rang. My aunt called me from the head of the stairs. "Clark, your mother."

No, I said, I hadn't seen him, I didn't know anything about it. She was crying. What can I tell them? my mother wanted to know. She'd been downtown, looking for our own apartment. We were going to stay in Winnipeg, that had been the plan. *We'd agreed; we'd try to settle down. For Clark's sake.*

He was gone, all right. Shirts, suits, shoes and car; the salesman's clearing out. My mother was already reframing it for her mother and sisters: "Leo decided he could do better in the States. He's following a lead in... (I made it up, blocking out all alternatives)... Denver. He'll send for us when he finds an apartment." I even believed in Denver; I looked up a city map and tried to memorize the grid. Years later, pursuing my own studies of another Franco-American whose life—given a different dominance in our family, I might have crossed—I again encountered those heroic late-40s and 1950 Denver streets of Neal Cassady and Jack Kerouac; madness to push this further, though a message to me seems to linger. Kerouac and Cassady were my father's world, the one he never escaped, of booze and fights and women and endless travel, and he died back inside it, buried in a plot of New Hampshire called "*le petit coin du Canada*," as desolately as Kerouac did in his mother's transplanted Lowell kitchen in Florida. Jack's father's name was also Leo.

On the sheet of notebook paper I found drafts of a letter. It said more or less what we expected: he'd gotten a lead, it looked good, and he always did better if he could interview in person. If he got it, we'd live better than we ever had. My mother, too, gazed out over the roof, up Stiles, at that one. No need to say the obvious.

She didn't care about the rest of the paper, which wasn't a proper letter at all. It was a page of signatures. His signature: Lee R. Blaise, it said, up and down several rows. No more a Blais, that quiet little burp of a name between "blay" and "bligh" that I couldn't pronounce anyway.

"Lee Blaise," I said to myself. Yes, yes, Clark Blaise. It looked right. It balanced. It was anchored.

Section IV
Identity

How do we determine our identity? Which language do we choose for self-expression? And are we merely a collection of our cultural attributes, or can we select those we most want to keep?

Moving among places, mobile children gather phrases and expressions, attitudes and gestures. Language is the most portable cultural landmark. It facilitates communication, eases transitions, and connects newcomers with existing social groups. It informs the senses and secures one's place in the world. It is through language that one forges identity. With words as their medium, children create memories, ideas, selves. Like patchwork, they stitch their lives story by story, binding together various experiences with the thread of language.

More than just a collection of words, language anchors its speakers in a common cultural understanding. Thoughts, beliefs, and attitudes are immersed in the language that expresses them. Language reflects values, humor, history, pride—all the unspoken assumptions that form a sense of self—an identity—and lead to bonds between speakers. In using a particular language, the speaker is also expressing affiliation. The ability of international children to simultaneously hold more than one worldview is closely tied to their understanding of the nuances of language and the values and assumptions of its speakers.

Many mobile children are gifted in the use of more than one tongue. They are polyglots, facile with wordplay, enticed by new languages. Bilingual or even multilingual, they learn languages quickly and often adapt to other cultures quite easily. Some of the authors in this section move freely among identities, able to comfortably choose personas that reflect the cultural values and the language in which they find themselves immersed. Others are able to create multiethnic personalities, incorporating the various influences on their lives rather than choosing among them. They find an expressive language to speak and write that enables them to synthesize their many selves.

Yet while language can unite its fluent speakers, it can also exclude the halting ones. A strong accent can isolate the nonnative speaker from the mainstream, and this can be devastating to the developing child. Some tell of lonely childhoods lived on the border of language, with confused identities that are not secured until adulthood.

For Peter Ruppert, whose childhood was shattered by war and displacement, identity is forged in personal memory and the language that calls it forth. Severed from family history by his parents' refusal to look back and remember the painful past, he must define for himself who he is. Each forced relocation requires learning a new language, yet every language learned "maps the world differently; each construes time and space and memory in different ways." Who, then, is he? And where does he belong? Struggling to rid himself of an accent "that makes it impossible to forget your past," he comes to view language as "the barbed wire of the global community" and himself as a perpetual outsider. Eventually, he takes comfort identifying with "hyphenated Americans," composites of their varied histories, languages, and cultures.

Writing, and the articulation of one's personal history, is a way to claim one's place in the world. To Lisa Suhair Majaj, "we are the stories we tell; our words map the spaces of home." But she feels homeless as a child, shuttled between her mother's Iowa and her father's Lebanon, unable to choose between her American and her Arab loyalties. For years, she retreats into an anxious, lonely silence. It is in adulthood, when Majaj is able to come to terms with her dual identity, that she finds a voice that embraces her mixed heritage and speaks out for Arab Americans the world over.

Ariel Dorfman learns early in his life that language is laden with cultural implications. A name, that first identifier, can be used to include or exclude its owner. In an unwelcome transit from his familiar life in New York to a new home in South America, he chooses to preserve an American identity by securing an English-sounding name. "What did my name mean?" he writes. "It means that I can't conform, that I can't make believe I'm from here." Years later, when he more closely identifies with Chilean political and cultural life, he sheds his North American identity and name and becomes Ariel.

For Carlos Fuentes, identity is not as much a choice as it is a merging of selves, a blending of influences. The enthusiasm and practicality that make him feel thoroughly American as a child are interwoven with an alternate, almost mythical identity with his Mexican heritage. Traveling in the Americas and Europe, studying the great writers from around the world, he concludes that "no culture...retains its identity in isolation; identity is attained in contact, in contrast, in breakthrough." His decision to write in Spanish symbolizes his acceptance of his multihued cultural background.

Like many of the authors in this collection, Marie Arana struggles with a dual identity as an "American Chica." Learning several languages, trying on identities, she finds "a new kind of independence" in her chameleon-like self-transformations. Ultimately, she refuses to choose among the strands of her mixed heritage, preferring to consider herself a bridge between cultures. She calls her composite self a "New World fusion."

In the end, it is the use of language, both oral and written, that allows these writers to contemplate their values, their place in the world, their characters—their very natures. They turn to reading and, later, to writing to sort out the complexities of their lives, to shelter them from the loneliness of so many moves, and to discover for themselves those cultural guides that help define who they are.

Peter Ruppert examines the role of language and memory in creating identity. Born in Hungary just before the invasion of the Nazis, he was shuttled from one refugee camp to another, suffering family separation and reunion, sorrow and silence. By the age of ten, when he was finally relocated to the United States, he had lived in six countries and learned four languages. He attributes a lifelong problem with stuttering to the near-constant postwar displacements and to the many languages and identities he had to acquire.

His parents emphasized learning new languages as a way to fit in, to forget the past, and to adopt a new identity, but his accent and his stutter forever marked him as an outsider. Ruppert realized early that "history and language also shape us," no matter how we try to ignore the past. Intensely uncomfortable as a child, it is only as a graduate student that he comes to accept his otherness, creating for himself a composite identity, similar to the way his mother tongue, Mucsingrish, is a composite of German, Hungarian, Slovene, and French.

Ruppert is currently a professor of modern languages at Florida State University in Tallahassee.

Displacements

Peter Ruppert

I was born in Hungary in 1941, one year before the Nazis occupied my homeland. When the war ended four years later my family was behind the Iron Curtain and there were Russian soldiers in our house. From the time I was six until I turned seven, we were shuffled from one refugee camp to another—from Hungary to Austria to East Germany to France to West Germany. At seven I found myself learning German on the Rhine. At ten I was in America studying English on the shores of Lake Michigan. Though I never learned French, I managed four languages in six countries within the first decade of my life. Each new language displaced the previous one, just as each new country gave way to the next.

This was a decade of turmoil, upheaval, displacement, and separation, not just for my family, but for millions of Middle Europeans. In this context the refugee learns quickly to move on, to avoid attachments, not to look back, not to remember. But the fact is that one is the child not only of one's parents; history and language also shape us. They nurture us or deprive us of nurture. In one way or another they leave their mark, traces that we can never quite escape, no matter how hard we try. After all, it is only the mother-tongue that we speak without an accent, and it leaves traces on every language we subsequently learn.

My relation to Hungary is best summed up in my relation to the two languages I spoke as a child. I no longer speak Hungarian, my native language, and I have to travel to Wisconsin or Illinois or Toronto to speak "Mucsingrish," a mishmash of German, Hungarian, Slovene, and French, named after Mucsi, the town of my birth. These were the languages that I spoke without an accent and, I presume, without an affliction that has caused me more hardship, more personal grief and anxiety, than anything else in my life. Though I have no scientific evidence for this, I attribute my near lifelong struggle with stuttering to the emotional and physical stress I experienced in acquiring my third and fourth languages. No one really knows for certain why some people stutter. We do know that about one person in a hundred is a stutterer, that it affects four times as many men as women, that there's a greater chance of you stammering if a close relative has a speech problem. I know that a stammer never goes away. It may disappear for a while, and you may think it's gone for good, when it suddenly returns with a vengeance. Speech therapists claim that its source almost always lies in childhood, in the past.

My parents avoided the past. In the dialectic of remembering and forgetting they opted for the latter. When we lived in Germany they encouraged me to study German so I would fit in. When we arrived in America, they emphasized English, so we wouldn't stand out. After we left Hungary, they spoke Hungarian only when they were alone or when they didn't want my younger brother to understand what they were saying. For a while I could understand them. But since I never learned to read or write Hungarian and never got beyond the vocabulary of a six-year-old, it's not surprising that I forgot my native language in the course of time. We continued to speak Mucsingrish at home, perhaps because it was a better fit, perhaps it sounded more "Western," or perhaps because of my father's resentment of the way he was treated after the war. But this language, and the singularity of its speech-world, is dying out. Mucsingrish is spoken by only a handful of people today, the scattered remnants of a destroyed community. Soon this language will no longer articulate dreams, express poetry, tell meaning-making stories. My brother, who is four years younger than I am, does not understand it. Depending on how long I live, I may be the last person on the planet to speak this language. A professor of linguistics at Creighton University has published a complete phonetic transcription of Mucsingrish, including its grammar, syntax, and vocabulary. Each human language, he argues, is worth studying because it maps the world differently; each construes time and space and memory in different ways. So when a language dies, a possible world dies with it.

Today, more than a half a century after the war, the line separating memory from history has become obscure and uncertain. While memory has gained in value and public interest, history has become a signifier of the inauthentic, designating what is left when memory has been vacated by the living. But how authentic are my memories? I was four when the war ended, seven when we left Hungary, ten when we arrived in America. When I say I remember Hungary what I mean is that I remember the last time I told my memories of Hungary. The truth is that what I remember about Hungary is contained in the stories that my parents and grandparents told me, especially my grandmother, who was the oral historian of the family. Because of her, I know that my father's vineyards had names: *salács, szabadság, közoshegy*; but I don't recall what they mean. Do I really remember the German soldiers who stayed with us toward the end of the war, or just my grandmother's stories about them? I think I remember the Russians soldiers who came when the war was over. What I mainly remember are the Hungarian dishes my mother cooked: juicy dumplings filled with plum jam, milk soup, cherry soup, noodles sautéed in bread crumbs, and of course *nockerli* with chicken paprikás or *perkölt*. I remember playing in my father's vineyards at harvest time and watching him as he played cards. I know I remember gooseberries and red currants, the apricots and peaches that fell ripe from the trees in our orchard. The apricots had seeds that tasted like almonds. But I have no recollection of when I first started to stutter.

We left Hungary in 1947, two years after my grandparents and most of my aunts, uncles, and cousins had gone West—to Austria, Germany, America, Canada, England. My father stubbornly refused to leave in 1945 because he couldn't abandon his

vineyards, his wine cellars, the house he built. When my grandparents left they were not allowed to take anything, but they had
visas, passports, documents. By the time my father decided to
leave, the harsh years of Soviet communism had begun and those
papers could only be obtained by bribes. We left on foot, taking
what we could carry. But what I remember most is waiting in train
stations, in cattle cars, in refugee camps. When we started out,
it was Russian-speaking soldiers who interrogated us, then came
the German-speaking officials, then the Austrians, the French, the
Americans. They asked my parents many questions, sometimes
with a translator present.

Months later we arrived by train in East Germany. I remember
the town was called Falkenstein. It was here that I first noticed
that my parents argued a lot, in Hungarian, and that my father was
capable of anger. I learned later that he had been assigned to work
in a coal mine. Unable to come to terms with this, he must have
been dreaming of his vineyards when he decided to go west, crossing the border illegally, abandoning his wife and three children. I
didn't see my father for three months after that. Then one day my
uncle Peterné showed up with forged documents. He spoke very
fast, with a stutter, and took me on a long train ride west. When
we arrived in the town of Eltville on the Rhine in the middle of the
night, my father was waiting at the train station. I was happy to
see him again, but I didn't realize that I would be separated from
my mother for six months. My aunt Nanscinéne took care of me.
She told me later that I cried for six months and started walking in
my sleep. My father seemed less angry because he had found a job
working the beautiful vineyards on the Rhine.

Three months later my little brother arrived with a different
uncle, Jakobpacsi, who also had forged documents. It was at this
point that I apparently stopped talking altogether. No one could get
me to say a word until my mother and sister arrived in the spring
of 1948. Like my father, they crossed the border illegally, on foot,
bribing their way, with many setbacks. They arrived on the Rhine
by train. I remember Nanscinéne holding me in her arms when I
spotted my mother on the platform. For weeks after that I clung

to my mother, would not leave her side, even in bed where I slept between her and my father. When my father tried to put me in my own bed, I apparently cried and had tantrums. My mother claimed that it was at this point she first noticed my stammer.

The rest of that year is a blur. We moved from one refugee camp to another, Wiesbaden, Frankfurt, Cherbourg, other places. I remember that the food was better in these camps, and I remember that my little brother was often lost. He would simply walk out of the camp and try to attach himself to someone outside, to someone better off than we were, no doubt. I also remember the first time I saw a black American GI; he gave me a whole pack of Juicy Fruit gum. I saw my first American movie, John Ford's *Stagecoach*, in one of the camps. And I think I remember seeing a dead horse, on its side in the rubbled streets of Frankfurt. Some of it had been butchered for meat. Later I saw a similar scene in a Rossellini film, so I can't say whether this is an authentic memory or just a movie memory. I don't recall having any speech problems during this time.

By October of '48 we were back on the Rhine, living in a two-room, third-story flat with an outdoor bathroom. My parents, my little brother, and I slept in one room; my sister had the smaller room to herself. My father was back in the vineyards, laughing again, singing Hungarian songs, playing cards with his friends on Sundays. My sister, not yet thirteen, was working at the M/M champagne distillery. I remember that my mother, brother, and I spent many idyllic days together harvesting peas, lettuce, and potatoes in the fields. Food was still rationed, but at least there was some food to ration now.

My troubles began toward the end of October when I started first grade at the Gutenberg Grundschule. The German language was no obstacle—at seven languages are a snap—but my foreignness and my stutter proved insurmountable. Children are remarkably resourceful when it comes to identifying someone's weak points, and I gave them enough ammunition to supply an army. My clothes and my accent stigmatized me as a "dirty DP," and that made it difficult for me to fit in. But my stammer made it impossible; it was the audible equivalent of being foreign. I remember standing in line with twenty other boys in gym class waiting to call out their names, dreading my turn, knowing that there would be ridicule, laughter, sarcasm. I used to get angry at the fact that my last name came toward the end of the alphabet. If my last name were Anders or Aaron, I could at least get it over with. Unless you've experienced it yourself, it is impossible to imagine the abject terror of worrying about every single word that comes from your mouth. Rare was the day that I didn't get into a fight with one of my classmates. Three years of bloody noses, scabs on my knees and elbows, building up scar tissue on top of scar tissue. Herr Horvay, my teacher, was a former member of the Hitler Youth. His way of dealing with my affliction was to rap me on my hand with his dreaded stick every time I stammered. As you might imagine, I began to hate the German language, though I understood it well. I didn't like its literalism, its tinker-toy accumulation of compound nouns, its separable verbs and prefixes. Whenever I heard it spoken, it always sounded pushy to me. I thought of it as a good language to shout in.

Learning English proved less traumatic. We arrived in the U.S. on December 22, 1951, at Ellis Island, where we were finger-printed before we got on a train to Chicago. Two months later we moved to Wisconsin. In February my parents enrolled me in third grade at St. Francis Elementary, an inner-city school on the edge of Milwaukee's black ghetto. Today we would call it multicultural. Here everybody was a hyphenated American, so it was difficult to stand out, even if you wanted to. My teacher, the antithesis of Herr Horvay, was a patient and gentle Franciscan monk, who wore sandals without socks, even on the coldest Wisconsin days. He assigned one of my classmates to tutor me in English in the lunchroom when it was not in use. I remember her name was Judy. She had freckles and blue eyes, just like the girl in the primer we were using. She was also the smartest girl in class and my first true love. I loved her because she didn't seem to notice my stammer and because she had such beautiful white teeth. Perhaps she thought all Hungarian boys talked the way I did. I have preferred smart girls ever since. Judy made English easy, except for pronunciation. I had a hard time with words like *through, tough,* and *bough,* with distinguishing *red* from *read* (I have read the book), and it took me a long time to get the sound of *th*. I learned to play basketball and I played it well. For the first time in my life I had friends—Jam Rosy, Red Leffier, Vinnie Lampone. But I still felt tongue-tied and my stammer got worse. I skipped classes, wandered around department stores during the day, watched television in the appliance section, stole small items from dime stores. I went to the movies when I had money. I liked westerns and science fiction films, and I liked the fact that at the movies you were not supposed to talk. The tribulations of learning a new language and adjusting to a new culture were nothing compared to my struggles with stuttering. Some women have told me that they find a stammer attractive, a sign of sensitivity and vulnerability. But no teenage girl ever told me this.

As a result my teenage years were filled with a mortifying fear of talking. Stammering, I realized, was not a disguisable affliction. I was embarrassed by images of stammerers in the movies: invariably they were portrayed as crooks, perverts, idiots, or simply objects of ridicule. There was little solace in knowing that Marilyn Monroe had a discernible stammer. So I opted for silence. I was reluctant to join any group, except for the basketball team, where actions spoke louder than words. Though I was accepted, even popular, the years between ten and eighteen were utter hell. Every phone call had to be worked out in advance, every request carefully calculated. I became monosyllabic, taciturn. I avoided telling jokes because I always seemed to lose it at the punch line. I gravitated toward words I knew well, or at least words I could easily pronounce, and tried to avoid all words that began with the dreaded letter *m*. I even cultivated a kind of bluntness, like the tougher kids on the playground. If I sounded tougher than I looked, then maybe people would leave me alone, stop laughing at me, talking about me behind my back.

By the time I started high school in '56, the Hungarian Uprising was taking place—one of the many unsuccessful revolutions that identify Hungarian history. By this time, though, I had managed to look and sound (when not stuttering) like any other Midwestern American boy, interested in cars and girls and basketball. I forgot where I came from because it seemed irrelevant. I remember a refugee family that stayed with us for a few months after the uprising was put down by Soviet tanks. They spoke only Hungarian, so I took little notice of them, except for the ten-year-old boy who watched television all day. One day, after watching *Superman*, he tied a red blanket around his neck and jumped off the second-story porch. He suffered only a few scratches. When his father tried to explain to me what had happened, I couldn't understand a word. My sister had to translate. It came out that the boy had been "lost in translation."

As a graduate student in the sixties I came to terms with my stammer. I accepted it, like a badge or a symbol, the sign of a certain kind of "otherness." Otherness was now in, and so the importance of my stammer faded from my life, like comic books, baseball cards, basketball, and my Hungarian homeland.

Since leaving Hungary in 1947, 1 have been back twice: in the spring of '93 my wife and I visited Mucsi, the Lake Balaton area, and Budapest; in the fall of '96 we spent ten days in Budapest. It would be wonderful if I could say that I felt at home instantly, that I was able to speak Hungarian like a native, that my stammer stopped miraculously. None of these things happened. On our first visit we spent a day and a half in Mucsi, visiting relatives, cemeteries, war memorials. We returned to my father's house, which had my name etched in the glass portico under the eave. As the eldest son I was in line to inherit it one day, along with my father's vineyards. But the vineyards were gone, replaced by communal corn fields, and the house looked shabby. Before the war, Mucsi was a multilingual community of over five thousand; now there were about seven hundred people left, and most of them spoke Hungarian exclusively. There was nothing here that resembled anything I had known in my memory. I felt like a tourist, detached, disinterested. I tried to relive the emotions I felt as a seven-year-old boy. But it didn't work. The visual memory was gone. The language was gone.

Our second visit was more fruitful. We spent ten days in Budapest, at the Hotel Victoria, on the Buda side of the river. This time I read about Hungarian history, the history of the language, the failed revolutions—something I had not done before, even though I majored in history as an undergraduate. We visited many historical sites—Heroes' Square with its immense sculptures of men on horseback, the art museum, the national museum, the city park—and we read Hungarian literature—Petőfi, Estherházy—in translation. It may have been the official doctrine, I said to my wife, but socialist realism never took hold here. I felt good using the few phrases of Hungarian that I remembered. It felt right somehow. Though I didn't feel at home, I began to feel an attachment to the city. Like many great cities that have a river running through them, Budapest is stunningly beautiful, especially at night, when the Parliament and the Fisherman's Bastion are lit up. It was comforting to hear Hungarian spoken around me. I have often heard people say that Hungarian is an impossible language, outside the Indo-European family of languages, too difficult for anyone not born into it. I was born into it. My father always said that it was a good language for cursing and invective. But to me it sounded like a wonderfully expressive language, with many vowels, diminutives, and terms of endearment.

I told my wife that I had never felt at home anywhere—not in Austria, not in Germany, not in America—but that I was beginning to sense what it means to find a place where you feel you belong. I wonder if I would have developed a stammer if Hungarian had remained my only language. If my father had decided not to abandon his vineyards in '47, I imagine that I would be writing this in Russian now instead of English. I try to think about all that that would entail. Perhaps I would be speaking Russian with a Hungarian accent. Maybe that wouldn't be so bad. The central function of speaking with an accent, I think, is that it makes it impossible to forget your past.

On our last night in Budapest, my wife and I walked along the Danube. Though it was not exactly blue, the lights reflecting on the water made it spectacular. We talked about my parents and their avoidance of the past, about my father who died in 1986, three months before we adopted Anne. He did not live to see our daughter, and he did not live to see a postcommunist Hungary. But I think he would have been pleased with the role that Hungary played in allowing East German refugees to use its territory to escape to the West. And I think he would have returned after "the Change," as Hungarians refer to the fall of Communism, if only to see his house again and spend an afternoon in one of his wine cellars. My mother died in 1995, six years after "the Change." We all urged her to return to Hungary for a visit, to see her friends and her few remaining relatives. But she was adamant in her refusal. There was nothing in Hungary that interested her in the slightest, she said. When I asked about the people she knew who were still alive, she said she had forgotten them, that, as far as she was concerned, they had disappeared off the face of the earth. For my mother, survival after the war depended on forgetting the past. She had done a good job of it.

As we crossed the Erzebeth Bridge on our way to the Pest side, I explained that Erzebeth translates as Elisabeth, my mother's name. For some people, my wife said, the past is too painful to remember, but it is also too important to forget.

We walked on in silence as images from the past came to me with a kind of hallucinatory intensity. I remembered being in a bomb shelter with my parents. It must have been toward the end of the war. On one wall there was a statue of the Virgin Mary with many candles. My mother was there, on her knees, praying the rosary with other women. Leaning on the other wall were men, drinking and cursing. My father's voice was among the loudest. We could hear explosions in the distance, shaking the earth around us like an earthquake. They must have been Allied bombs, though I can't imagine why anyone would want to bomb the vineyards of Mucsi. I also remembered our German "guests." They were polite, distant, ordinary, and they stayed for only a few days. My father told me they were on their way home from the Russian front. Soon after that the Russians came. They stayed much longer. They were huge, noisy, and sang wonderful songs, and I remember saying to my mother that I liked them a lot more than the Germans. They taught me how to sing their songs and some Russian words that my father said were obscene. I recall that my father did not like them because they took things from him—his horses, his vineyards, his house—and they drank his wine. My mother and grandmother cooked for them, and they liked the food so much they asked my mother to go with them. She didn't want to go, but they insisted. Finally they let her stay, because they were fond of children and she was pregnant with my brother.

On our way back to London, my wife and I stopped in Kaposvár to visit my cousin Imre and his family. The last time I saw him, forty-eight years ago, we were both seven years old. My mother told me that we often played together in the vineyards and that we were inseparable friends. I had anticipated a language barrier, but I found it to be worse than I had imagined. We struggled to communicate in Mucsingrish, our only common language. He had forgotten more than I had, even though Kaposvár is only a few miles from Mucsi. I translated into English for my wife; he translated into Hungarian, and sometimes into Russian, for his wife and son. It's the Tower of Babel all over again, I thought to myself. Linguists have estimated that there have been more than twenty thousand languages spoken on this planet, sometimes separated by only a few miles. Here I was struggling to communicate with someone who was born across the street from where I was born. I wondered why human beings, so uniform in all respects, subject to identical biological and environmental constraints and possibilities, speak thousands of mutually incomprehensible tongues. The material, economic, and social advantages of using a single language seemed so blatantly obvious to me. Languages, I said to my wife at one point, are the barbed wire of the global community.

At dinner we talked about "the Change." My wife said that we were like a miniature UN with all the simultaneous translation that was going on. As near as I could determine, my cousin felt that things were a lot simpler during the Cold War. Now that Europe has reverted to a multiplicity of nation-states, to a kind of pre-World War I system, he was afraid that all the old racial stereotypes would reemerge. The old regime is gone, he said, and everyone wants to believe they're better off because now even the poorest can dream of great wealth (*gazdaság nagy*, he translated for his wife). The old system, he went on, was a joke. But everyone knew it was a joke. It worked and people laughed a lot. Now, he said, everyone is serious, and there's little to laugh about, unless you can laugh about the new right-wing parties, ethnic cleansing, anti-Semitism. But what about democracy? I asked. *"Ah igen, demokrácia?"* he said and shrugged his shoulders. When was there ever demokrácia? After the war we had the Russians, before the war there was Horthy and the fascists, before that the Austrians. At this point his teenage son, who had been silent the whole time, interrupted him and said that he would die for his Hungarian homeland (*"En meghalnek magyar hazamert"*). See, my cousin said, no one would ever have said such an idiotic thing under the old regime.

For the rest of the evening we talked about Mucsi, our parents, how our personal histories had been changed by public events. At one point I asked him if anyone on his side of the family had ever had any speech problems. He said that his brother, Istvan, who was now an agricultural engineer in Mexico City, had had a terrible stammer as a teenager. We decided to call him long distance so that he too could share in this family reunion. On the phone I blocked on the word *Mexico*.

All my life, the words I have dreaded most were those that begin with *m—murder, marriage, money, mute, mother, memory*. They have all wreaked havoc on my life. Later, when I looked them up in an English-Hungarian dictionary, I discovered that in Hungarian they all begin with a vowel.

The "hybrid child" of a Palestinian father and an American mother, **Lisa Suhair Majaj** *was raised in Jordan, Lebanon, and the United States. Disparaged by each side of the family for the foreignness of the other, she retreats into silence as a way to escape the pressures and anxieties of her daily existence, seeking solace in the narratives of the books she adores. Eager for acceptance from family and friends, she learns to use silence as a way to fit in and as a shield against terrors that threaten to overwhelm her. She lived through the 1970 civil war in Jordan, the 1967 and 1973 wars with Israel, and the 1982 invasion of Lebanon.*

But she finds in silence a betrayal of self she cannot tolerate. "Who are we," she asks, "if we cannot speak about what we have undergone, learned, become?" She discovers that it is only through reclaiming her voice that she is able to face her fears and overcome them, and to accept her dual identity. Majaj has edited three anthologies of literary criticism and currently resides in Cyprus, writing poetry and essays about the Arab American experience.

Beyond Silence

Lisa Suhair Majaj

But when we are silent
we are still afraid.

—Audre Lord

I have tried to name the things that have frightened me in my life. Spiders. Shadows under my bed. The angry voice of my father. Air-raid sirens. My mother's weeping. Jet bombers overhead. The rising noise of arguments late into the night. A lamp lit during blackout. Recurring nightmares. The half-eaten body of my cat's first kitten. A cloudless sky black with explosions. The sharp sound of bullets striking rock. An Israeli soldier's command, "Come to one side." A man whose hand brushes my hips or breasts, grabs at my crotch. Rows of tanks rolling across a border. The sharp look, the slight double take when I mention my Palestinian identity. Subtly hostile questions, indecipherable silences. A door that remains closed despite my desperate pounding, the stillness of death within. Proclamations of war. Racist scrawls across my posses-sions. Anonymous phone threats, anonymous mail. Red splashes of paint on the sidewalk marking spots where a rape has occurred: red paint at every corner. A man cursing women. A Jew cursing Arabs. An American cursing foreigners. Neo-Nazis brandishing swastikas. The sound of blows behind a wall. An airport overflowing with refugees. A man in a uniform, any uniform.

I could separate these fears into categories: those inspired by my troubled family life, by the implacable forces of war, by sexism, racism, violence. Thus separated, they seem more manageably distinct, more subject to control. The child screaming from a nightmare of terrible insects fears only her imagination, unlike the student knocked breathless by a bomb's enormous reverberation. The girl so trained in silence as to be rendered speechless is merely shy, unlike the frightened young woman called aside for strip-searching and questioning because her name marks her as Arab, whose silence emerges from a politically circumscribed and historically grounded unease.

Yet these distinctions are too simple; they neglect the subtle connections between violence and repression, the myriad tendrils interweaving victimization and the ways in which we learn to inhabit our lives as victims. Besides, the visceral experience of fear respects no such distinctions. The autumn I turned ten I was troubled by a recurring dream of falling. In my dream I would slip off the rocky edge of a cliff and hurtle downward, air hurtling past my gesticulating limbs, my vision clouded with the yellow film of nausea. I would wake to radio static, disembodied voices floating across the room, the distinctive retorts of guns and mortars beyond the windows, and the nausea would return. This was Amman, Jordan: Black September, 1970. The Jordanian army had moved to expel the Palestinians. Our house was unpropitiously located between a building held by the army and an empty lot occupied by Palestinian fighters. Chips of stone littered the pavement below our window where bullets had struck the house. We huddled for weeks below window level without water or electricity, eating canned food and drinking our diminishing stock of warm Pepsi. To awaken from a dream of falling to this shrouded darkness punctuated with gunfire, the urgent, surreal cadence of radio broadcasts, my parents' worried murmurs, the muffled breathing of sleeping relatives who had fled their exposed second-floor apartment to shelter with us, was to continue falling.

That October my mother, sister, and I left Amman for the quiet safety of my mother's Iowa hometown of Hawarden. Excited, at first, by the endless grocery aisles of colorful junk foods, the countless television channels, I soon grew silent before the sea of strange faces in my fifth-grade classroom, the curious, pitying eyes of adults in church, the looks that marked me *waif, stranger.* My first day at school I stood motionless while children swirled round me, shouting questions that blurred into taunts: Did I live in a tent? Ride a camel to school? Eat with my hands? When the confusion calmed, I settled into a routine of classes and recess and lunch, Saturday morning cartoons and Sunday morning church, ballasted by my grandfather's steady presence at the kitchen table, where he drank one can of beer a day and listened to the corn index.

Eventually I made friends with two girls in my class. We played marbles, tag, tetherball; traded comics and fifth grade jokes; wrote in each other's autograph books. I never spoke of Jordan, of the bullet holes in the wall above my grandmother's bed, the burned-out rooms of her home, the mortar shells we collected in the streets during ceasefire. Certainly I never mentioned my memories of the 1967 war with Israel, which these more recent events inevitably evoked: the pressure of my mother's frantic hands pushing my head into her damp apron as we huddled beneath the sink, the fierce whine of the air-raid siren piercing the dusty summer air, the acrid taste of fear flooding my mouth. Anxious for acceptance, I joined instead in chatter about marbles and Barbie dolls, choir practice, and sledding, allowing the indecipherable outlines of my life to fade into a haze of silence.

Nine or ten months later, when school was out and the war was over, I returned to my circumscribed life amid the dusty rosebushes and low stone homes of Amman, the city the ancient Romans had called *Philadelphia, city of brotherly love.* I heeded that year's injunction to silence well; my return to Jordan reinforced the lesson. Although Palestinian life after 1970 was indelibly marked by the massacres and expulsions of that year, I managed to maintain a level of ignorance due not just to my parents' careful protectiveness of my childhood but also to my own resistance of unsettling knowledge. I did listen with awe to stories of hungry families setting their starving pets loose to forage in the streets. But I juxtaposed these tales with reassuring memories of a quiet Hawarden year, a winter of snow, two new friends. Before I left Hawarden, my friends and I had exchanged addresses and promised to keep in touch. For a few years we wrote faithfully—their letters arriving months late, by boat, because they kept forgetting to send them air mail, their script large and round and clear, reminding me of the calm pace of Hawarden life. But then the letters stopped—around the time that one of them became pregnant, rumor had it, by her uncle or cousin. She was married off shortly before her fifteenth birthday. I did not hear from her, or from my other friend, again.

Teen pregnancy and sexual assault were as implausible to me then as gunfire ravaging Hawarden's quiet streets would have been. I was a girl who did not easily understand or accept violence; I wanted not to speak of such things, as I had not spoken of Black September, of the war. I wanted my life to be like a book, possessing coherence and closure. But by retreating into silence I rendered myself unable to articulate, and therefore to confront, the chaotic forces that pressed imperceptibly, irrefutably, upon my life. It is an old betrayal, silence, one too frequently chosen for reasons we may or may not understand. When my friend stopped writing to me, did she stop speaking as well, thinking that wordlessness could protect her, cradling speech inside her like the child she was too young to carry? Her imposed or self-imposed silence was in its own way as stark a violation as the incest or rape, which abducted her into a life with no horizon. I wonder, sometimes, if she ever reclaimed her voice, or whether that sheen of calmness sank her altogether.

Perhaps I only arrived at some semblance of adulthood when I began to understand the ways in which the quiet patterns of our daily lives are built upon semiwilled ignorance of the agony of people in different streets, different cities, different countries. This century has defined itself through massacres and expulsions: Armenians, Jews, Palestinians, Kurds, Bosnians, Rwandans—vast numbers of people exiled, murdered, leaving behind the translucent rubbish of ravaged lives. As an Arab American I find myself particularly attuned to Middle Eastern sufferings: Lebanese and Palestinian children riven by occupation and war; Iraqi children killed by bombs, by sanctions' hunger and disease; Lebanese villages crushed by Israeli air raids; Palestinian refugees still homeless after a half century of despair. What messages of fear will these children carry with them into their futures, scripted into the ligaments of their bodies, the shadows that hollow their eyes? And anguish knows no boundaries: a fierce current courses from South Central Los Angeles to South African townships, Sarajevo and Sebrenica to Khan Yunis and Gaza City. An undertone of horror echoes from women in Serbian rape camps, eyes and bodies taut with an unspeakable anguish, to deceptively ordinary American homes where someone whispers threateningly, "Don't tell."

Don't tell. It has taken me a lifetime to begin to understand the ways in which such words corrode, crushing palpable lives beneath the stone weight of fear. But who are we if we cannot speak out about what we have undergone, learned, become? We are the stories we tell; our words map the spaces of home. Our experiences etch themselves into our faces, the lines of grief and joy becoming sharper with age; our lives are timbered with a resonance underscored by the surprisingly fragile bass note of sorrow. To remain silent is to deny the embodied selves that bear us, rooted stalks, into the world: to become complicit in our homelessness. It is to deny, as well, those other narratives that inhabit us—the people crushed by tanks or bombs or guns or simple despair, the eyes and hands and voices whose pleas bind us to our jointly human state.

My attempts at writing are haunted by the Palestinian and other Arab lives so rarely given media space in human, personal terms. Voices I do not know press upon me, reminding me of the betrayal of silence. But the task of confronting, on both a personal and political level, the outrages of history requires a measure of personal confidence difficult for one schooled in silence. Like other Arab Americans, I have experienced hostility upon speaking out: threatening phone calls, anonymous mail, destruction of property, racist accusations. When I attempt to testify to the lives beyond the brief images of despair or anger flashed across the screen, I stumble over my own wariness of an environment so resistant to acknowledging Arab concerns, grievances, homelessness.

This silencing not only reinforces my sense of exile as a Palestinian but also makes it difficult to explore other aspects of Arab American experience. The imperative of speaking out about political realities often claims precedence over more personal negotiations. But important as it is to challenge the daily litany of violence, the burden of testimony can become a means of avoiding a more personal self-confrontation. There are unspoken stories caught beneath our tongues: words we don't always understand, a mixture of Arabic and English welling up from deep within, frightening in its intensity. We are Arab American—but what guides can help negotiate this confluence of cultures? "I feel sorry for my Arab American students," an educator tells me. "They don't know who they are. They aren't American, they aren't Arab. They're nothing." I used to introduce myself as "half Palestinian, half American," moving in and out of these dual identities with the same rapidity and surreptitious fear with which I still tuck my Palestine map necklace inside my clothing when I wish to avoid confrontation, or pull it out when I am weary of avoidance. Though I now insist on the facets of my identity as integrally interrelated, my articulation of selfhood against this landscape of homelessness is a matter of constant negotiation and renegotiation.

If I could, would I rewrite myself? Born in Iowa to an American mother and a Palestinian father, I grew up in Jordan as a hybrid child, absorbing diverse and contradictory cultural nuances: both from the American Community School, where mixed heritage children were often disparaged by the "pure" Americans, and from my Arab relatives and neighbors, who viewed my limited Arabic, my relatively fair skin and hair, and my American-inflected manners as marks of foreignness. Despite the fact that English was our language of communication, in my family behavior was judged by Palestinian norms. Repeatedly told by my relatives and by others that I was Palestinian, that identity is bequeathed from one's father, I was also told—often by the same people—that I was American, different, an outsider. Chastised for not speaking Arabic, teased

when I did speak it, I learned to keep quiet, drawing as little attention to myself as possible. In yellowing childhood snapshots, I peer
warily out at the camera, thick plastic glasses obscuring the expression in my eyes, one tip of my wiry braid in my mouth. I lived on
the edge of language, surrounded by a swirl of Arabic and English,
but came to words slowly. Even in my teens I lisped, my mouth
moving awkwardly around *s*'s as if they were foreign creatures.
My own name pulled my speech out of alignment, and so I avoided
naming myself whenever possible.

At some point I began to take solace in the written word.
Though much of my childhood is a blur, certain memories emerge
unbidden: lying sprawled on a hot tile sidewalk, absorbed in a
thick edition of *Moby Dick*; crouching in the crook of a cherry
tree, too transfixed by a Narnia tale to heed my cramped limbs or
my mother's repeated call to lunch. I loved reading, the magical
cadence of words, the narratives that lifted me up and away from
the anxiety of daily existence. Perhaps part of my pleasure came,
too, from the sheer physicality of English, its square letters so distinct from the fluid forms of Arabic script, its sounds clear and
plain—in contrast to the infinitely subtle differentiations of Arabic
consonants, the difficult, arching *'ein* that coated the throat like
dibbes (grape molasses). Unlike Arabic, which seemed far too complex—something that attracts me now—English seemed simple, its
possibilities hemmed in by a reassuring certitude. Overwhelmed by
my uncertainty about where I belonged, I turned longingly to the
structures of English for a sense of home.

Besides, reading—and later, writing—offered a means of nego-
tiating the fears that had started to rise within me: my anxieties
about the familial tensions regulating our lives, the insecurity
instilled by Christian missionaries who convinced me I was not
"saved," my incomprehension about my budding, swiftly repressed
sexuality, my fear of the political events that erupted like fireballs
in my childhood sky. In the fall of 1970, I read and reread *The
Diary of Anne Frank*, lying on the floor away from the windows,
oblivious to the muted spiral of my parents' tension. When gunfire
started riddling our days, and the protected back room filled with

unwashed bodies rustling incessantly through the long nights, I returned again and again to Anne's diary, clinging to the amazing durability and resilience of language I found there, the evidence that homelessness and fear could be narrated, and through narration, transformed. During the long evenings I sat cross-legged just outside the circle of lamplight, where the adults played endless games of pinochle and gin rummy, telling stories to myself as I formed figurines out of candle wax, turning instinctively to narrative to ward off the edging knowledge of darkness.

Looking back, however, I see the seeds of my adult alienation in the disjunction between my reading life and my actual environment. The books that wooed me in those early years were the classics of any American girlhood: *Black Beauty; The Lion, the Witch and the Wardrobe; Anne of Green Gables.* My mother, secretary/librarian at the American school, would bring home stacks of newly arrived library books; I read these eagerly, turning the pages carefully so as not to dispel the aroma of newness. By the time I was twelve, I had exhausted the school library. But these books merely reinforced my longing to be "really" American. They offered, moreover, no reflection of my own Jordanian life, no hint of a world east of Europe, of the land and culture that both bound me by its restrictions and claimed me, however tenuously, as its own. The American curriculum my teachers so assiduously followed taught me next to nothing about the Middle East. When my parents took us to see the ruins of Crusader castles at Karak and Ajloun, their massive stone structures invading the horizon, I knew the Western narrative of the Crusaders' invasion and conquest, but I could not begin to imagine what that epoch of history had meant for Arabs.

My knowledge about Palestinian issues was similarly limited. Palestine was never mentioned in my American classrooms, and my Palestinian relatives did not speak to me about their past. It may have been too painful, or perhaps they assumed that I would absorb Palestinian history by osmosis—something that did not happen, since their political discussions not only excluded me as a child and a girl but also took place in Arabic. Much to my present dismay, the first book I read about the Palestinian-Israeli conflict was Leon Uris' *Exodus*. Oblivious to its distortions, I was riveted by the novel's sensationalism. It never occurred to me to search for an Arabic novel in translation, a book of Palestinian history, an Arabic poem. Perhaps I should not have been so irritated, recently, with an Arab American student who replied, when I mentioned an anthology of Arabic poetry, that he "didn't know Arabs *had* poetry." After all, the gaps in his education are no starker than those in my own.

If this alienation occurred in Jordan, I can only guess at what growing up in the United States would have been like, where my identity as a Palestinian would have been even more tenuous. When I was a child I longed desperately to come to the United States, where I assumed I would "belong." Would I have had the fortitude to withstand the taunts of "terrorist," "sand nigger," "camel jockey"; the profound silences or open hostility with which attempts at discussing Palestinian history are still met? Or would I have attempted to slough off my Palestinian identity altogether, becoming ever more silent in an attempt to prevent disclosure?

When I write or speak, I embark on a complex negotiation with the multiplicity of selves I carry with me, the silence so profoundly ingrained in me. Often I feel like a well-educated foreigner who is not quite fluent in her adopted language and culture—whether that culture is Arab or American. Each part of my identity—Palestinian, American, woman—requires acknowledgment, affirmation, making it both possible and necessary to speak. Yet each one of these identities has silenced me at various junctures of my life. Marginalized by my American identity in Jordan, my silence was reinforced by a sense of shame as I began to understand the role the U.S. has played in Middle Eastern history. As a Palestinian in the United States, my attempts at articulation have been met with hostility, incomprehension, ostracism. In both cultures I have been silenced as a woman—a silencing not necessarily more repressive in Arab culture, merely different. And though in the Middle East I experienced war and political violence, in the

U.S. I fear sexual and physical assault in a manner I never did in Amman or Beirut.

I have wondered who I am writing for: Arabs, Americans, Arab Americans? But perhaps the question is better put: where am I writing from? For too long Arabs in the United States have had to stress what we are not: not ignorant peasants, bloodthirsty terrorists, wandering nomads; not harem girls, oppressed wives, seductive bellydancers; not oil-rich sheiks or evil emirs; not anti-Semites or anti-Christians. It is time, in contrast, to begin exploring who we are: women and men, straight and gay, artists, scientists, teachers, grocers, lawyers, carpenters, doctors, singers, gardeners: individuals only partially contained by any category or label, whose lives challenge the easy simplicity of identification. Beyond the stereotypes that cling with a terrible tenacity lies the fluid, subtle complexity of lived experience. Only when we begin to speak of our realities will our own voices finally welcome us home.

Recently I participated in a "high ropes course," an activity that involved traversing a series of rope bridges and cables strung thirty feet in the air between trees. I began by scrambling up a bridge, balancing in a tree while switching to a safety rope. Then I turned to face a cable stretched through space across which I was expected to walk, and felt fear detonate within me: my body limp with nausea, my voice a congealed mass in my throat. I do not remember how I got myself onto, and across, that cable; I recall only my partner's voice calling up to me, distant yet comforting, "I'll catch you if you fall." And the fierce recognition, solid as a fist in my belly, that *I had paid too much already to fear.*

Silence does not disperse fear, does not eliminate it. Rather, it is our voices and actions in the face of fear that are transformative. Coming to language is a process not unlike walking that cable high in the air with nothing but space below. I write by feeling my way along words that shape the silence around them, impelled by a fierce awareness of the voicelessness that precedes me, the huge price I have already paid to fear. The farther I go the more I understand that words are not the tightrope on which we balance, but the steps themselves that carry us forward into the headiness of motion, toward the articulation of home. On one side of me lies the abyss of historical tragedy, against which my own voice threatens to disappear. On the other side is the trench of personal indulgence into which I can too easily fall. I move tentatively, testing my fragmented weight against voices that articulate the silence. As I move forward these voices become clearer. Many are Arab American, some only recently familiar: Elmaz Abinader, Diana Abu-Jaber, Etel Adnan, Naomi Shihab Nye, Joseph Geha, Lawrence Joseph, Nathalie Handal, Joanna Kadi, Pauline Kaldas, D.H. Melhem, Deborah Najor, Therese Saliba, David Williams. Others are older companions, familiar and challenging: Gloria Anzaldua, Mahmoud Darwish, Joy Harjo, Sahar Khalifeh, Maxine Hong Kingston, Audre Lorde, Toni Morrison, Adrienne Rich, Leslie Marmon Silko. With so many voices weaving the air into a shimmering mesh, who would not dare move forward into sound?

*The son of a United Nations economist, **Ariel Dorfman** lived in New York, Argentina, and Chile, depending on the vicissitudes and politics of his father's employer. Language became a way to carry place within him, a refuge from loneliness, and a home. Inventing and reinventing himself through language, Dorfman created new identities with each move, assuming one self when English was the dominant language and another when the language was Spanish. He learned to preserve his personal history in journals, which he was able to take with him as he moved from country to country.*

The first time Dorfman became aware of the power of language, he was three or four years old, living in a United Nations enclave in New York City. He locked himself in the bathroom and refused to come out until his Argentine parents spoke to him in English. Years later, he recognized in this act the central fact of his life: he can determine his identity through the language he speaks and, later, writes. And his first conscious choice is as an English-speaking American.

It is an identity he must carry with him when, at the height of Cold War fears in the United States, his "Russian-infatuated" father takes his family on a business trip to Europe before being transferred to Chile. Dorfman writes, in this excerpt from his memoir, of his decision to rid himself of his hated Russian name and of the gift of a journal that would change his life. Aboard ship, the young Dorfman begins the first of many self-transformations, securing his American identity by changing his name. He also discovers his lifelong passion: literature; writing; the putting down, in the words and language of his choosing, those parts of his life he wants to hold on to.

A Bilingual Journey

Ariel Dorfman

I hated being called Vladimiro, but hated Vlady even more. The kids at school deformed my name without mercy: Bloody, Floody, Flatty—and especially the terminal insults, Laddie and Lady, names for dogs. Kids are cruel. But adults, who are not inevitably cruel—at least not to children—would also make me feel thoroughly self-conscious about who I was. Where did you get that name? What does it mean? My parents, absurdly, had told me to allege I was named after the pianist Vladimir Horowitz. And I obeyed. What was I supposed to proclaim in red-baiting America? That my dad worshipped Lenin and was glad that Uncle Joe Stalin had the bomb so he could defend socialism against the imperialists? What did my name mean? It means that I can't conform, that I can't make believe I'm from here, that's what it means.

Slowly, when I was alone, I had begun to call myself by another name. A fantasy that many children indulge in—we are not really the offspring of our parents, we were exchanged as babies, we are princes and princesses, our lineage secretly royal. The name I chose for myself, accordingly, was Edward, a name I had first come across in the Classic Comics edition of Mark Twain's *The Prince and the Pauper*—though later, as obsessively it became my favorite story, I managed to ingest the Errol Flynn film version and also read over and over again an abridged edition of the text. I was fascinated by the tale of the two physically identical boys born the same day in

Renaissance England, one to poverty and hardship and the other to opulence and power, and how they switched places, the beggar and the Prince of Wales. It may have been the first time I came across the idea of the doppelganger that was to haunt my literary work, the certainty that out there (in here?) somebody just like us suffers and watches and is waiting for his chance to take over our lives. Or the opposite idea: we may seem marginal and power-less to ignorant eyes, but someday our majesty will be recognized and the world will bow down before us. Twins, doubles, duality, duplicity, there at the start of my life. So I told myself that in real-ity I was Edward the Prince, but not content, like most children, to secrete my fantasy within my own closeted world, I decided to force the world to acknowledge, if not my princehood, at least my Edwardliness. With the same deranged determination with which I had succeeded in coercing my parents into speaking English back to me, I now carefully planned the demise of Vlady and the crown-ing of Edward.

I was not so far gone that I deluded myself into believing that I could manage this metamorphosis ensconced in my regular sur-roundings: the only way to force my mom and dad to accept a change in designation was to spring it on them in a location where I controlled how I was called. So when my father announced one day that he would have to spend many months in Europe on United Nations business and wanted the whole family to come along—London, Paris, Geneva, Italy, and then a visit to Argentina on home leave before returning to the States—I was delighted: no school for half a year, the legendary Old Continent of castles and adventures, the home of the Grand Masters of Painting. But more important, here was my chance to throw Vlady into the sea, drown the sonofabitch, and baptize myself with my true and princely title. I did not inform my parents of my intentions when we boarded the French ship *De Grasse* in June 1951. First I carefully spread my new English name among the other children on the ship, then engaged their parents, the crew members, the waiters, the stewards, until everybody was calling me Eddie. I would have preferred the lofty and lordly Edward, but what the hell—a small price to pay, that tacky diminutive, for getting rid of the detested Vladimiro. By the time my parents began to realize what I had wrought, it was too late....

It was on that French ship that I made the real transition and I could not have conceived of a more appropriate locale: a floating hotel in the middle of nowhere, a site of exile where you can craft your identity any way you want, where you can con everybody into believing anything because there is no way of confirming or denying your past.

And it was also on that ship that I was to begin a different sort of transition, one which was to prove far more crucial in the decades to come in defending the self I had come to identify with English. A transition to what might well be called the biggest con game ever invented by humanity: literature. The game I am still engaged in right now, the reader believing in the truth of my perishable, sliding words, lending faith to them without a shred of proof that I am not making everything up, inventing a self in this book as I invented (or so I say) a name for my future on that vessel.

But that was not the reason, at least not initially, not then, why literature entered my life so forcefully so early. During those six months in Europe, a rehearsal for the more permanent departure I was envisioning, literature was revealed to me as the best way to surmount the question of how to hold on to the language that defined my identity if I did not inhabit the country where it was spoken.

This discovery of how the literary imagination could protect me had humble origins: a small notebook, bound in red leather, presented to me by my parents when we boarded the *De Grasse*. They suggested that I record there, and therefore keep forever (I remember that word, *forever*), my recollections of the trip. It was in that diary—unfortunately lost in the coup in Chile many years later—that I first tentatively anticipated the specific marvels of writing. After the day's harrowing conglomeration of activities, I would sit myself down and watch my hand painstakingly preserve what otherwise would have become ephemeral; I fixed time, stopped it, calmed it; I read over the next evening what I had written and found it wanting, crossed out one word, put in another one, tested it, forced myself to work. Nobody would ever read this, I said, but once in a while I would show my mother what I'd written (always looking for approval, obsessed with contacting others) and I realized that I could be absent in my body and still be there, with her, or anybody else for that matter, through my words. More important, perhaps, than replicating myself in others was the intuition that writing was first of all a private act whose audience was primarily one's own self, so that loneliness did not need to be mastered by escaping from it into the outer world of performance, demanding the frantic fraternity of others, but by journeying with written words into the loneliness itself. A dangerous discovery: because I think I began, from that moment, to live in order to record life, that the register of that life started to be more essential than life itself. It was then that I began formulating the expression of what was happening while it was happening, often before it happened. But I was unaware of that peril: by expressing my English entirely independent of the oral or, more crucially, of performance, I took a pivotal step toward answering the question of how to keep alive the language I had adopted as my own if I was to leave the United States. In that diary, for the first time, I created an imaginary space and self outside the body and, perhaps as fundamentally, beyond geography, a dialogue with language which could be deepened regardless of where that body happened to be, what contingent geography surrounded me.

These faint glimmerings of literature's power and how that power could answer my specific needs were reinforced and in fact received a boost from an unexpected quarter.

One morning, my father stopped me as, hurly-burly and zany as usual, I rushed by him on the deck of our steamer headed for Le Havre.

He pointed to a man, gaunt I remember him somehow, his back to us, holding the hand of a woman, standing at the bow.

"That's Thomas Mann," my father said in a hushed tone I had rarely heard from him. We were not religious in my family: at that point I don't think I had stepped inside a church or a synagogue.

Though in a few weeks' time I was to discover the interior of the great cathedrals of France and England, and the quiet that greeted me there, the lowered voices of my parents as they crossed the threshold, would remind me of the sacred awe that had overcome my father as he spoke of Thomas Mann.

"He's a great novelist, perhaps the greatest in the world," my father whispered. "Do you want to say hello to him?"

I nodded.

We went up to him. Thomas Mann was looking forward, in the direction of the Europe where he had been born, to which he was returning for the first time since he had fled the Nazis in 1938. Mann turned from his vision of the homeland that awaited him, scrutinized me intensely, shook my hand. I was unabashed and looked right back. I don't remember what petty phrases we exchanged, probably about the trip, the weather, some such nonsense....

I would be mythifying grossly if I stated that our brief and vapid exchange of pleasantries altered my life, disclosed to me in a flash my true calling. It is true that for one intense moment, confronted with the brooding, famous, implausibly eternal bulk of Thomas Mann, I suddenly knew what I wanted in life: to be him, be Thomas Mann. I wanted that power to reach all humanity. I wanted the world to admire me the way they admired him, the way my parents admired me when I came running with my minor artistic wares in search of adoration, the way my parents admired him even if he was not their son.

Far more essential to my transition to literature, and specific to Thomas Mann's providential and ultimately evanescent presence on that ship, far more interesting than that accidental flicker of envy at success, was a question, provoked by Mann's thick, strange accent in English, that I fired at my father as soon as we were out of earshot. "In what language does he write?"

The answer, that Mann's language was German and that he had continued to produce extraordinary works in his native tongue when he had been forced to flee the Nazis, was simple enough and would have meant nothing to me a year before, but I was to return to it often in the following months as I traveled through Europe, rehearsing for that other, longer voyage that I saw coming.

And when it did arrive, when another ship, three years later, approached the port of Valparaiso, a twelve-year-old boy found himself ready to confront the terrors of Spanish and Latin America, armed with literature as his ultimate defense. It would take me less than a decade to start thinking of myself as a Chilean. The distance that the politics of the Cold War had created inside me would grow into a divorce from North America. But English's alliance with writing, its merging with literature, that was to be another matter. By the time I disembarked in Chile, English had become the efficient instrument of my intimacy, the inner kingdom I could control, and also the foundation for what I already called my profession, convinced as I was that my place in the world and in history would be determined by the way in which I affected and shaped that language permanently.

Carlos Fuentes *was born in Panama City, the son of a Mexican diplomat to the Panama Canal Zone, but he spent most of his childhood in Washington, D.C., and his adolescence in Chile and Argentina. "I am Mexican by will and imagination," he asserts early in this essay. Identity is a deliberate choice for Fuentes, of language and culture and home, a choice made with conscious consideration.*

Raised in an atmosphere of optimism and ease, he grew up identifying with all things American, despite his father's insistence that he understand Mexican history and tradition. Comfortable in his surroundings, he believed he was "part of that world." But on the day Mexico nationalized its oil holdings, his American friends suddenly ostracized him. He learned what it meant to be "other"; his very sense of self was challenged.

"The shock of alienation and the shock of recognition are sometimes one and the same," he writes. His initial passage from writing in English to Spanish occurred in Chile when, as an ambitious fourteen year-old bent on writing a novel, he accepted the Spanish language and Latin American culture as his own. Years of travel and study confirm his belief that cultures attain comparative identities through reading, writing, and learning. Fuentes has published more than sixty books and has become one of Latin America's most important authors.

How I Started to Write

Carlos Fuentes

I was born on November 11, 1928, under the sign I would have chosen, Scorpio, and on a date shared with Dostoevsky, Crommelynck, and Vonnegut. My mother was rushed from a steaming-hot movie house in those days before Colonel Buendia took his son to discover ice in the tropics. She was seeing King Vidor's version of *La Bohème* with John Gilbert and Lillian Gish. Perhaps the pangs of my birth were provoked by this anomaly: a silent screen version of Puccini's opera. Since then, the operatic and the cinematographic have had a tug-of-war with my words, as if expecting the Scorpio of fiction to rise from silent music and blind images.

All this, let me add to clear up my biography, took place in the sweltering heat of Panama City, where my father was beginning his diplomatic career as an attaché to the Mexican legation. (In those days, embassies were established only in the most important capitals—no place where the mean average year-round temperature was perpetually in the nineties.) Since my father was a convinced Mexican nationalist, the problem of where I was to be born had to be resolved under the sign, not of Scorpio, but of the Eagle and the Serpent. The Mexican legation, however, though it had extraterritorial rights, did not have even a territorial midwife; and the minister, a fastidious bachelor from Sinaloa by the name of Ignacio Norris, who resembled the poet Quevedo as one pince-nez resembles another, would have none of me suddenly appearing on the legation parquet, even if the Angel Gabriel had announced me as a future Mexican writer of some, albeit debatable, merit.

So if I could not be born in a fictitious, extraterritorial Mexico, neither would I be born in that even more fictitious extension of the United States of America, the Canal Zone, where, naturally, the best hospitals were. So, between two territorial fictions—the Mexican legation, the Canal Zone—and a mercifully silent close-up of John Gilbert, I arrived in the nick of time at the Gorgas Hospital in Panama City at eleven that evening.

The problem of my baptism then arose. As if the waters of the two neighboring oceans touching each other with the iron fingertips of the canal were not enough, I had to undergo a double ceremony: my religious baptism took place in Panama, because my mother, a devout Roman Catholic, demanded it with as much urgency as Tristram Shandy's parents, although through less original means. My national baptism took place a few months later in Mexico City, where my father, an incorrigible Jacobin and priest-eater to the end, insisted that I be registered in the civil rolls established by Benito Juárez. Thus, I appear as a native of Mexico City for all legal purposes, and this anomaly further illustrates a central fact of my life and my writing: I am Mexican by will and by imagination.

All this came to a head in the 1930s. By then, my father was counselor of the Mexican embassy in Washington, D.C., and I grew up in the vibrant world of the American thirties, more or less between the inauguration of Citizen Roosevelt and the interdiction of Citizen Kane. When I arrived here, Dick Tracy had just met Tess Truehart. As I left, Clark Kent was meeting Lois Lane. You are what you eat. You are also the comics you peruse as a child.

At home, my father made me read Mexican history, study Mexican geography, and understand the names, dreams, and defeats of Mexico: a nonexistent country, I then thought, invented by my father to nourish my infant imagination with yet another marvelous fiction: a land of Oz with a green cactus road, a landscape and a soul so different from those of the United States that they seemed a fantasy.

A cruel fantasy: the history of Mexico was a history of crushing defeats, whereas I lived in a world, that of my D.C. public school, which celebrated victories, one victory after another, from Yorktown to New Orleans to Chapultepec to Appomattox to San Juan Hill to Belleau Wood: had this nation never known defeat? Sometimes the names of United States victories were the same as the names of Mexico's defeats and humiliations: Monterrey. Veracruz. Chapultepec. Indeed: from the Halls of Montezuma to the shores of Tripoli. In the map of my imagination, as the United States expanded westward, Mexico contracted southward. Miguel Hidalgo, the father of Mexican independence, ended up with his head on exhibit on a lance at the city gates of Chihuahua. Imagine George and Martha beheaded at Mount Vernon.

To the south, sad songs, sweet nostalgia, impossible desires. To the north, self-confidence, faith in progress, boundless optimism. Mexico, the imaginary country, dreamed of a painful past; the United States, the real country, dreamed of a happy future.

The French equate intelligence with rational discourse, the Russians with intense soul-searching. For a Mexican, intelligence is inseparable from maliciousness—in this, as in many other things, we are quite Italian: *furberia*, roguish slyness, and the cult of appearances, *la bella figura*, are Italianate traits present everywhere in Latin America: Rome, more than Madrid, is our spiritual capital in this sense.

For me, as a child, the United States seemed a world where intelligence was equated with energy, zest, enthusiasm. The North American world blinds us with its energy; we cannot see ourselves, we must see *you*. The United States is a world full of cheerleaders, prize giving, singin' in the rain: the baton twirler, the Oscar awards, the musical comedies cannot be repeated elsewhere; in Mexico, the Hollywood statuette would come dipped in poisoned paint; in France, Gene Kelly would constantly stop in his steps to reflect: *Je danse, donc je suis.*

Many things impressed themselves on me during those years. The United States—would you believe it?—was a country where things worked, where nothing ever broke down: trains, plumbing, roads, punctuality, personal security seemed to function perfectly, at least at the eye level of a young Mexican diplomat's son living in a residential hotel on Washington's Sixteenth Street, facing Meridian Hill Park, where nobody was then mugged and where our superb, furnished seven-room apartment cost us 110 pre-inflation dollars a month. Yes, in spite of all the problems, the livin' seemed easy during those long Tidewater summers when I became perhaps the first and only Mexican to prefer grits to guacamole. I also became the original Mexican Calvinist: an invisible taskmaster called Puritanical Duty shadows my every footstep: I shall not deserve anything unless I work relentlessly for it, with iron discipline, day after day. Sloth is sin, and if I do not sit at my typewriter every day at 8 A.M. for a working day of seven to eight hours, I will surely go to hell. No siestas for me, alas and alack and *hélas* and *ay-ay-ay*: how I came to envy my Latin brethren, unburdened by the Protestant work ethic, and why must I, to this very day, read the complete works of Hermann Broch and scribble in my black notebook on a sunny Mexican beach instead of lolling the day away and waiting for the coconuts to fall?

But the United States in the thirties went far beyond my personal experience. The nation that Tocqueville had destined to share dominance over half the world realized that, in effect, only a continental state could be a modern state; in the thirties, the USA had to decide *what to do* with its new worldwide power, and Franklin Roosevelt taught us to believe that the first thing was for the United States to show that it was capable of living up to its ideals. I learned then—my first political lesson—that this is your true greatness, not, as was to be the norm in my lifetime, material wealth, not arrogant power misused against weaker peoples, not ignorant ethnocentrism burning itself out in contempt for others.

As a young Mexican growing up in the U.S., I had a primary impression of a nation of boundless energy, imagination, and the will to confront and solve the great social issues of the times without blinking or looking for scapegoats. It was the impression of a country identified with its own highest principles: political democracy, economic well-being, and faith in its human resources, especially in that most precious of all capital, the renewable wealth of education and research.

Franklin Roosevelt, then, restored America's self-respect in this essential way, not by macho posturing. I saw the United States in the thirties lift itself by its bootstraps from the dead dust of Oklahoma and the gray lines of the unemployed in Detroit, and this image of health was reflected in my daily life, in my reading of Mark Twain, in the images of movies and newspapers, in the North American capacity for mixing fluffy illusion and hard-bitten truth, self-celebration and self-criticism: the madcap heiresses played by Carole Lombard coexisted with the Walker Evans photographs of hungry, old-at-thirty migrant mothers, and the nimble tread of the feet of Fred Astaire did not silence the heavy stomp of the boots of Tom Joad.

My school—a public school, nonconfessional and coeducational—reflected these realities and their basically egalitarian thrust. I believed in the democratic simplicity of my teachers and chums, and above all I believed I was, naturally, in a totally unself-conscious way, a part of that world. It is important, at all ages and in all occupations, to be "popular" in the United States; I have known no other society where the values of "regularity" are so highly prized. I was popular, I was "regular." Until a day in March—March 18, 1938. On that day, a man from another world, the imaginary country of my childhood, the President of Mexico, Lázaro Cárdenas, nationalized the holdings of foreign oil companies. The headlines in the North American press denounced the "communist" government of Mexico and its "red" president; they demanded the invasion of Mexico in the sacred name of private property, and Mexicans, under international boycott, were invited to drink their oil.

Instantly, surprisingly, I became a pariah in my school. Cold shoulders, aggressive stares, epithets, and sometimes blows. Children know how to be cruel, and the cruelty of their elders is the surest residue of the malaise the young feel toward things strange, things other, things that reveal our own ignorance or insufficiency. This was not reserved for me or for Mexico: at about the same

291

time, an extremely brilliant boy of eleven arrived from Germany. He was a Jew and his family had fled from the Nazis. I shall always remember his face, dark and trembling, his aquiline nose and deep-set, bright eyes with their great sadness; the sensitivity of his hands and the strangeness of it all to his American companions. This young man, Hans Berliner, had a brilliant mathematical mind, and he walked and saluted like a Central European; he wore short pants and high woven stockings, Tyrolean jackets and an air of displaced courtesy that infuriated the popular, regular, feisty, knickered, provincial, Depression-era little sons of bitches at Henry Cook Public School on Thirteenth Street N.W.

The shock of alienation and the shock of recognition are sometimes one and the same. What was different made others afraid, less of what was different than of themselves, of their own incapacity to recognize themselves in the alien.

I discovered that my father's country was real. And that I belonged to it....

In 1939, my father took me to see a film at the old RKO-Keith in Washington. It was called *Man of Conquest* and it starred Richard Dix as Sam Houston. When Dix/Houston proclaimed the secession of the Republic of Texas from Mexico, I jumped on the theater seat and proclaimed on my own and from the full height of my nationalist ten years, "Viva México! Death to the gringos!" My embarrassed father hauled me out of the theater, but his pride in me could not resist leaking my first rebellious act to the *Washington Star.* So I appeared for the first time in a newspaper and became a child celebrity for the acknowledged ten-day span. I read Andy Warhol *avant l'air-brush:* Everyone shall be famous for at least five minutes....

In the wake of my father's diplomatic career, I traveled to Chile and entered fully the universe of the Spanish language, of Latin American politics and its adversities. President Roosevelt had resisted enormous pressures to apply sanctions and even invade Mexico to punish my country for recovering its own wealth. Likewise, he did not try to destabilize the Chilean radicals, communists, and socialists democratically elected to power in Chile under the banners of the Popular Front. In the early forties, the vigor of Chile's political life was contagious: active unions, active parties, electoral campaigns all spoke of the political health of this, the most democratic of Latin American nations. Chile was a politically verbalized country. It was no coincidence that it was also the country of the great Spanish American poets Gabriela Mistral, Vicente Huidobro, Pablo Neruda.

I only came to know Neruda and became his friend many years later. This King Midas of poetry would write, in his literary testament rescued from a gutted house and a nameless tomb, a beautiful song to the Spanish language. The Conquistadors, he said, took our gold, but they left us their gold: they left us our words. Neruda's gold, I learned in Chile, was the property of all. One afternoon on the beach at Lota in southern Chile, I saw the miners as they came out, mole-like, from their hard work many feet under the sea, extracting the coal of the Pacific Ocean. They sat around a bonfire and sang, to guitar music, a poem from Neruda's *Canto General*. I told them that the author would be thrilled to know that his poem had been set to music.

What author? they asked me in surprise. For them, Neruda's poetry had no author; it came from afar, it had always been sung, like Homer's. It was the poetry, as Croce said of the *Iliad*, *"d'un popolo intero poetante,"* of an entire poetizing people. It was the document of the original identity of poetry and history.

I learned in Chile that Spanish could be the language of free men. I was also to learn in my lifetime, in Chile in 1973, the fragility of both our language and our freedom when Richard Nixon, unable to destroy American democracy, merrily helped to destroy Chilean democracy, the same thing Leonid Brezhnev had done in Czechoslovakia.

An anonymous language, a language that belongs to us all, as Neruda's poem belonged to those miners on the beach, yet a language that can be kidnapped, impoverished, sometimes jailed, sometimes murdered. Let me summarize this paradox: Chile offered me and the other writers of my generation in Santiago both the essential fragility of a cornered language, Spanish, and the protection of the Latin of our times, the lingua franca of the modern world, the English language. At the Grange School, under the awesome beauty of the Andes, José Donoso and Jorge Edwards, Roberto Torretti, the late Luis Alberto Heyremans, and myself, by then all budding amateurs, wrote our first exercises in literature within this mini-Britannia. We all ran strenuous cross-country races, got caned from time to time, and recuperated while reading Swinburne; and we were subjected to huge doses of rugby, Ruskin, porridge for breakfast, and a stiff upper lip in military defeats. But when Montgomery broke through at El Alamein, the assembled school tossed caps in the air and hip-hip-hoorayed to death. In South America clubs were named after George Canning and football teams after Lord Cochrane; no matter that English help in winning independence led to English economic imperialism, from oil in Mexico to railways in Argentina. There was a secret thrill in our hearts: our Spanish conquerors had been beaten by the English; the defeat of Philip II's invincible Armada compensated for the crimes of Cortés, Pizarro, and Valdivia. If Britain was an empire, at least she was a democratic one.

In Washington, I had begun writing a personal magazine in English, with my own drawings, book reviews, and epochal bits of news. It consisted of a single copy, penciled and crayoned, and its circulation was limited to our apartment building. Then, at age fourteen, in Chile, I embarked on a more ambitious project, along with my schoolmate Roberto Torretti: a vast Caribbean saga that was to culminate in Haiti on a hilltop palace (Sans Souci), where a black tyrant kept a mad French mistress in a garret. All this was set in the early nineteenth century and in the final scene (Shades of Jane Eyre! Reflections on Rebecca! Fans of Joan Fontaine!) the palace was to burn down, along with the world of slavery.

But where to begin? Torretti and I were, along with our literary fraternity at the Grange, avid readers of Dumas *père*. A self-respecting novel, in our view, had to start in Marseilles, in full view of the Chateau d'If and the martyrdom of Edmond Dantès. But we were writing in Spanish, not in French, and our characters had to speak Spanish. But, what Spanish? My Mexican Spanish, or Roberto's

Chilean Spanish? We came to a sort of compromise: the characters would speak like Andaluslans. This was probably a tacit homage to the land from which Columbus sailed.

The Mexican painter David Affaro Siqueiros was then in Chile, painting the heroic murals of a school in the town of Chillán, which had been devastated by one of Chile's periodic earthquakes. He had been implicated in a Stalinist attempt on Trotsky's life in Mexico City, and his commission to paint a mural in the Southern Cone was a kind of honorary exile. My father, as chargé d'affaires in Santiago, where his mission was to press the proudly independent Chileans to break relations with the Bedin-Rome Axis, rose above politics in the name of art and received Siqueiros regularly for lunch at the Mexican embassy, which was a delirious mansion, worthy of William Beckford's follies, built by an enriched Italian tailor called Fallabella, on Santiago's broad Pedro de Valdivia Avenue....

This Gothic grotesque contained a Chinese room with nodding Buddhas, an office in what was known as Westminster Parliamentary style, Napoleonic lobbies, Louis XV dining rooms, art deco bedrooms, a Florentine loggia, many busts of Dante, and, finally, a vast Chilean vineyard in the back.

It was here, under the bulging Austral grapes, that I forced Siqueiros to sit after lunch and listen to me read our by then 400-page-long opus. As he drowsed off in the shade, I gained and lost my first reader. The novel, too, was lost; Torretti, who now teaches philosophy of science at the University of Puerto Rico, has no copy; Siqueiros is dead, and, besides, he slept right through my reading. I myself feel about it like Marlowe's Barabbas about fornication: that was in another country, and, besides, the wench is dead. Yet the experience of writing this highly imitative melodrama was not lost on me; its international setting, its self-conscious search for language (or languages, rather) were part of a constant attempt at a breakthrough in my life. My upbringing taught me that cultures are not isolated, and perish when deprived of contact with what is different and challenging. Reading, writing, teaching, learning, are all activities aimed at introducing civilizations to each other.

No culture, I have believed unconsciously ever since then, and quite consciously today, retains its identity in isolation; identity is attained in contact, in contrast, in breakthrough.

Rhetoric, said William Butler Yeats, is the language of our fight with others; poetry is the name of our fight with ourselves. My passage from English to Spanish determined the concrete expression of what, before, in Washington, had been the revelation of an identity. I wanted to write and I wanted to write in order to show myself that my identity and my country were real: now, in Chile, as I started to scribble my first stories, even publishing them in school magazines, I learned that I must in fact write in Spanish.

*As a young child, **Marie Arana** accepts her dual identity, assuming she is Latina when she lives with her father's family in Peru and gringa when she stays with her mother's family in Wyoming. But reentering a culture thought to be familiar can confuse the nomadic child with false expectations and cause her to question who and what she is. In this excerpt from her prize-winning memoir, Arana discovers that the mannerisms she learned in Wyoming, which she thought so all-American, are incomprehensible to her new friends in New Jersey.*

Her mother is ecstatic to be back on home turf in New Jersey; her father feels homesick, out of place, dependent on his children to translate the fast-paced English. Arana initially feels disconnected from the culture at large and tries hard to fit in with her schoolmates, hoping they will not notice her differences, but she soon realizes she will never be "a full hundred percent." She will always be a "fifty-fifty," a bilingual, bicultural child shuttled between heritages.

As an adult, after years of studying linguistics, "trying on languages like so many dresses," Arana comes to embrace her dual identity. She sees herself as a bridge between two cultures, "neither here nor there…happy to be who I am, strung between identities."

American Chica

Marie Arana

Not Paramonga, not Cartavio, not Rawlins could have prepared me for Summit, New Jersey. Mother chose it for the excellence of its schools, but she might as well have chosen it for its polarity to everything we'd known. Moving from Lima to Summit was like wandering into Belgrade from Bombay, the differences were so marked.

It was a small-town suburb of New York City, bedroom community for company presidents and businessmen. Split between Anglos and Italians, the residents were largely prosperous, but there was a hierarchy to that prosperity I was slow to see. The rich were the commuters, WASPs who had graduated from the Ivy League, played golf at the Beacon Hill Country Club, shopped at Brooks Brothers, and sent their children to prep schools nearby: Pingry, Lawrenceville, Kent Place. The less rich were the Italians—merchants, landscapers, restaurateurs, mechanics—who serviced the town. There was another notable category: scientists who worked in nearby Bell Labs or Ciba-Geigy, and their brainy, musical children. But there were no indigents: no beggars in the streets, no señoras hawking fruit.

Ours was the only Hispanic family. There were few Jews. The relative sizes of the town's churches told the story. Summit Presbyterian was the largest, most prestigious. That imposing stone structure sat squarely in the middle of town, and the rich could be seen strutting in and out of it in their finery. The Catholic Church of St. Theresa, with steps sweeping up to its portals as if they led to salvation itself, was situated several blocks away, next to its own school. The Episcopal, Methodist, and Baptist churches were scattered about town, signaling lesser lights.

By June we were in Troy Court, a cluster of brick apartment buildings on New England Avenue. It was a modest district, on the other side of town from the mansions, and it would have been clear to anyone but us children that it was home to people on the fringes of society. There were strings of apartments up and down the avenue, where transients came and went, and old ramshackle houses, where nurses and waitresses lived.

Mother had her eye on a house in the middle range of the Summit spectrum, but it would be months before the owners vacated it. She had decided we would be wise to wait. When we moved into the apartment, it was empty save for an upright piano, the one thing we had bought on Route 22. We took our meals on it, plinking while we chewed, sleeping on the floor, waiting for our crate to arrive.

Within a week, we had re-created Lima on New England Avenue—*huacos* on the shelves, llama skins draped through the rooms. The display looked odd, even to us. The Lima we had come from had been a jumble, a place where Spanish and indigenous objects mixed freely—where modern and ancient accompanied each other, where a rich man's house might be flanked by a tenement—but here, in this quiet, suburban setting, our possessions looked out of place. When the truck finally pulled away, two neighbors came over to see.

They were ten and eight, as sunny and frisky as Dutch maids on a roadside billboard. "You new?" said the older one. *"We're* new. We just moved in a few days ago."

[Suzi and Sara] were from Westfield, a few towns over. George and I told them we were from Peru, but they puckered their mouths, rolled their eyes, and allowed as how they didn't know where that was.

While George and I were running up and down the driveway behind those apartments, working to seal a friendship with these girls, Mother was humming through our rooms, settling into the life she had dreamed of for so long. She'd whisk outside from time to time, smoothing her hair, trotting to a cab, pointing to our big sister's face in the window. "You mind Vicki, you hear?" When we asked where she was going, she'd reply, "To Summit Food Market!" Or "Off to your school!" Or "Off to see about the house!" Off!

She seemed enraptured with her new life, was a bundle of energy. I watched her cook meals, wash dishes, scrub floors—do tasks I had never seen her do before—but she dug in with relish, singing as she went, looking up joyfully when I walked in, pushing the hair from her eyes.

If it had never been clear before, it was crystal clear now: my mother had been a sad woman in Peru. There was nothing sad about her now. It didn't seem to matter that she wasn't with the Clapps. She did not visit them [her family], nor did she call or write them, as far as I knew. She didn't seem to need them at all. It began to dawn on me that it wasn't *them* she had missed in Peru; she'd missed these American streets and her freedom to roam around in them.

Papi was another story: he dragged out to the train station earlier and earlier in the morning, shuffled home beat at the end of the day. He grew more and more disengaged. He missed his Peruvian family and his *compadres*. You could see it in the way he slumped through the door, headed for his chair, heaved himself down with a sigh. "Write to your *abuelita*," he'd tell me day after day, pointing to the stack of letters from her. "She wants to know how you are."

In town, he had trouble understanding the fast-talking, slang-slinging suburbanites; he'd cast a weary look my way to signal me to translate. At first, I was as puzzled by accents as he was. But his reliance on me made an impression. In Peru I had always thought he and I were similar, that Mother was the different one. But here in Summit, I felt more kinship with my mother, my father the odd one out. "You kids are turning into gringos," he'd say, staring at us in amazement. But I knew our mother was the only gringo among us, a full hundred percent. My father was the only Peruvian; he, too, was one hundred percent. They were wholes. They were complete. They were who they were. They would never *become* anything like the other. We children, on the other hand, were becoming "others" all the time, shuttling back and forth. We were the fifty-fifties. We were the cobbled ones.

Summit was nothing like Mother, really, nor was it anything like the American school in Lima, nor like Rawlins, Wyoming, whose lingo we heard in our dreams. At first, we swaggered around, George and I, like cowboys, a-yawin' and a-struttin', thinking we knew what America was. But when Easterners looked at us, they drew their chins into their necks, pocketed their hands, and sidled away. We trotted down Springfield Avenue, hiking our jeans, jiggling our heels, only to find that the places that drew these gringos were Roots haberdashery and Summit Athletic. Not bars with decapitated fauna. Not general stores with buckshot and beans. There were men in hats, plenty of them, but they were scurrying out of the Summit train station with their faces pulled down and their collars pulled up, repairing to Brookdale Liquors, then tearing home with their wives behind the wheel. On weekends, a different breed swept down Main Street: in pastel cardigans, with bags of charcoal briquets, golf clubs, and Roots merchandise dangling from their hands, pennies winking out of their shoes.

It was the way they spoke that was most puzzling. Why didn't it sound like English we'd heard before? It certainly didn't sound like Nub, or Grandpa Doc, or Old Joe Krozier. "Ah'll take a pack uh this here Juicy Fruit, mister," I drawled to Summit's version of a cornerstore Wong, a scrubbed little man in a white jacket and spectacles behind the counter at Liss Pharmacy.

"Beg your pardon, miss?"

I cleared my throat and tried again, raising my voice this time. "This here Jee-you-see Fah-root, mister. How much yew want?"

"Oh, ho! No need to shout, my dear. That'll cost you...a nickel."

"Nekel? *Qué quiere decir* nekel?" I whispered to George.

'That big *moneda* there," he hissed, pointing into my palm. "The five-cent one."

"Oh." I surrendered it to the man. He pursed his lips.

"Y'ever chaw weed?" I asked Suzi, sitting on the stair step of our apartment, looking out at the pristine grass where children were not to go.

"Chaw weed?"

"Yip. My cousin Nub, he's a cowboy, and he learned me how."

"Taught me how."

"O-keh, o-keh. Taught me how. Have you ever done it?"

"No, I haven't. Gee, Marie, you gotta stop talking weird. You say things all wrong. And I don't know why; I hear your mother talking just like everybody else. If you don't talk right, you'll never fit in school. Kids are gonna make fun of you, for sure."

Suzi and Sara became our tutors, whiling away summer days until fireflies bumped our faces, teaching us what to say. You said *okay*, not *o-keh*. You went to a *movie*, not a *cinema*. You caught *colds*, not *constipations*. You wrote on a clean, spanking new *sheet* of paper. Not a fresh *shit*. It was clear we had entered a new phase, far from our dirt-lot hankerings on Avenida Angamos. We weren't hoping to be thought of as better. We just hoped we wouldn't be made "fun of." We hoped not to be noticed at all.

Many years later, when I was studying at the British University of Hong Kong—linguistics to be precise, after I'd studied Chinese, after I'd studied Russian and French, trying on languages like so many dresses—I came across a theory claiming that bilingualism can hurt you. This was not one of those theories about the educational process or the capacities of the brain. It was a slender little monograph, not particularly well written, which claimed that in operating as two distinct personalities with two distinct tongues, a bicultural person will be highly suspect to those who have only one culture. The bicultural person seems so thoroughly one way in one language, so thoroughly different in another. Only an impostor would hide that other half so well. A liar.

An African American friend of mine, Carol, once told me that this happens to blacks in a white culture, too: you talk like a white in the workplace, like a black in your neighborhood. You use two dialects, two personalities, two senses of humor, two ways of shaking a hand, two ways of saying hello—one for the world you're trying to make a way in, another when you're home with your kin. Now, Carol was a very sedate woman—elegant in bearing, cautious with words. I came upon her unexpectedly one day as I elbowed my way through a party: There she was, in a group of black women, swiveling her hips, flinging her hands, carrying on in another lingo, so that I hardly recognized her. She laughed about it later, but I could see it was nervous laughter. She confided that she'd always thought that whites who saw her in her other context wouldn't understand it. She worried they wouldn't trust her when she resumed standard English, they might conclude she was insincere. I mentioned the linguist's monograph. She and I agreed that, however different our backgrounds were, the fear of being called a faker, an impostor, had meaning for both of us.

But the monograph doesn't begin to tell the story. The truth about biculturalism is more complicated. That others doubt you is not the point. The doubt creeps into you, too. What Carol was saying was that not only did she fear people would think her a two-face, she was confessing that *she* was afraid she was. I understood it, because I, too, had doubted my own trustworthiness. I had been fooling people for years. Slip into my American skin, and the playground would never know I was really Peruvian. Slip into the Latina, and Peruvians wouldn't suspect I was a Yank. But even by the age of ten, I had gone one giant step past Carol: I was flitting from one identity to another so deftly that it was just as easy to affect a third. I could lie, I could fake, I could act. It was a way for a newcomer to cope in America. You can't quite sound like your schoolmates? Never mind! Make it up, fashion a whole new person. *Act the part,* says the quote under my school photo, *and you can become whatever you wish to become.* Invention. It was a new kind of independence.

I love to walk a bridge and feel that split second when I am neither here nor there, when I am between going and coming, when I am God's being in transit, suspended between ground and ground. You could say it's because I'm an engineer's daughter and curious about solid structures. I've always been fascinated by the fit of a joint, the balance in trestles, the strength of a plinth. Or you could say it's because I'm a musician's daughter, who knows something about the architecture of instruments. I've pulled string over a bridge on a violin, stretched it tight, anticipated sound.

It could be, perhaps, because I am neither engineer nor musician. Because I'm neither gringa nor Latina. Because I'm not any one thing. The reality is I am a mongrel. I live on bridges; I've earned my place on them, stand comfortably when I'm on one, content with betwixt and between.

I've spent a lifetime contemplating my mother and father, studying their differences. I count both their cultures as my own. But I'm happy to be who I am, strung between identities, shuttling from one to another, switching from brain to brain. I am the product of people who launched from one land to another, who slipped into other skins, lived by other rules—yet never put their cultures behind them....

I, a Latina, who—to this day—burns incense, prays on her knees to the Virgin, feels auras, listens for spirits of the dead.

I, an Anglo, who snaps her out of it, snuffs candles, faces reality, sweeps ash into the ash can, works at a newspaper every day.

I, a north-south collision, a New World fusion. An American *chica*. A bridge.

For Further Reading

Bell, Linda. 1999. *Hidden Immigrants: Legacies of Growing Up Abroad.* Notre Dame, IN: Cross Cultural Publications.

Thirteen voices respond to chapter introductions by the author, providing insight into what it means to feel migratory, to suffer culture shock upon immersion in one's "own" culture, to learn how to form relationships and identity on "home" turf.

Corbitt, J. Nathan. 1998. *Global Awareness Profile (GAPtest).* Yarmouth, ME: Intercultural Press.

This inventory tests knowledge in six geographic regions and six subject areas as a measure of global perspective and knowledge of other countries, both important to cross-cultural success.

Fenzi, Jewell, with Carl L. Nelson. 1994. *Married to the Foreign Service: An Oral History of the American Diplomatic Spouse.* New York: Twayne.

An oral history that explores the roles and experiences of the spouses of U.S. Foreign Service officers in the twentieth century, the manner in which those roles have been redefined to reflect the profound social changes of the twentieth century, including such issues as the women's movement, divorce, and terrorism.

Fuller, Alexandra. 2003. *Don't Let's Go to the Dogs Tonight: An African Childhood.* New York: Random House.

"My soul has no home" writes Fuller about the confusion of identity she suffered growing up Scottish in Africa. She writes honestly about loss, racism, alcoholism, and her mother's break with reality.

Grearson, Jessie Carroll, and Lauren B. Smith, eds. 1995. *Swaying: Essays on Intercultural Love.* Iowa City, IA: University of Iowa Press.

Essays on the experience of falling in love with and marrying people of other nations. It explores connecting, adjusting, settling, and enduring—or not.

Lewis, Tom, and Robert Jungman. 1986. *On Being Foreign: Culture Shock in Short Fiction, An International Anthology.* Yarmouth, ME: Intercultural Press. (Out of print.)

Classic authors—Borges, Camus, Conrad, Crane, Hesse, Kipling and others—illustrate six stages of cross-cultural adjustment in this collection.

McCluskey, Karen Curnow, ed. 1994. *Notes from a Traveling Childhood: Readings for Internationally Mobile Parents & Children.* Washington, DC: Foreign Service Youth Foundation.

A collection of essays and poetry by and about children raised overseas. Includes parenting tips and guidelines, short autobiographical pieces, and descriptive profiles of global children.

Meyers, Margaret. 1995. *Swimming in the Congo.* Minneapolis: Milkweed Editions.

Coming of age during Congo's independence is a strange, complex, and sometimes pleasurable experience for a white missionary kid.

Michaux, Phyllis. 1996. *The Unknown Ambassadors: A Saga of Citizenship.* Putnam Valley, NY: Aletheia Publications.

A group of Americans living abroad address issues of citizenship, bilingualism, raising children overseas, taxes, voting, and representation for American expatriates. Includes a useful list of organizations for Americans living overseas.

Orr, M. Elaine Neal. 2003. *Gods of Noonday: A White Girl's African Life.* Charlottesville: University of Virginia Press.

While awaiting a kidney transplant in the United States, Orr relives her early years in Nigeria, the daughter of medical missionaries. A dynamic journey in two directions.

Piet-Pelon, Nancy J., and Barbara Hornby. 1992. *Women's Guide to Overseas Living.* 2d ed. Yarmouth, ME: Intercultural Press. (Out of print.)

Careful preparation for moving overseas helps women take advantage of "one of life's greatest opportunities," whether they are single, married, with or without children, or seeking a job.

Pollock, David C., and Ruth E. Van Reken. 2001. *Third Culture Kids: The Experience of Growing Up Among Worlds.* Yarmouth, ME: Intercultural Press.

Maps boldly and clearly what happens to children raised outside their parents' home country as it explores the effects of such a childhood on maturing, developing identity, and adjusting to the passport country.

Romano, Dugan. 2001. *Intercultural Marriage: Promises and Pitfalls.* 2d ed. Yarmouth, ME: Intercultural Press.

The impact of an intercultural marriage can be joyful and adventurous if couples can overcome the obstacles that such a marriage presents, including raising bicultural children and dealing with death, divorce, and other trouble spots.

Shames, Germain W. 1997. *Transcultural Odysseys: The Evolving Global Consciousness.* Yarmouth, ME: Intercultural Press. (Out of print.)

Cross-cultural encounters can expand worldviews, as told through the testimonials of individuals and families.

Smith, Carolyn D. 1991. *The Absentee American: Repatriates' Perspectives on America and Its Place in the Contemporary World.* New York: Praeger.

This book is based on more than three hundred responses to a questionnaire the author mailed out and which is reprinted in an Appendix. Smith addresses the experience of American citizens living abroad, as well as reentry issues—identity, reacculturation, worldviews of adult global nomads, and more.

Smith, Carolyn D., ed. 1996. *Strangers at Home: Essays on the Effects of Living Overseas and Coming "Home" to a Strange Land.* Putnam Valley, NY: Aletheia Publications.

Another collection of essays and descriptive pieces, including some sociological research about military brats and third culture kids, cultural identity, and reentry issues.

For Further Exploration

In addition to the many notable autobiographies, memoirs, and biographies of internationally mobile children, the following resources offer publications, Websites, and other sources of information pertinent to unrooted childhoods.

Aletheia Publications
www.members.aol.com/AlethPub
46 Bell Hollow Road
Putnam Valley, NY 10579

Publishes several books about Americans abroad, maintains a links page to military brats sites and other areas of interest.

The Foreign Service Youth Foundation
www.fsyf.org
P.O. Box 39185
Washington, D.C. 20016

Publishes a half-dozen books about traveling childhoods and repatriation issues; maintains a Website with subjects including publications; youth clubs around the world; an extensive links page; a resource page for children, families, and repatriation; and education issues.

Intercultural Press
www.interculturalpress.com
P.O. Box 700
Yarmouth, ME 04096

Publishes an extensive collection of books, videos, games, simulations, training materials, and other resources about crossing cultures.

Websites of Interest

www.overseasbrats.com

www.alumni.net

www.military-brats.com

www.aauw.org (American Association of University Women)

www.ifuw.org (International Federation of University Women)

www.gnvv.org (Global Nomad Virtual Village)

www.livingabroad.com (Living Abroad: The World Online—International Resource Center)

Notes on Contributors

Isabel Allende was born in Peru, raised in Chile, Bolivia, and Lebanon, and currently lives in California. She has written for newspapers and for the theater, and her fiction includes children's works, short stories, and novels. She is known around the world as the author of *Paula, The House of the Spirits, Aphrodite: A Memoir of the Senses,* and *Portrait in Sepia.*

Kathleen Anderson is an assistant professor of English at Palm Beach Atlantic College, Florida, specializing in Victorian literature and gender. Anderson also writes creative nonfiction. Her work has appeared in the *Journal of the Fantastic in the Arts, Persuasions: The Jane Austen Journal Online, Victorian Periodicals Review,* and *Harvard Book Review.* She spent parts of her childhood living in Palestine, Japan, and England and is at work on her memoir as well as a scholarly work on nineteenth-century British narratives.

Marie Arana sees herself as a bridge between two cultures, those of her father's genteel Peruvian relatives and her mother's Wyoming ranching family. She has served on the board of directors of the National Association of Hispanic Journalists and the National Book Critics Circle. Formerly a book editor at Harcourt Brace Jovanovich and vice president at Simon & Schuster, she joined the *Washington Post* in 1992, where she is currently editor of the *Washington Post Book World.* She lives in Washington, D.C. Her award-winning memoir, *American Chica,* was published in 2001.

Tara Bahrampour, Iranian and American, grew up balanced precariously between two nations and cultures, and watched them clash on the nightly news. At age eleven she experienced the Islamic revolution in her architect father's Iran, and refugee life in her singer mother's America. The fourth generation of her family to attend the University of California at Berkeley, Bahrampour then went on to graduate with an M.A. from Columbia University's School of Journalism. Her memoir, *To See and See Again: A Life in Iran and America*, was published in 1999. She has written for *The New York Times Magazine*, *The Wall Street Journal*, the *New Republic*, and *Travel and Leisure*. She lives in New York City.

Clark Blaise was for many years the director of the International Writer's Workshop at the University of Iowa, before moving to San Francisco, California. Born in the United States of Canadian parents, he grew up in both countries. Among his works are *Resident Alien, I Had a Father,* and *A North American Education: A Book of Short Fiction*. He is coauthor with Bharati Mukherjee of *Days and Nights in Calcutta* and *The Sorrow and Terror*.

Pat Conroy is author of numerous articles and essays and has written several books, including *My Losing Season, Prince of Tides, The Great Santini,* and *The Lords of Discipline*. He was raised the son of a Marine Corps pilot, moving more than twenty times on bases around the United States.

Ariel Dorfman is the son of a United Nations economist. He is a Chilean expatriate but was raised between Argentina and New York. Dorfman resides with his family in Durham, North Carolina, where he holds the Walter Hines Page chair at Duke University. He is the author of many books, including *Blake's Therapy; Heading South, Looking North;* and *Death and the Maiden*.

Eileen Drew lives and writes in Sebastopol, California. The daughter of a U.S. Foreign Service officer, she was born in Casablanca, Morocco, and lived in Nigeria, Guinea, Ghana, Korea, and Washington, D.C., then returned to Africa as a Peace Corps volunteer in Congo. She is the author of *Blue Taxis: Stories about Africa* and *Ivory Crocodile: A Novel* and a contributor to *Living on the Edge: Fiction by Peace Corps Writers*.

Anora Egan was raised around the shores of the Mediterranean in the 1960s. A student of Arabic, Italian, French, Latin, Spanish, and Chinese, she sought personal identity in many different cultures. Her work has been published in *Swaying: Essays on Intercultural Love* and in *Global Nomads, International Quarterly, Pan Gaia*, and *SAS Quarterly*. She is currently working on three projects: essays on coming into being, a collection of fairy tales, and a collection of essays reflecting on daily life.

Faith Eidse grew up in Congo/Zaire, Canada, and the United States, the daughter of Mennonite missionaries. Her *Oral History of the Apalachicola River and Bay* was solicited by the University Press of Florida. Her memoir, *African Soil*, won the 1995 Ann Durham Award for Outstanding Master's Thesis; her writing portfolio won a full scholarship Kingsbury Award; and her dissertation, *Occupied Territories*, was nominated for the Bellwether Prize. Her work appears in *International Quarterly, Q Magazine, Penumbra, Al-Kalima, Rhubarb, Swaying: Essays on Intercultural Love*, and the e-journal *J'Ouvert*.

Carlos Fuentes, son of a Mexican diplomat, was raised in Washington, D.C., and Latin America. He has published more than sixty books, including *The Years with Laura Diaz, Aura, The Buried Mirror: Reflections on Spain and the New World*, and *The Death of Artemio Cruz*.

Nancy Henderson-James calls herself "American by birth, Afro-Portuguese-Anglo by culture." She was a missionary kid, raised in Angola and schooled in Rhodesia. She commemorated the cease-fire in Angola's forty-year war by returning to her childhood home and searching for Tez. She is raising a family in Durham, North Carolina, where she is at work on her memoir.

Pico Iyer was born in England, to parents from India, and moved to California at the age of seven (while continuing his education in England). He is a long-time essayist for *Time* and the author of many books about his travels, including *The Global Soul, Tropical Classical: Essays from Several Directions,* and *Cuba and the Night: A Novel.* His novel, *Abandon: A Romance,* was published in 2003.

Lisa Suhair Majaj, daughter of a Palestinian father and an American mother, was born in Iowa, grew up in Amman, Jordan, spent nineteen years in the United States, and now lives in Nicosia, Cyprus. She is a poet, essayist, and independent scholar. Her poetry has appeared in numerous journals and collections, including *Unsettling America, Visions International,* and others. She is coeditor of *Going Global, Intersections,* and *Etel Adnan.* The essay in this collection was taken from *Homemaking.*

Peter Ruppert was born in Hungary in 1941. A refugee at the end of World War II, he lived in Austria, East Germany, France, and West Germany before his family emigrated to the United States in 1951. He is a professor of modern languages at Florida State University, Tallahassee, author of *Reader in a Strange Land: The Activity of Reading Literary Utopias,* and editor of two volumes on film studies. He is currently writing a memoir.

Nina Sichel was born in the United States and raised in Venezuela. After graduating from college with a degree in English literature, she worked in book editing and publishing, taught English as a second language, and counseled migrant farm workers and refugees from Mexico, Central America, and the Caribbean. She lives in Tallahassee, Florida, with her family and is working on a book of humorous poetry for children.

Sara Mansfield Taber, daughter of a U.S. Foreign Service officer, was raised in Taiwan, Japan, East Malaysia, Vietnam, the Netherlands and the United States. She is a cross-cultural development specialist and author of three books of literary nonfiction: *Bread of Three Rivers: The Story of a French Loaf, Of Many Lands:*

Journal of a Traveling Childhood, and *Dusk on the Campo: A Tour in Patagonia.* She was educated at Carleton College, the University of Washington, and Harvard University and earned a master's degree in social work and a doctorate in cross-cultural human development. She lives, writes, and teaches writing at Johns Hopkins University and at Bethesda Writer's Center.

Camilla Trinchieri, an Italian native, lives with her husband in Greenwich Village, New York City. As Camilla T. Crespi, she has published seven HarperCollins mysteries in The Trouble With series, which features food-loving Simona Griffo, a transplanted Italian ad executive. The series includes *The Trouble with Thin Ice, The Trouble with a Hot Summer, The Trouble with a Bad Fit,* and *The Trouble with Going Home.*

Ruth Van Reken, the daughter and mother of missionaries in Africa, is the author of *Letters Never Sent* and coauthor with David Pollock of *Third Culture Kids: The Experience of Growing Up Among Worlds.* She lives and writes in Indianapolis, Indiana, and serves with Interact, a TCK outreach program.

Mary Edwards Wertsch, born to a career army family in 1951, is the author of the nonfiction *Military Brats: Legacies of Childhoods Inside the Fortress,* which analyzes the effects on children of growing up in the military culture. She is also cofounder of Operation Footlocker, a movement to help American military brats now in adulthood reclaim their cultural identity through shared memories. She lives in St. Louis, Missouri, with her husband and two children, where she runs a youth project, Students for Civic Action, and is project director of the Initiative for Science Literacy.